nd upon Tha ~~Poliakoff~~ Libra
~~...~~ ys: 3

Caught on a Train, Coming in to Land, Close My Eyes

Caught on a Train has established itself as a classic TV film: 'Recognisibly in the train film genre: young man in trans-continental express, unsettled by high-handed old lady and more or less hostile passengers . . . Hitchcock out of Kafka. And it certainly winds up the suspense, with inventive plotting from Poliakoff. But what emerges is a piece that goes farther, and in an unexpected direction . . . Through the night-long journey, Poliakoff steadily revolves the psychology.' *Guardian*

Coming in to Land: 'Very effectively, it reminds us that our perception of Eastern Europe is blurred by propaganda and fiction and that lingering foreign notions of England as a land of grace and freedom have little connection with our spiralling decay.' *Guardian*
'Poliakoff is not a naturalistic writer, and the confrontations in his plays are simply the means by which he can release energies within his characters that might otherwise lie latent and untested. And *Coming in to Land* is not a literal-minded melodrama about a woman fighting to stay in England, but an impassioned account of the obsessional resiliance of the thwarted individual.' *Independent*

Close My Eyes, winner of numerous awards including *Evening Standard* Best British Picture of 1992: 'Burns with an off-beat lustre and intensity rarely encountered in recent British cinema . . . Incest is not Poliakoff's chief concern. Alert to social nuances and London's labyrinths, he uses the siblings' sultry encounters as a weapon for probing Britain's sexual fears, class fissures and greed: the legacy of the eighties . . . a script full of subtleties and terse comic phrasing.' *The Times*

Stephen Poliakoff, born in 1952, was appointed Writer in Residence at the National Theatre for 1976 and the same year won the *Evening Standard*'s Most Promising Playwright award for *Hitting Town* and *City Sugar*. He has also won a BAFTA award for the Best Single Play of 1980 for *Caught on a Train*, the *Evening Standard* Best British Film award for *Close My Eyes* in 1992 and the Critics' Circle Best Play Award 1996 for *Blinded by the Sun*. His plays and films include *Clever Soldiers* (1974), *The Carnation Gang* (1974), *Hitting the Town* (1975), *City Sugar* (1975), *Heroes* (1975), *Strawberry Fields* (1977), *Stronger than the Sun* (1977), *Shout Across the River* (1978), *American Days* (1979), *The Summer Party* (1980), *Bloody Kids* (1980), *Caught on a Train* (1980), *Favourite Nights* (1981), *Soft Targets* (1982), *Runners* (1983), *Breaking the Silence* (1984), *Coming in to Land* (1987), *Hidden City* (1988), *She's Been Away* (1989), *Playing with Trains* (1989), *Close My Eyes* (1991), *Sienna Red* (1992), *Century* (1994), *Sweet Panic* (1996), *Blinded by the Sun* (1996), *The Tribe* (1997), *Food of Love* (1998) and *Talk of the City* (1998).

STEPHEN POLIAKOFF

Plays: 3

Caught on a Train
Coming in to Land
Close My Eyes

introduced by the author

Methuen Drama

METHUEN CONTEMPORARY DRAMATISTS

This collection first published in Great Britain 1998 by Methuen Drama
Random House, 20 Vauxhall Bridge Road, London SW1V 2SA

Methuen Publishing Limited
11-12 Buckingham Gate
London SW1E 6LB

Caught on a Train first published in a volume with
Favourite Nights in 1982 by Methuen London Ltd
Copyright © 1982 by Stephen Poliakoff
Coming in to Land first published in 1986 by Methuen London Ltd
Copyright © 1986 by Stephen Poliakoff
Close my Eyes first published in 1991 by Methuen Drama
Copyright © 1991 by Stephen Poliakoff
Collection and Introduction copyright ©1998 by Stephen Poliakoff

Transferred to digital printing 2006

The author has asserted his right under the Copyright, Designs and Patents Act, 1988,
to be identified as the author of this work.

Methuen Publishing Limited Reg. No.3543167

A CIP catalogue record for this book is available from the British Library

ISBN 0 413 72320 8

Typeset by Delatype Ltd, Birkenhead, Merseyside
Printed and bound in Great Britain by
Cox & Wyman Ltd, Reading, Berkshire

Contents

Chronology
of first performances

Day With My Sister, Traverse Theatre, Edinburgh   1971
Pretty Boy, Royal Court, London   1972
Berlin Days, Little Theatre, London   1973
Sad Beat Up, Little Theatre, London   1974
The Carnation Gang, Bush Theatre, London   1974
Clever Soldiers, Hampstead Theatre, London   1974
Hitting Town, Bush Theatre, London   1975
Heroes, Royal Court, London   1975
City Sugar, Comedy Theatre, London   1976
Strawberry Fields, National Theatre   1977
Stronger Than the Sun, BBC   1977
Shout Across the River, Royal Shakespeare Company,
    London   1978
American Days, ICA, London   1979
The Summer Party, Crucible Theatre, Sheffield   1980
Caught on a Train, BBC   1980
Bloody Kids, Black Lion Films   1980
Favourite Nights, Lyric Theatre, London   1981
Soft Targets, BBC   1982
Runners, film   1983
Breaking the Silence, Royal Shakespeare Company,
    London   1984
Coming in to Land, National Theatre, London   1987
Hidden City, film   1988
She's Been Away, BBC Films   1989
Playing with Trains, Royal Shakespeare Company,
    London   1989
Close My Eyes, film   1991
Sienna Red, Peter Hall Company, touring   1992
Century, film   1994
Sweet Panic, Hampstead Theatre, London   1996
Blinded by the Sun, Royal National Theatre   1996
The Tribe, film   1997
Food of Love, film   1998
Talk of the City, Royal Shakespeare Company, Stratford 1998

Introduction

In 1978 I travelled from London to Vienna by train. I was twenty-five years old, full of optimism and ambition – indeed the purpose of my trip was to see three of my plays performed in a new theatre in Vienna, the first time my work had been produced in Europe.

But the whole journey was ruined by an elderly Viennese woman who wanted my window seat on the Ostend-to-Vienna express, the seat I had specially booked for myself with uncharacteristic foresight. I was never to discover the woman's name, or in fact anything about her at all, but she declared silent war on me for the whole journey, fixing me with a stare of deep hatred from the other side of the compartment. As we travelled for hour upon hour in this state, the story of *Caught on a Train* began to unfold in my mind, while outside the window I had so carefully defended, a night-time Europe flashed past. A Europe that began to seem more and more hostile and unwelcoming.

The three works in this volume span twelve years, from 1979 to 1991, years, of course, of momentous change in Europe. The collapse of Communism, the melting of the Iron Curtain, naturally affects *Coming in to Land* most fundamentally, but the passing of time has had an interesting effect on all three works.

Caught on a Train, despite its genesis, was written not to exorcise a troubling travel experience, but to reflect the deep feelings of unease, we, the British, have about Europe. When it was written we had only relatively recently voted to stay in the Common Market, and the mood in the country remained highly ambivalent. Indeed looking back at *Caught on a Train* now, it can almost be taken as a graphic metaphor for Euroscepticism. It has remained over the last eighteen years one of the most popular works I've written, and I've often wondered if this is the reason why – it somehow speaks to our instinctive fear about mainland Europe. This would be very ironic, as I am passionately in favour of closer ties with

Europe. But one of the recurring themes of my work is how we have cut ourselves off, again and again through this century, both emotionally and intellectually from events in Europe. This is explored most fully in my 1998 play *Talk of the City*, and definitely has its seeds in *Caught on a Train*.

Peter, the ambitious but emotionally dead central character in *Caught on a Train*, evolves directly into Neville in *Coming in to Land*, indeed they could well have been acquaintances of each other. *Coming in to Land* was written during the last gasp of the Reaganite/Thatcher Cold War, Russia was the Evil Empire, glasnost, though about to happen, had as yet not been heard of, Solidarity was still being repressed in Poland.

The play obviously does closely reflect its period, in fact it is perhaps the only contemporary play I've written that could now be called a period piece. But it does also express a situation that will never date – the hunger of people wanting to enter this country from some repressive regime colliding with the ennui and complacency that we often feel as we loll about in our affluent freedom. Neville's *fin-de-siècle* staleness of mind, his lack of emotional engagement, is only punctured when Halina refuses to enter an arranged marriage with him because she sees him as the worse of two evils. She prefers to try to lie her way into the country by providing a powerful story for the immigration authorities, to show she will be in danger if she returns to her native land. A high risk strategy that very nearly works.

I wanted to portray the awful sensation of being stateless, the extreme vulnerability of the immigrant's position, and I also wanted Neville, the successful English professional, to experience what that would be like, when he suddenly finds himself under the searchlight of the immigration service. For a moment he is faced with the hallucinatory situation of being questioned as if he is a foreigner, and has to confront the possibility of being chucked out of his native land.

Coming in to Land represented quite a daring experiment in form for me, in that it was determinedly retrogressive, taking the shape of a boulevard play – or that wonderful phrase 'a well-made play' – the kind of drama I spent most of my career reacting against. (Interestingly this sort of structure was soon to become fashionable among some of my contemporaries, a move which seemed to coincide with the rehabilitation of Terence Rattigan's reputation.)

My reason for adopting this structure was to enable me to subvert the expectation of the audience to maximum effect, and provide an initial feeling of comfort and complacency that reflected Neville's state of mind. That at least was the intention, and by and large I feel it worked, the story proved involving and the mess and unhappiness of Halina's predicament leaked through the neat structure. But 'neatness' is not something normally associated with me, and in my later work I have returned to my more free flowing style.

Close My Eyes has a direct link to the comfortable London that is portrayed in the early scenes of *Coming in to Land*. Richard is much more emotionally alive than Neville, but he is seemingly also trapped in a successful world that he wishes to break out of, he needs to take risks to make his life more interesting. But Richard's motives are very different to Neville's. He is much more sensitive, and his pursuit of an incestuous relationship with his sister is due to a sudden crisis of confidence.

The genesis of *Close My Eyes* lies in my 1975 play about a brother and sister, *Hitting Town*. The action of the play all took place on one winter night, during which the brother and sister, Clare and Ralph, slept together. She was recovering from being left by her lover, he from the shock of being near the Birmingham bombs when they went off. The play was about people retreating into a private melancholy, away from the urban desolation all around them. It also tried to catch the uncertain, ugly mood of the mid seventies, following so soon after the exuberance and confidence of the sixties.

Ever since I had finished the play I'd had a desire to explore the central relationship more deeply. The idea kept coming back to me over the years, troubling me. But I could not recapture those earlier characters, nor did I particularly want to. Instead of merely revisiting the play I wanted to create a new story involving a brother and sister that would reflect some of the anxieties that pursued us in the nineties. In particular I wanted to explore sexual worries, the reality that sex is much more complicated and dangerous than it was when I wrote the original play and how that would affect one young man leading a reasonably active heterosexual life. But the play and the film do share a common purpose, a desire not to shock the audience, but to make them accept the central relationship as almost natural, for it to unfold with a beguiling momentum of its own, which discourages all moralising about it.

In 1975, *Hitting Town* inhabited a brutal, concrete and neon world. *Close My Eyes* is set against a wider landscape full of nineties contrasts, the rebuilding of London and the lush, prosperous, disquietingly beautiful Home Counties. Both stories show characters trying to escape from the present and, in Richard's case in *Close My Eyes*, very nearly succeeding. The present in *Hitting Town* was a dirty, lonely, hideous place. In *Close My Eyes* it is more seductive, but it is also a lot more dangerous.

Interestingly when *Close My Eyes* first came out it was taken as a metaphor for the dying fall of eighties greed, the sleek landscape of Thatcher's southern Britain, the moment before the cracks began to appear. But actually, and rather disturbingly the story seems to make perfect sense in the shadow of the Millennium Dome. In the film, and script, Canary Wharf is seen rising, half-built, clad in blue plastic. A vast symbol of the over-confidence and insensitivity of the times. If I was to make the film now, using the same locations, Richard would be working right next to the Dome, as it swelled above him.

It is facile to suggest that nothing has changed, but the feelings expressed in *Close My Eyes* are lingering on for longer than I anticipated.

Stephen Poliakoff
February 1998

Caught on a Train

Caught on a Train was first transmitted on BBC2 on 31 October 1980 with the following cast:

Frau Messner	Peggy Ashcroft
Peter	Michael Kitchen
Lorraine	Wendy Raebeck
Preston	Michael Sheard
Kellner	Ingo Mogendorf
Dietrich	Louis Sheldon
Hans	Michael Kingsbury
Small Man	John Dolan
German Guards	Christopher Frederick
	Ken Shaw
Belgian Guard	Terry Gurry
Fat Man	Baron Casanov
Belgian Youth	Martin Phillips
Porter	Richard Merson
Waiter	Lex Van Delden
Steward	Sean Barry-Weske

Directed by Peter Duffell
Produced by Kenneth Trodd
Designed by Derek Dodd
Original music by Mike Westbrook

Exterior: Ostend railway station: Mid-afternoon:

A large diesel engine staring directly at the camera — the driver in a leather jacket is visible staring through the windscreen.

We pan across the front of the other platforms with the engines pointing directly out towards us. One of the locomotives is roaring, ready to move.

On the soundtrack a voice is babbling fast in various languages.

We cut to the main hall of the station. Sunlight is pouring in from the big windows.

Peter *is walking towards us through the bunches of people. He is twenty-seven years old, dressed immaculately in an expensive jacket and light trousers. He has dark hair, a pale slightly pinched face, very sharp blue eyes. We move with him as he approaches the camera, across the concourse of the station up to the barrier.*

The sound of announcements in French, then in German. They are garbled fast. In front of him is a girl, **Lorraine**, *extremely attractive in a sleek, air hostess way. she is carrying two large suitcases.* **Peter** *watches her. The announcements change to musak.* **Peter** *is up to the ticket barrier.*

The ticket collector is a small man with round owl-like glasses, one of which is cracked. He motions to **Peter** *to produce his ticket, without speaking.* **Peter** *hands over a large Euro-rail ticket, the size of a booklet. The man looks at the ticket very, very carefully, almost as if inspecting for a forgery, flicking through its different sections. He glances up at* **Peter** *and gives him a piercing look through his spectacles then back at the ticket.*

Peter (*surprised at this caution*) What on earth's wrong with it?

Shot of **Lorraine** *receding towards the train.*

The ticket collector tears out part of the ticket, reluctantly gives it him back, clipping it with a short stabbing movement.

We move with **Peter** *along the platform. He glances with idle curiosity towards another train on the far side with its board announcing it is going to Moscow, its engine roaring.*

Lorraine, *in front of him on the platform, is struggling with her suitcases.* **Peter** *is following several paces behind, watching her.*

There is a sudden noise from the far end of the platform. From **Peter**'s *point of view we see a group of kids, about seven of them, ranging from thirteen to eighteen years old, running across the railway tracks outside the station towards the platforms. They are swinging bags and shouting in German 'Wait. Wait.' They are clutching various tourist-like belongings and football scarves, suggesting they have been across to England for a football match.*

One of them is blowing a loud and extremely high-pitched whistle. They jump and run across the lines as a porter shouts at them furiously in French. The noise of the engine is building to a roar. The leading boy, **Dietrich**, *a blond boy, with a sharp pointed face, reaches the train, but remains on the track in front of it. They shout back at the porter, and realise it is the wrong train, so most of them clamber on to the platform. But two kids remain on the track in front of the train,* **Peter** *moving all the time closer to get a better look. He glances at his ticket, and moves along the side of the train he is about to board, past notices saying: 'Ostende-Bruxelles-München-Wien'.*

Dietrich *rushes past him and barges into* **Peter** *as he does so.*

There is no one on the train except, from one window, a small girl stares with large, blank eyes. She is eating a hot-dog. He pauses for a second and looks at her. She does not smile back.

Peter *climbs aboard the train.*

Interior: Train: Afternoon:

Peter *moves through the carriage. The sun is pouring through the windows, throwing some of the carriage into deep shadow.*

Peter *moves through a carriage with an open gangway down the middle. The carriage is totally empty. Newspapers and magazines lie on the seats, some party hats and a half-smoked cigar on a table. On one seat lies a pair of black tights.* **Peter** *leans down and picks them up.*

As he reaches the end of the carriage there is a noise behind him. **Lorraine** *is at the other end of the carriage carrying one of her heavy suitcases and pushing the other one along in front of her, stumbling and straining, preoccupied with the effort.*

Peter *watches her for a second with a slight smile on his face. She is almost up to him before she notices, when she starts slightly and looks up. She stares straight at him; sharp intelligent eyes. She is dressed casually but expensively. She has long brown hair.*

Peter (*a slight smile*)   I was about to offer to help.

Lorraine (*politely*)   I can manage, thank you.

She moves to push past him but he takes one of the suitcases firmly away from her. He is carrying a small bag of his own.

Lorraine   That's very kind.

She moves through the empty train in front of him. He follows behind her carrying the enormous suitcase, truly surprised by its excessive weight. From his point of view we watch **Lorraine** *move through the empty train. The sun is shining in, there are empty compartments wherever he looks.*

Peter   It's not exactly overcrowded is it! Where is everybody?

As he moves after her, she talks without looking back at him.

Lorraine   I'm glad to be here – little boys kept on pinching me on the boat. Coming up behind and poking me and things. (*She suddenly stops, looking back and staring at him.*) Were you on the boat?

Peter   Yes. but I wasn't one of them.

They have moved in to the couchette carriage. It is split into different compartments. Sun is still pouring through the windows. **Lorraine** *glancing into the empty compartment as she moves.*

Lorraine   I'm in 'F'.

She stops by the compartment.

Peter   I think . . . I'm pretty sure . . . (*He puts down the* *case, looks at his ticket.*) We're sitting in the same compartment.

Lorraine (*a polite smile*)   Are we? That's nice. (*She moves into the compartment, looking at him.*)

Peter (*heaving the suitcase up*)   Yes – we're opposite. You going far?

Lorraine (*looking at him*)   To Nuremberg. And you?

Peter   Even further.

*He finishes putting **Lorraine**'s immensely heavy suitcase on the rack.*

Lorraine (*smiles*)   Thanks. (*Indicating the cases.*) I haven't got much for once – managed to travel lightly for a change. (*Her manner is totally ambiguous, impossible to tell if she is joking or not.*)

*They are both standing in the compartment. **Peter** looks down at the tights he is still holding, and smiles charmingly.*

Peter   I don't usually travel with these.

Lorraine   Don't you?

Peter   I just found them back there.

Lorraine (*taking the tights from him, glancing at them, matter-of-fact*)   I wonder what they were up to this morning.

Peter (*moves back into the corridor glancing around him*)   We seem to be entirely alone. (*Looking down the corridor: he smiles.*) It would be extraordinary to have a whole train completely to oneself. Fourteen carriages. Nobody else at all. (*He glances back into the compartment from the corridor.*) I take it we're on the right train? We're not going to quietly end up in Poland?

Lorraine (*totally matter-of-fact*)   Yes. God, it's so hot isn't it? Excuse me.

Lorraine *turns away from him. She is standing in the compartment, he in the corridor. She pulls her sweater off: her blouse* *underneath rides up her back, showing her bare back. He watches involuntarily for a moment.*

The engine of the train roars into action, whines savagely for a second and dies: both of them have looked startled.

Peter *(smiles)* Obviously only a trial run.

Lorraine *joins him in the corridor. She moves up to the window: outside we can see Ostend station, some people are milling on the platform.*

Lorraine *(staring out)* You know that feeling when you don't want other people to get on?

Peter Yes – but I think they're going to. These are all reserved.

He flicks the metal reserved signs outside the couchette compartment, sliding one half out then flicking it back.

Lorraine Perhaps they won't show up or maybe we can stop them getting in here.

Peter *(moving up to her by the window, smiling)* How?

Lorraine Look hostile. I'm very good at this back home. Used to think up lots of different ways of keeping people out. *(She leans out of the window,* **Peter** *watching her.)* Blow smoke at them – or you can spit at them of course. You have to really concentrate.

Peter *leans out of the window beside her. A shot of* **Frau Messner** *moving with a porter across the station, talking rapidly to the porter.*

Peter I like trains. *(He is leaning out of the window.)* I haven't been on a huge train journey for years.

Lorraine Look.

Peter *looking sideways down the train.* **Preston** *is moving along the side of the train looking determined.*

Peter I have a feeling *that* one is going to try to get on.

A sudden loud noise behind them while they watch **Preston**.

The door at the end of the corridor opens, and an extremely fat and large man struggles into the corridor.

Lorraine   Come on.

They both move back speedily into their compartment and slide the door back.

Lorraine *stretches herself out on the seat.*

The **Fat Man** *passes in the passage, his stomach brushing the glass, and moves on.*

Peter   I thought he was going to puncture himself.

Lorraine (*staring across at* **Peter**)   It would be incredible if we really were alone.

Peter (*smiles slightly*)   Wouldn't it?

Immediately their door slides open and **Preston** *stands in the doorway.* **Preston** *is in his late thirties, but has an ageless asexual quality. He is going bald: an egg-shaped head. He is wearing a huge windcheater and carrying a large all-purpose bag which he almost throws onto the luggage shelf with a sharp movement. The windcheater crackles with a grating noise every time he moves. He is wearing gym shoes. As soon as he sits he crosses his legs and does up his laces, which are already fastened, very sharply and purposefully.*

Peter (*as* **Preston** *enters, to* **Lorraine**)   You weren't concentrating hard enough.

Preston, *who is sitting by the corridor window, glances round the compartment. He notices some sweet papers over the floor, and an old newspaper – he looks straight at* **Peter**.

Preston   Is this how you found the compartment? In this condition?

Peter (*surprised*)   Yes.

Preston   You did? Fair enough.

The door slides back, **Kellner** *enters. He too is in his thirties. He has bright red hair and heavy spectacles. He is dressed in a pin-striped suit, but a very expensive one. He carries a shiny executive suitcase – a pile of papers very carefully folded under his arm. He* *has a broad smooth face. He glances for his seat number and sits between* **Preston** *and* **Lorraine**, *facing* **Peter**.

Peter *looks hard at* **Lorraine**.

Kellner (*as he sits, nods at* **Peter**) Gut. (*He places his papers – all of which are financial papers –* Wallstreet Journal, Financial Times, *etc. – beside him.*) Gut.

Peter (*to* **Lorraine**, *lowering his voice*) Do you think that's the lot?

Lorraine Maybe.

Preston *glances up, his windcheater crackling.*

Lorraine (*also lowering her voice*) Do you want some chocolate?

Peter (*smiles*) Chocolate? Yes . . .

Lorraine (*produces out of her bag a large bar of dark chocolate*) I couldn't stop myself, it was so large. (*She holds out the chocolate to* **Peter** *who takes some.*) So come on, have lots.

Peter No, just a bit.

She breaks some off and drops it into his hand: They look at each other and put the very dark chocolate into their mouths. **Peter** *flinches as he tastes it.*

Lorraine (*looking at* **Peter**, *not raising her voice*) Christ, it's really bitter.

Peter It's not exceptionally sweet.

Lorraine (*leaning towards him*) You're being very English and polite.

Peter (*staring back at her*) It's revolting. (*Then lowering his voice even more.*) I think we may have got off lightly. (*Very quiet to* **Lorraine**.) I wonder how far they're going.

A loud noise in the passage – the sound of arguing – we hear a **Porter**'*s voice shouting in French.*

Frau Messner *appears in the passage, confronted by a small and* *excited* **Porter** *who is holding her luggage.*

She stares back at him. She is in her seventies, neatly and very well dressed, but with a lot of clothes, as if it were winter. She has a strong face, a sharp abrupt and unmistakably Viennese manner. Her English is impeccable.

Porter   Ce n'est pas assez.

He repeats this several times, holding out his hand for more, then in disgust he gives her back her small tip.

Frau Messner   Aber ich habe nichts mehr!

The sound of the engine roaring again. It drowns them.

Peter *turns away, his nose pressed up against the glass – an amused smile on his face.*

The engine continues roaring – but quieter. Somebody is talking to **Peter** *in German: He does not turn round.*

During the voice-over we stay on **Peter**.

Frau Messner (*voice-over*)   Entschuldigung, Sie haben meinen Platz.

Peter *turning:* **Frau Messner** *is standing right over him.*

Frau Messner (*polite smile*)   Are you English or not?

Peter   Yes.

Frau Messner   Then you can understand. You are sitting in my seat where I have to sit.

Peter   I'm sorry – this is my seat.

Frau Messner   I asked for a window seat specially. I have to sit where my ticket says. (*She waves her ticket.*) You understand and I have to sit here.

Peter (*looking straight back at her, defiant smile*)   But I'm afraid this is my seat – and *I* have to sit here.

Frau Messner   Can I see your ticket please?

Peter *glances at* **Lorraine**, *then at* **Frau Messner**. *He hands* *over his ticket.*

Frau Messner (*sharp*) You should be sitting in E.

Peter I am sitting in E.

Frau Messner Did you ask for a window seat?

Peter No, but . . .

Frau Messner There, I thought so. I asked for one specially. I always do.

Preston (*suddenly staring hard at* **Peter**, *accusingly*) Sometimes the letters get changed around.

Frau Messner (*a polite steely smile*) As you see you are in my seat. (**Peter** *does not move.*) Do I have to say it again? I don't want to have to cause trouble.

Peter I'm very sorry but I want to sit here and I'm going to.

Frau Messner (*staring straight at him. More steely*) I don't think you understand me. I have to sit by the window. Are you going to move?

Peter No – I am not.

Silence.

Frau Messner *stares back at him in total surprise. A piercing look.*

Peter (*defiant back*) That is your seat – if you want to know.

He points to the seat opposite **Preston.**

Frau Messner (*still looking at him*) Somebody must have made a mistake mustn't they? (*She moves opposite to* **Preston.**) I will sit here! I can never travel comfortable unless I'm by the window. Never mind – I will not call the guard.

Kellner *looks very embarrassed,* **Lorraine** *looks out of the window.*

Preston (*leaps to* **Frau Messner**'s *aid, picking up her two* *suitcases*) Let me help you. Terrible breed porters, aren't they? Always causing trouble, the world over. It's impossible to find a helpful one. I think they have become extinct.

Frau Messner   It's very kind of you. How peculiar of them to make a mistake isn't it? It has never happened before. But I won't call anybody. I will just sit here the whole journey.

A moment's silence. The sound of train doors banging.

Peter *not looking at her.*

Preston *stares at him again.*

Frau Messner *is rustling about in her hand luggage: a very loud rustle.*

Frau Messner   How stupid! How very stupid of me . . . I seem to have forgotten my magazines. (*She looks at the whole of the compartment.*) I usually have a big pile of magazines to read and in the rush I have forgotten them. (*She suddenly leans over and looks at* **Peter**.) You don't think you could be so kind and get them for me?

A look of disbelief on **Peter**'s *face.*

(*Totally unabashed.*) You just have to go over to the big bookstall and get them for me. (*The sound of train doors slamming in the distance.*) It would be a great help to me, my legs, you see, are not very strong.

Peter (*disbelieving smile*)   But the train is about to go!

The sound of more train doors banging.

Frau Messner   No, no, it's not. Not for ten minutes.

Preston   Not for thirteen minutes, to be precise. They're never off on time.

Peter *gives* **Preston** *a savage look.*

Frau Messner   Of course you won't miss the train – it'll take you one minute. You won't even have to run.

Peter But . . .

A whistle blows loudly – **Peter** *looks round automatically.*

Preston That isn't us.

Frau Messner I have a list. (*She produces it.*) I always give them a list at the shop. (*Polite smile.*) I just have to have something to read you see.

Peter *looks up.* **Lorraine** *is looking out of the window.* **Kellner** *is staring at him, as is* **Preston***: straight at him.*

A distant but urgent train announcement in the background.

Nobody says anything.

Peter Give me the list . . .

Frau Messner That's so kind of you. I must give you money too of course. Here – there we are. (*She places the money in his hand, as she does it she looks at him.*) It is a great help to me.

Peter You are absolutely sure I've got time.

Preston You've got all the time in the world.

Peter Because there isn't another train for a day and a half. .

Frau Messner You can't possibly miss it – if you go now. (**Peter** *moves out of the compartment and slides the door shut. She looks up as he does so.*) We won't let the train go without you.

Exterior: Station: Afternoon:

Peter *moves briskly, rather than runs down the side of the train. He glances back. A receding shot of a couple of passengers leaning out of the train window watching him go.*

Peter *passes the ticket collector with cracked glasses who watches him in surprise.*

Peter (*smiling as he goes*)   I'll only be a moment.

Cut to **Peter** *standing in a queue at a news-stand. The person at the front of the queue is talking and gesticulating.*

Over the loudspeakers **Peter** *can hear trains being called. He glances up very impatiently. The sound of whistles. A loudspeaker above his head suddenly blares out brass band music.*

We pan over the magazines on the news-stand, glossy Euromagazines, Stein, Paris-Match, *the Italian magazines: a mixture of terrorists and bare-breasted girls polishing cars.*

Peter *gets to the front of the queue and hands the* **Man** *behind the counter the list. He languidly begins to collect the magazines.*

We keep very close on **Peter.** *He turns his head urgently to his right, leaning against the wall quite close to him. A policeman in dark glasses is staring at him suspiciously.*

The sound of a whistle blowing very shrilly again and again, and an announcement booms over a loudspeaker, totally inaudible except for the word 'Depart' but sounding very urgent.

He glances at his watch, it says six o'clock. He glances up at a clock on the wall of the news-stand. It says seven-thirty.

The **Man** *behind the counter comes back with a very thick pile of magazines.* **Peter** *pushes* **Frau Messner***'s money into his hand. The sound of doors slamming. The* **Man** *behind the counter looks down at the money.*

Man (*muttering crossly*)   Ce n'est pas assez!

Peter   Oh Christ! That's all she gave me . . . can't you . . .

He reluctantly but hastily pulls out some more money. The **Man** *takes the note with a look of annoyance and starts pawing over the cash register trying to find the change.*

The noise of a train moving out of the station as a further whistle goes.

Peter   Keep the change.

He lifts the heavy wodge of magazines and pushing past the queue is about to move out of shot.

Somebody in the front of the queue calls at him and waves a couple of magazines he has left behind.

Peter   Forget it!

He runs back towards the barrier across the main hall, dodging people as he goes. A luggage 'train' rattles past as he nears the barrier. Whistles are blowing loudly. We track fast behind him as he comes up to the barrier. The ticket collectors have shut the barrier and wave at him that he is too late, but he confidently pushes past them and gives the barrier a shove. It swings open on the second attempt. He runs up to the train, his manner confident, not desperate, though highly annoyed. A couple more magazines drop onto the platform as he runs. People lean from the train, a couple of kids, and shout down at him, encouraging him. He climbs aboard the train amid much shrieking and whistles.

Interior: Train corridor: Afternoon:

The first thing **Peter** *sees as he climbs onto the train, is three of the German eighteen-year-old boys whom he had seen running across the tracks earlier. They are the only people in the corridor. The leader of these three,* **Dietrich**, *is a boy of immense nervous energy, with bright blue eyes, charismatic looks and a very loud voice.*

Dietrich *stares at him as he moves down the corridor and into the compartment.*

Interior: Train: Afternoon:

Peter *slips back the glass door and enters the compartment.* **Frau Messner** *looks up.*

Frau Messner (*polite smile*)   You see. You did have time.

The train is pulling out of the station: the noise of its lumbering across the points outside the station.

Peter . All the time in the world . . .

Preston   You must have gone to the wrong bookstall.

Peter *hands her the huge pile of magazines.*

Frau Messner   Thank you. That was so kind of you. (*Very slight pause, then she glances up.*) Was there any change for me? Do you have my change?

Peter *has remained standing, facing her, keeping his balance as the train begins to pick up speed.*

Peter   Not exactly. You didn't give me nearly enough in fact.

Frau Messner   I didn't give you enough money? (*Concerned tone.*) I must give you some more at once. Immediately. (*She shuffles in her bag.*) Oh. I only have this! (*She is holding a large banknote – looking straight back at him.*) Can you change me a one thousand schilling note? This is all I've got. I'm afraid all my change has completely gone. (*To the rest of the compartment.*) You have to give away so much money all the time now.

The note is stretched out towards **Peter**. *He stares at it.*

Peter   No, I can't.

Frau Messner (*innocent*)   What are we going to do?

A very slight pause. **Preston** *watching.*

Peter (*sharp*)   It's all right, we'll forget it, for the moment. (*He sits as the train jolts on and then begins to run more smoothly.*)

Preston   They're off on time for once! Only fifty seconds late. They'll never keep it up.

Frau Messner (*checking her magazines*)   And you've got *almost* all of them – that is good.

Peter (*glances up at* **Lorraine**, *opposite him*)   I'm exhausted. I haven't run like that for years.

Lorraine   You've still got your seat though haven't you?

The afternoon sun is on **Lorraine** *as she lies back in her seat staring at him.*

Preston *suddenly leaning towards* **Frau Messner**.

Shot of the Belgian countryside through the window in the afternoon light.

Preston   The coffee of course will cost a fortune on this train. And it'll be undrinkable. Don't bother to try it.

Peter *looks back at* **Lorraine** *as* **Preston***'s voice continues –* **Peter***'s eyes half close, then open.*

Preston (*voice-over*)   On the boat, just now, how much do you think I paid for a cup of coffee and a piece of cake, like that, no bigger than a matchbox, with a piece of green icing on the top, and a packet of peanuts. How much?

Frau Messner (*voice-over*)   How much? You tell me?

Preston (*voice-over*)   No you have to have a guess.

Peter*'s eyes wander across* **Lorraine***'s body, up her legs, her blouse, the buttons slightly undone, her brown neck, the long smooth hair – up to her face. Afternoon light. He closes his eyes, as the train really picks up speed.*

The screen goes to black as the noise of the train becomes much louder, hurtling forward.

Dim shapes of other passengers from **Peter***'s point of view begin to come into focus.* **Preston***'s voice burbling on.*

Then onto **Peter***'s eyes, as they open.*

It is evening now, stormy sunlight outside.

Peter*'s point of view. The camera pans up the pair of legs in front of him, up the stockings, up the skirt, up to the face.* **Frau Messner** *is staring back at him with a polite smile, sitting in* **Lorraine***'s seat.*

Peter*'s head swings round.* **Lorraine** *is sitting in* **Frau Messner***'s seat, staring into the corridor.*

Silence: as he stares at **Frau Messner**.

The sound of the train cracking along.

Frau Messner   She let me change places. Wasn't it kind of her. (*There is a steely gleam in her eye. A close-up of the pile of magazines completely untouched.*) It makes me feel a lot better.

Peter (*sharply*)   Good . . .

The sound of a bell ringing down the corridor and the sound of somebody calling for bookings for dinner – his voice is some way off still.

Frau Messner   Have you had a good sleep?

Peter   I was only asleep a moment.

Frau Messner   Oh no. (*Looking at him.*) You were asleep for a long time. Nearly an hour. Maybe more.

Peter   Really? I don't believe you.

He glances at **Lorraine** *who is looking out of the window.*

Frau Messner (*not looking away*)   Are you going a long way?

Peter (*reluctantly*)   Yes – I am.

Frau Messner   So am I. I'm going all the way to Wien. I will be here the whole journey.

Peter (*smiles to himself*)   I imagined as much.

He glances towards **Lorraine** *who is still staring out into the corridor.*

The door flies open and the steward is flourishing a handful of red tickets.

Frau Messner   No I don't want any.

Peter   Merci.

The steward flicks him a ticket.

Lorraine   Could I also . . .

The steward flicks her a ticket and is out of the compartment in seconds, pushing the door loudly shut behind him.

While **Frau Messner** *speaks* **Kellner** *is adding something on a pocket calculator;* **Preston** *is staring ahead with a glazed expression.*

Frau Messner (*to the whole compartment*)   I have brought my own food. I always travel with my own, somebody prepares it for me. I never go anywhere without them. Little chickens cooked in breadcrumbs. (*Slowly.*) Since before the war, since I was only small, I have always travelled with them. (*She indicates a delicious-looking pile of food in a wooden basket covered in silver foil.*)

Preston   Quite right – the dining cars on these trains are hell on earth. You feel much worse when you come out than when you go in. Also, you can get bad food poisoning. Dreadful.

Frau Messner (*smiles*)   Like everything, it gets worse. (*Pulling her money out of her purse.*) I just have to count this now. (*The train is really rattling along.* **Frau Messner** *turns and looks at* **Kellner**.) You don't mind if I turn my back on you for a moment, I just must see how much I've got left. (*She starts to count the money.*)

Kellner (*smiles, a broad, good-humoured smile*)   No please, don't mind me. I'm used to the sound of money. I hear it every day from seven o'clock in the morning. (*He grins.*) Every day except Sundays – then I hear it at home.

A close-up of banknotes going through **Frau Messner**'*s fingers,* **Peter** *watches her count, as he takes out a packet of cigarettes and puts a cigarette in his mouth. As the cigarette actually goes into his mouth* **Frau Messner** *looks up.*

Frau Messner (*very firmly, smiles*)   Do you think if you want to smoke, you could smoke outside in the passage.

Peter *looks up in astonishment.*

Frau Messner   If you could go into the passage because we're going a long way, I asked for a non-smoker but for some reason this seems to be a smoker.

Peter   That's unfortunate. (*Icy*.) But if you don't like it I suggest you find somewhere else to sit.

Frau Messner (*ignoring this completely*)   I think the whole carriage must be a non-smoker. I'm sure it says so on the tickets.

Peter   I'm afraid it doesn't.

Frau Messner   You don't have to go far – the passage is just out there.

Lorraine *gets up and walks into the corridor. She does not turn round but stands with her back to them.*

Peter   And what happens to me if I don't?

Frau Messner *looks back at him. He lights the cigarette.*

Frau Messner (*still staring at him*)   Neither of these gentlemen are smokers, you see.

Preston   No. On a long journey it can get unpleasant. One wakes up at night with ash all over one's body.

Peter *blows smoke across the room.*

Frau Messner (*sharp*)   When I was young the men always smoked in the passage. They used to stay out there the whole journey – hanging their heads out of the window.

Peter   Did they?

Frau Messner (*politely*)   I am not going to ask you again.

Peter, *surprised at this, glances out at* **Lorraine** *in the passage, then straight into* **Frau Messner**'s *eyes.*

Peter   I'll be back in a second.

Interior: Train corridor: Afternoon:

Peter *goes out into the corridor. He glances back through the glass.* **Frau Messner** *is back sorting her money. He turns in surprise to* *look at the corridor. It is now chock-a-block, mostly kids, some standing up or sitting on their suitcases, or the small side-seats. They stare back at* **Peter.** *At the end of the carriage he can see* **Lorraine** *standing by the end window that stares directly onto the track.*

Peter *moves down the corridor, picking his way amongst the kids. We see the* **Fat Man** *sitting all alone. The blinds are pulled down, but* **Peter** *catches a glimpse through a gap in the blinds.*

In another compartment girls have stretched their legs out, kicked their shoes off, and are already fast asleep.

Half-way down the passage **Dietrich** *is leaning up against the wall, smoking, talking loudly in German. Two English schoolgirls with podgy white faces are sitting on their suitcase near* **Dietrich.**

Peter *reaches* **Lorraine** *at the end window. They stand next to each other for this sequence, staring directly out, the train moving fast along a curving scenic track.*

Peter (*moving up to her*) I think this is going to end in tears.

Lorraine (*not looking at him*) How do you mean?

Peter I can't sit there with her behaving like that. (*He smiles.*) I really might hit her – do her an injury.

Lorraine She's just old, you don't have to worry.

Peter I'm going to have to find another seat.

Lorraine (*still in profile, not looking at him*) You'll never find another one. The whole train's chock-a-block.

Peter *stares at the people on suitcases, in jeans, pale faces, holding beer cans.* **Dietrich** *is holding forth in rapid German. One of the other kids blows the football whistle loudly.*

Peter Where did they all suddenly spring from?

Lorraine You were asleep.

Peter I had no idea it would be so full. They must be all going home. They don't look particularly cheerful.

Lorraine (*glancing back*)   Why are they making so much noise?

Peter   We must be getting near the German border. (*Turning back to* **Lorraine**.) I should have flown. I nearly always do fly everywhere. (*An ironic smile as the kids lark around in the back of the shot.*) I wanted a change.

Lorraine (*staring out of the window*)   There you are then.

Peter (*more urgent*)   I can't sit with that old woman any more. I've really got to find another seat.

Lorraine   It's totally impossible.

Peter   Come on – we could try. (*He takes her sleeve.*)

Lorraine (*suddenly looking at him. Slight smile*)   You could.

Peter (*surprised*)   Yes.

Lorraine *turns back to the window.* **Peter** *glances at her face, her blouse.*

Lorraine   It's going to rain. It's hardly stopped raining since I've been in Europe. First in England and now here. On and on.

Dietrich *suddenly shouts at them, in German, teasingly lewdly down the length of the corridor.*

Lorraine   What's he saying?

Peter   I don't know.

Lorraine *moves away from* **Peter** *back down the corridor.* **Peter** *follows her. They stand in the corridor next to their own compartment, next to* **Dietrich** *in the corridor.*

Peter *glances at* **Frau Messner**. *She is leaning back in her seat, seemingly sleeping, but then she looks up for a second straight at him.*

Peter (*suddenly louder to* **Lorraine**)   Why on earth did you give up your seat for her?

Lorraine   Because she really needed it so badly.

Peter   Don't you realise that's exactly what she wanted to happen?

Lorraine   No it wasn't.

Peter   What do you mean?

Lorraine (*looks at him*)   She wanted *your* seat. (*Straight at him.*) And you should have given it to her – you really should.

Peter   Why? Why should people like that get exactly what they want all the time? It's what she's used to.

Lorraine   It was rude of you. She's an old lady.

Peter *stares at* **Frau Messner** *through the glass. As he talks about her the camera moves across* **Frau Messner**'s *face.*

Peter   Do you think she knows, we're talking about her?

Lorraine   She looks like she's dozing.

Peter   Yes ... she can probably hear everything we're saying. No doubt she can hear perfectly through glass. I expect she can hear through reinforced concrete. She's obviously not going to forgive me for the whole trip. (*He smiles.*) For defying her.

Frau Messner *moves in her seat but does not open her eyes.*

Boy (*in broken English, to both of them*)   Have you ... a cigarette?

He seems very nervous, preoccupied, flicking his hair away from his face.

Peter   Yes. OK. Here.

Boy   Thank you.

Peter (*smiling at his nervousness*)   You can have two or three if you like.

The **Boy** *takes them and goes into the compartment on the right-hand side of theirs and sits by the door.* **Peter** *can see him through the glass.*

Peter (*softer to* **Lorraine**)   Maybe I'll go and explore on my own then.

Shot of **Frau Messner** *sleeping, through the glass.*

Lorraine (*slight smile*)   You could always get off the train couldn't you – if you don't like being here.

Peter   No I can't. I've got to be in Linz at ten o'clock tomorrow. (*He smiles, jokey.*) I could pull the communication cord and get her taken off.

Lorraine   What cord?

Peter (*points*)   There. The lever. (*They look up at it.* **Peter** *stretches up to it.*) This actually is much more difficult to pull than you think. They're very stiff. You have to really tug at them. (**Peter** *touches it with the tip of his finger.*) It's sticky.

As he touches it, the train brakes savagely. They are all thrown violently sideways in the passage.

Lorraine   What's happening? Did you do that?

Peter (*smiles*)   Unfortunately, no. We've reached the border. (*He pulls out his passport.*) Passport checks and everything.

The train brakes again. A loud whining screech. The noise cuts out and then returns three times until the train finally comes to a halt.

Peter   Sounds as if it's in pain doesn't it?

As the train is stopping **Lorraine** *takes* **Peter**'s *passport.*

Lorraine   Can I see?

The rain starts during the following speech, streaking down the window.

Very hard rain playing on the roof and spattering down the window.

A shot of **Guards** *moving down the track outside the train.*

Peter *bending over his passport as she looks at it: charming smile.*

Peter   I work for a publisher's. Public relations. Coaxing successful authors out of bed and on to television. Not that they really need encouragement of course. Some of them get incredibly nervous. I have to pour drink down them in the taxi.

The door at the end of the carriage slides open with a crash. Border **Guards** *in uniform, glistening Mackintosh capes, move through. They wear guns. They begin to check passports at the other end of the train. One is very young. The other an old man in his sixties.*

Peter   These are the Belgians. Then we're in Germany.

Dietrich *suddenly snatches* **Peter**'s *passport. Another kid takes it, and it is returned to him in a flash.*

Dietrich (*grins at* **Peter**)   You like to see my pictures. (*He produces photographs and presses them up to* **Peter**'s *face.*) My parents. (*Pictures of prosperous Germans with Mercedes.*) My car . . . and me taking drugs. (*A picture of* **Dietrich** *sitting on a wall inhaling something through his nose.*) I'll show this one to the police.

Peter: *slight uneasy smile as the photographs are whipped away from him as the* **Guards** *get up to* **Dietrich**. **Dietrich** *waves the picture of himself taking drugs in the* **Guards**' *faces as they look at his passport, and jabbers in German. They take no notice as he does this.*

Peter *notices the* **Young Guard** *pull back the door of the* **Fat Man**'s *compartment.*

The rain is much louder, beating on the roof and down the sides of the train.

The **Fat Man** *is clearly visible hunched up in a large black overcoat. His compartment looks empty though* **Peter** *can only see half of it through the glass.*

Peter   I think he's all alone in there you know. Got the whole compartment to himself! I wonder how.

He glances at the kids sitting on the suitcases in the passage. The **Guards** *are picking their way amongst them.*

We pan with his point of view across his own compartment – with **Frau Messner** *looking up.*

Peter (*voice-over*)   Maybe if we're very lucky they'll send her back to Ostend.

*Across to the right, in another compartment, he can see the **Boy** who asked for a cigarette sitting restlessly by the door nervously chain-smoking, lighting the second cigarette with the end of the first. Slight track in on him as **Peter** stares at him fascinated. The **Boy**'s face is extremely tense and scared.*

Peter   Look at that boy there.

Lorraine   Which boy?

*Close up of the **Boy**'s face.*

Peter (*voice-over*)   There.

Lorraine (*voice-over*)   Why?

Peter (*voice-over*)   He's frightened, I think.

Lorraine (*quietly*)   Look – his socks don't match.

Young Guard (*pushes up to **Peter***)   Passport . . . (*He glances at **Peter** and snaps his passport, returning it.*) Merci . . .

*The **Young Guard** then pushes back the door of the compartment the **Boy** is in and stands over him. Real close-up, through the glass, of the **Boy**'s face. We see the panic and his effort to stop it showing. The **Boy** looks at the floor. The **Young Guard** is about to give back the passport, when he suddenly stops himself, and looks closely. The **Boy** is almost biting on his cigarette.*

Young Guard (*sharp*)   Ce passport n'est pas le vôtre.

Boy (*without real conviction*)   C'est le mien.

*The **Young Guard** talks to him rapidly. It is only half-audible from where **Peter** watches.*

Young Guard   Venez ici.

*He takes the **Boy** and leads him out into the corridor. The **Boy** begins to babble, people stand up in the carriage half-obscuring **Peter**'s view.*

Peter   I told you.

The **Young Guard** *calls sharply to the* **Older Guard** *to join him, and then places the* **Boy** *up against the window and frisks him.*

The rain is playing loudly on the roof.

Someone in the passage is cat-calling, but quite sheepishly. The **Boy**'s *face is sullen, but anxious.*

Older Guard (*moves up to* **Peter** *and* **Lorraine**)   Could you move into your seats please! Take your seats.

Lorraine *and* **Peter** *remain in the corridor.*

The **Boy**'s *head goes back and suddenly he starts shouting, though it is unintelligible.*

Interior: Train compartment: Afternoon:

Peter *watching from the corridor.*

Frau Messner (*looking up*)   What's happening? Why are we being held up?

Preston   No doubt it's a forged passport. I've heard it often happens. Maybe he was not meant to leave the country – in trouble with the courts.

Peter *is watching the* **Boy** *who is near to tears. The* **Older Guard** *has left urgently, the* **Young Guard** *is standing with the* **Boy**, *holding him firmly by one arm.*

The **Boy** *has sat down in the passage, by just letting his legs sink under him and the* **Young Guard** *is pulling him to his feet and dragging him along the corridor.*

Peter (*to* **Lorraine**)   He looks just like I used to when I was being taken back to boarding school.

The **Boy** *passes* **Peter**, *his face very close to him.*

Frau Messner (*watches the* **Boy** *as he goes by*)   He doesn't look well.

Kellner (*suddenly very sharp and impatient*)   It is annoying to be kept waiting, isn't it? We must make up a lot of time now or we'll be very late. (*He glances at his watch, tense.*) *Come on* ... It has to start now ...

From **Peter***'s point of view we see, through the train window, the* **Boy** *being led across the railway lines against a large, dwarfing, industrial back-drop, towards waiting police cars.*

As they cross the lines the **Boy** *pulls half-heartedly away.* **Dietrich** *and other kids cat-calling from the train. When they are half-way across the lines* **Dietrich** *suddenly opens the door of the train and jumps out, racing across the lines towards them, shouting exuberantly in German. The police stop and shout threateningly back at him.* **Dietrich** *mockingly raises his hands above his head, taunting them as he does so, then runs back towards the train for all he is worth, as the other kids cheer him and laugh, and the train begins to move.*

Dietrich *grinning, leans against the passage wall looking flustered and excited. His eyes meet* **Peter***'s.*

Dietrich   Some fun eh?

Cut to overhead shot of the train speeding deeper into Germany.

The door of the compartment slides back and a **Small Man** *in a mackintosh enters. Water dripping off him. He moves towards the last seat.*

The compartment is now full and claustrophobic. It is now night outside.

Preston   Excuse me, that seat has been reserved by somebody. Are you that person?

The man nods and sits next to **Peter***, facing* **Frau Messner** *and* **Kellner***. His face is round, very white and flabby, and totally expressionless. He grunts at them, a hardly audible noise.*

He takes off his mackintosh and rolls it up into a ball. Muddy water leaks off it and runs across the floor towards **Frau Messner***, who slides her feet backwards and starts lifting her hand luggage off the floor and onto her lap and the seat. She stops for a second as she realises something is missing and begins to sort through bags, getting more alarmed as she does so.*

Peter *watches her. As her panic begins to spread, the noise of her wrestling with her bags fills the compartment.*

Frau Messner   My food . . . my picnic . . . (*She looks up.*) The poussins. It's vanished. They've gone.

Preston   They can't have done. Maybe they have fallen down the side here.

Preston *pushes his hand down the side of the seat.*

Frau Messner (*very concerned*)   They were here! I fell asleep for a few moments. Just a moment. And now they have gone.

Kellner *and* **Lorraine** *begin to look,* **Lorraine** *round her feet.*

Frau Messner   It was in a basket, all done up in silver paper. Everything I had for the whole journey. You all saw it – I showed it to you.

Kellner   I'll look up here.

He looks in the luggage rack. The **Small Man** *lifts his mackintosh. Everybody moves except* **Peter**.

Preston (*to* **Kellner**)   Here, lift up the seat – let's have a look underneath here.

They look underneath the seat. Just a few coins and a dirty magazine that have slipped down the seat stare back at them.

Waved on by **Preston**, **Lorraine** *and the* **Small Man** *in the mackintosh have moved into the corridor to allow more room.*

Lorraine *stands with her face right up to the glass, staring into the compartment watching* **Peter** *throughout the rest of the sequence. He glances at her with a knowing smile half-way through the sequence.*

As **Kellner** *and* **Preston** *have been lifting the seat,* **Frau Messner** *carries straight on.*

Frau Messner   Chicken legs in breadcrumbs and wurst. They were prepared for me specially. I have never travelled anywhere without them. We must find them.

She suddenly stops and looks at **Peter**, *who has not moved at all. He is sitting watching her.*

Frau Messner (*quiet*)   Have you seen any of them?

Peter (*with an amused smile, staring back at her*)   I haven't seen any of your chicken, no.

Frau Messner (*staring at him*)   In silver paper. It was wrapped in . . .

Peter   I know. I still haven't seen them.

The others all stop and look at him. Silence as the train rattles on. The rain is still streaking the window. **Peter** *glances at* **Lorraine** *who is staring at him icily.*

Frau Messner (*staring down at* **Peter**)   They didn't run away by themselves.

Peter   I wouldn't be so sure.

Frau Messner (*into his face*)   Could you just stand up for a moment please.

Peter   I don't think so.

Frau Messner (*her voice sharper*)   I just want you to stand up and show me. I won't be angry if they are here.

Peter (*a slight smile*)   Are you doubting my word? (*Pause.*) Maybe you haven't lost them at all.

Frau Messner (*very forcefully*)   I will not be angry with you, if you've been hiding them. Just stand up now.

Peter *stands up. They all crane forward to see: there is nothing there.*

Peter (*smiles*)   Of course, I could have swallowed it all already. Could be inside me.

He touches his stomach. They are both standing up.

Frau Messner (*a piercing look*)   I shall ask you just once – have you taken my food?

A shot of the others watching **Peter**.

Peter No I have not.

A bell goes down the passage and we hear the voice of a steward.

(*He smiles.*) Why should I – I have a ticket for the dining car. (*He waves it.*) Now if you'll excuse me.

He glances at **Lorraine**, *and smiles as he moves out of the compartment into the corridor.*

I'll see you in there!

Lorraine *has sat down again at the edge of the compartment, her face registering disapproval at his behaviour. She glances straight at him and then away, their eyes meet for a second.*

Frau Messner (*as* **Peter** *is leaving*) I won't ask to see his bag. We must believe he's telling the truth. I will just sit here all night with nothing to eat.

Peter *closes the door shut on this last line and stares back through the glass for a second.*

Dietrich *has been standing in the passage. The three other German boys, his friends, are further down the corridor amongst the other kids.* **Dietrich** *is standing by the two puffy-faced schoolgirls who are shyly sitting on their suitcases.*

Dietrich *looking at* **Peter** *as he comes out of the compartment, his manner is loud, volatile.*

Dietrich Are you an American? I think you're American.

Peter (*as he passes him, glancing back at* **Frau Messner**) Hardly, no.

Dietrich (*pulling the cigarette out of his own mouth*) This is an American cigarette. (*Glancing down at his sneakers.*) This is American shoe, I think you're American.

He turns away and starts talking excitedly in German to his friends down the carriage, laughing and raising his voice.

Peter *has moved down the corridor towards the dining car.*

Interior: Corridor: Night:

The corridor is lit by wall lamps – not very brightly. It is night outside. The train is travelling very fast. People are still sitting on suitcases. Beer cans are rattling on the floor.

The door of the **Fat Man***'s compartment is slightly ajar, the blinds are drawn down.* **Peter** *on a sudden impulse pushes back the door and steps in.*

The **Fat Man** *is sitting hunched up in his coat. The compartment is totally empty: he has covered the seats with objects, radio-cassette recorder, briefcases, etc., to make it look occupied.*

Peter   I'm sorry . . . I didn't realise . . .

Fat Man (*waving him away. In broken English*)   Full up. This is full up. They're all in the dining car, they will be back in a moment. They're just coming back.

Peter *grins to himself, leaves the compartment and glances at the kids sitting in the corridor. He moves on towards the door. There is a loud sound outside: heavy industrial noise.* **Peter** *stops by the window and stares out, a red glow on his face.*

Cut to outside exterior. Shots of a vast steel works, a huge industrial complex flooded by arc lights.

Cut back to **Peter** *as he is about to move out of the corridor. There is a noise behind him. He stares back along the corridor.* **Frau Messner** *is following him down the corridor, walking sharply towards him.*

Peter (*under his breath*)   Oh my God.

He walks through the next carriage. It has an aisle down the middle and no compartments.

The carriage is full of people lying sprawled over the seats asleep, or just staring ahead or playing cards. A transistor is on somewhere but the sound is terrible, bottles are stacked up on the table. Nobody is talking.

Peter *walks down the carriage. As he is about to leave* **Frau Messner** *appears at the other end of the carriage and moves* *towards him.*

He goes through the doors. There is a connecting bridge section into the next part of the train, joining the carriages together. We can hear the noise of the tracks, it is deafening. The floor moves underfoot.

Peter *crosses over gingerly for the train is moving fast. As soon as he has crossed the doors open behind him.*

Frau Messner *stands on the other side of the bridge section staring across at him.*

Peter (*has to raise his voice above the crushing noise of the train*) Where are you going?

Frau Messner   I am going to have my dinner.

Peter   You can't. You need a ticket.

He waves his red ticket.

Frau Messner (*stares at him and produces the red ticket*) I have one.

Peter   How on earth did you get that?

Frau Messner   The young girl gave it to me.

A close-up of **Peter**, *complete surprise on his face. He turns to go. She stands on the other side of the bridge section and then moves to cross it. It is wobbling around considerably. She looks at him, but* **Peter** *does not move to help her.*

For a moment **Frau Messner** *stands stranded and has to clutch to remain upright.*

Peter *reluctantly stretches out his hand.* **Frau Messner** *crosses. She walks past him into the bar.*

Interior: Bar: Night:

The bar area is small and crammed with people, the air is full of smoke.

It is impossible to get to the bar. There is a queue and people are leaning against it – kids and an old man.

Frau Messner *walks straight through, pushing past people.*
Peter *follows, letting her get out of sight. He glances at the faces of
the kids in the bar. One girl is curled up in the corner, on the floor.
She is wearing heavy eye shadow and looks very drunk. Somebody is
singing a song in the background: a pop song with German and
American words muddled together.*

Peter *moves through the bar into the dining car.*

Interior: Dining car: Night:

*The dining car is covered in mahogany panelling and has low-hung
lamps. Each table has a vase with three carnations in it. There are
only about nine tables and they are all full, except for one small table
half way down the carriage opposite the sideboard.* **Frau Messner**
is standing over this table.

Frau Messner   I will sit here.

She sits with much clatter and moving of chairs.

Peter   Goodbye then.

There are no other tables.

Peter *glances across the whole dining car. There are some students
huddled in groups and some older people eating in silence. Hardly
anybody has any food – there is one scraggy salad on the sideboard.*

*At the far end of the carriage, leaning against the door, stands a
large man staring back down the aisle.*

Peter   You would have thought there would have been
just *one* more free table.

Frau Messner (*looking up, having settled herself*)   You are
still here? Where are you going to sit? I suppose you can
sit here. But maybe you would prefer to stand.

Peter (*smiles*)   Yes, I think, maybe I would.

Frau Messner   Do as you wish. (*She looks with disgust at* *some used plates that have been left on the table.*) Really they should have cleared these things. I will have to call them.

The **Waiter**, *a very small, dapper man, with an ability to walk down the carriage without catching anybody's eye, moves straight down the aisle very fast and disappears.*

Frau Messner   Are you going to stand there the whole meal? If the train stops suddenly you will probably get your neck broken.

The train is travelling very fast.

Peter (*staring down at her*)   I think I'll take the chance.

Frau Messner   We're coming soon to a station, a big city.

The train lurches and **Peter** *topples forward slightly.* **Frau Messner** *watches unmoved.*

After the lurching the train need not be going very fast. We see the lights of the city looming up, moving past the window.

Peter *slides into the seat opposite her, the carnations between them.*

Exterior shot of **Peter** *sitting opposite* **Frau Messner** *in the dining car, beginning very close on the window, and pulling away to show the whole lighted carriage, sliding into the city, with kids hanging their heads out of the window.*

Frau Messner (*matter-of-fact*)   ˙There! I can keep a watch on you. (*She glances round.*) Now, we have no menus as you can see. (*She points at a group of kids over on the other side of the carriage.*) Can you get theirs? – They don't need them any more.

Peter (*not moving*)   Why can't you do it?

Frau Messner (*slight smile*)   Because I think you're nearer. (**Peter** *is not.*) I don't think you can be very hungry.

Peter *stretches for the menus. In doing so he notices the man standing leaning against the door at the far end of the carriage. He is staring down the aisle. The man is watching everything that is going on with a distant smile on his face.*

Peter (*dropping the menus in front of her*) There you are, and that is absolutely all I'm doing.

Frau Messner (*glances at a menu for a second and then snaps it shut*) There's nothing I can eat here, I don't think – they will have to prepare me something else.

Peter lights up a cigarette and looks at her through the carnations.

She moves the flowers.

Frau Messner Tell me what is your name? Do you have one?

Peter Yes.

He smokes and looks at her.

Frau Messner (*watching his eyes move*) My name is Frau Messner. (*Very slowly.*) Can you say that? Mess-ner.

Peter No I don't think I can.

Frau Messner I think you ought to try. English children can never speak any languages.

*The **Waiter** rushes straight past them not looking to right or left.*

Frau Messner (*sharply*) Ich möchte . . .

*The **Waiter** walks straight past.*

Frau Messner He is not attending. (*She lowers her voice and leans towards **Peter**.*) Look – you can see that girl's bosoms. You can see them quite clearly. (*She is looking at a girl who is wearing a tight-fitting T-shirt.*) I don't think all these people are meant to be here. They can't all have tickets to eat here! (*Her voice getting really loud.*) They have to have a ticket like this – a red *ticket*.

Peter Do you have to talk so loudly? – everybody can hear you. You really should have travelled first class, shouldn't you?

Frau Messner First class. How I could possibly afford it? It's so expensive!

Peter *looks down at the discreet but rich jewellery on her fingers and round her neck.*

Frau Messner *moves her head suddenly, looking round, her restlessness beginning to grow.*

Frau Messner   They have tried to make it look like an old carriage. You see? (*She indicates panelling.*) Before the war these dining carriages were so beautiful. They had fresh salmon here you know, lying here, and sometimes sturgeon. They have tried to make the carriages look old but none of it is real. It's all false. See this table? It's plastic.

She suddenly stabs at the panelling with her fork, and rubs the fork up and down the table.

You see! You can't scratch it. I can't scratch it at all. It's all false.

The fork makes a loud screeching noise on the table.

Peter (*looking away, embarrassed*)   Please, can we sit here with no trouble! Please.

The **Waiter** *passes down the aisle.*

Frau Messner (*loudly to him*)   Warum haben Sie uns nicht bedient?

He walks straight past her. Others are trying to get his attention, but he ignores all of them.

Did you see that? He didn't even stop.

Peter   No.

Frau Messner (*extremely restless*)   Next time he passes we will *stop him*. It is a disgrace this is still here. (*Indicating the dirty plates.*) Why are you pulling all the flowers to pieces?

Peter   Only one of them – (*He looks at her through the flowers which he has moved back.*) It makes me less tense.

Frau Messner (*quiet*)   Pick it up.

Peter *puts it in his buttonhole.*

Frau Messner   You are well dressed for a young man nowadays. (*She feels his jacket.*) This would be expensive. (*She looks straight at him.*) Are yo doing something important?

Peter   Could be.

Frau Messner   Where are you going?

She is looking directly at him, impassive.

Peter (*looks at her*)   I'm going to a bookfair in Linz, hundreds of shiny new books. They sell books like cars now.

Frau Messner (*still staring at him*)   And it is important?

Peter *smiles slightly, watching her warily.*

Cut to the lights of the city, growing in intensity and size.

Frau Messner (*looking straight at him*)   Is it important?

Peter (*a slight smile*)   Very, as it happens. I've got to meet two famous authors that we handle. Big European celebrities . . . medium-sized celebrities, 10.30 tomorow morning. It's the first time I've represented my firm abroad. (*Slight smile to himself.*) Naturally if I handle things well . . . (*Suddenly he looks up.*) You're *not* listening to me. You ask me questions and then you don't even bother to listen.

Frau Messner   I heard enough. (*She is looking about, extremely agitated.*) I have to find the waiter. I can't wait any longer!

The **Waiter** *approaches with food, and walks straight past them as* **Frau Messner** *calls out to him.*

Frau Messner   He didn't even look at me. Stop him.

The **Waiter** *gives the food to a group of students. The train is begining to slow down and draw into a station.*

Frau Messner (*leaning forward*)   Were those people here before or after us? I think they were here after. I am quite sure they haven't got the tickets. We should ask them.

They aren't allowed to eat if they haven't. Will you ask them if they have dinner tickets? Go on.

Peter   Don't be ridiculous...

Frau Messner *immediately leans over and asks them: half-audible.*

Frau Messner   They say they have. But they must be lying.

Peter (*staring at the man who is watching the carriage. He has not moved at all*)   He's watching you – you'll get us both thrown out any moment. I wonder who he is.

Frau Messner (*matter-of-factly*)   A policeman – secret policeman.

Peter   He's hardly very secret. He can't be a policeman. (**Peter** *stares fascinated. The man has one hand in his pocket.*) Maybe he's the chef...

Frau Messner (*wrestling in her seat, unable to sit any more*)   I can't bear this any longer. We will show them. There's a salad over there. (*She indicates the miserable salad.*) You could reach it if you tried. (*She stares at him.*) Why don't you try? Go on.

Peter   No.

Shot of the man, watching.

Frau Messner (*staring at him*)   You can reach it from your seat easily.

Peter   You really can't wait for anything can you? It's like a disease. I have never ever seen somebody quite so unable to wait their turn. It's almost as if the effort would kill you.

Frau Messner (*stares at him for a moment. Quietly*)   If you are going to be rude to me you can leave my table. (*Her tone changes, still quiet.*) I *cannot* wait. Ever. They have to give you service, that is what they are paid to do.

The **Waiter** *moves down the aisle, still not looking at any of his* *customers, his dapper figure moving fast.*

Frau Messner   Here he comes now. We will catch him.

As he passes her **Frau Messner** *catches the* **Waiter** *by the arm. The drink he is carrying spills. She holds him by the arm while remaining seated in her chair.*

Frau Messner   Wir haben zu lange gewartet.

The **Waiter** *whose arm is being held, is very quiet.*

Waiter   Bitte . . .

Everybody is watching. The conversation fades until the carriage is completely silent. The train has stopped.

Peter   Please, could you not . . .

He is looking at the tablecloth in embarrassment.

Frau Messner *(very sharply)*   Ich werde mich beschweren. *(To* **Peter.***)* I am going to report him. Give me a pencil please.

She is still holding on to the **Waiter.** **Peter** *is watching in amazement.*

Frau Messner *(really sharply)*   Come on, have you got a pencil? Will you give it to me?

Peter *(quietly)*   I haven't got a pencil and I won't give it to you.

Frau Messner   I am holding him here until I have taken his name.

She looks in her own bag with one hand. The **Waiter** *hands her a pencil sharply. The large man at the end of the aisle has not moved at all and is watching. The* **Waiter** *stands frozen.*

Frau Messner   Wie heissen Sie?

Waiter   Rutz.

Frau Messner *(writes it down)*   Rutz.

The **Waiter** *immediately moves away.* **Frau Messner** *picks up* *the dirty plates and holds them out across the gangway.*

Frau Messner (*calling after him*)   Warum haben Sie diese
sachen nicht weggenommen?

*The **Waiter** ignores her and disappears, leaving her still holding the
dirty dishes.*

Frau Messner *simply lets go of the dishes and they shatter in the
gangway, pieces of crockery going everywhere.*

Frau Messner   And now I will go.

*She gets up and walks out of the dining car. The dining car is very
silent.*

Peter *crouches down to begin picking up pieces of crockery: everybody
is staring at him. He looks embarrassed. He puts part of the broken
plate on his chair and leaves the dining car.*

Interior: Corridor: Night:

Frau Messner *is standing by the door of the carriage, as if
expecting him to follow her. As soon as he appears she starts talking
loudly.*

Frau Messner (*firmly*)   You have to make these people
understand you. See that when they do wrong, they will be
punished, and then they will never forget it. You just have
to do it.

Peter   It was a totally ridiculous thing to do and now I
can't get any supper. (*He glances back to the dining car.*) I am
quite incredibly hungry.

Frau Messner *is by the door trying to open it.*

Peter   Where are you going?

Frau Messner   The train is stopping here. They have
left the handle off this door – it won't open! There should
be a handle.

Peter   You can't even open the doors. Haven't you ever

learnt how to do this? You've probably always had doors opened for you!

He moves to the door and slides down the window.

Frau Messner   It stops here half an hour. I will find something to eat in the station. (*She opens the door and moves to climb out.*) I can show you where you can eat. Can you hold this?

Peter (*staring at* **Frau Messner**. *Slight smile*)   No, thanks.

Frau Messner   Are you hungry or not? Do as you wish.

She climbs out of the train. Close-up of **Peter** *looking famished. He stares back towards the dining car. The* **Waiter** *is still standing outside the dining car looking at him with extreme hostility.*

Exterior: Platform: Frankfurt: Night:

Cut to outside the train. **Frau Messner** *is walking down the outside of the train.* **Peter** *is behind her, walking very slowly.*

Peter   How do you know the train stops here half an hour?

Frau Messner   You should have a piece of paper. It tells you all the times.

Peter (*walking several paces behind her*)   Are you completely sure? You're positive it's half an hour?

Frau Messner   At least half an hour.

Peter (*looking to check on his ticket*)   We've got to keep in sight of the train.

He glances back. One or two people have got off the train and are standing on the platform having a smoke.

Frau Messner (*quietly*)   I am not interested if you come or not.

Receding shot of people on the platform.

The locomotive towers above **Peter**. *He stares up at the cab. A small boy stares back through the windscreen of the cab: a hard, very white face. He is the only person in the cab.*

Peter   I hope he hasn't been driving us.

They walk past a chauffeur standing with a pile of suitcases next to him. A fur coat is lying on top of the suitcases.

Frau Messner (*waves at it*)   The money people have now . . .

They walk across the huge concourse of Frankfurt station.

There are powerful lights shining down. There is a large puddle of water on the concourse, although it is a totally covered area.

Frau Messner *is walking purposefully in front of him and skirts the edge of the puddle.*

Frau Messner   The roof leaks of course.

Peter *stares around him at the large bright advertisements lit up along the wall. A receding shot of the front of the engine.*

Peter *is staring around him. There are no signs telling him which station it is.*

Peter   Which city are we in anyway?

Frau Messner *is walking across the station. He follows, a short way behind her, staring at her back, at her determined walk.*

Exterior: Station concourse: Night:

Along the edge of the walls of the huge concourse are some kids, lying in sleeping bags. Some are leaning against the wall smoking and watching them as they pass.

Frau Messner (*glancing over to them*)   They are probably all from good families.

Peter *stares at their pale faces. They stare right back at him: a glazed look.*

Peter   It's funny how people are attracted to stations.

The kids are leaning up against huge lighted advertisements and some posters for local elections.

Peter (*as he moves past them*)   Some people live for years in places like this, sleeping out here. Maybe they're going to try to jump a train.

The faces stare back at him, some of them are very young, staring out of the tops of sleeping bags.

A blond-haired boy is leaning against the wall with a guitar, half strumming it, singing an old sixties standard, singing a few English words, humming the rest.

The kids are a mixture of long-haired boys and much younger, more aggressive-looking kids. Two young girls with very short haircuts are leaning against a wall.

We see these kids as **Frau Messner** *walks purposefully across the great hall of the station. We track with* **Peter**, *just a pace behind her.*

Peter (*glancing up at the enormous clock*)   I'm taking regular time checks.

Frau Messner *is striding ahead.*

Peter   Where on earth are you going?

Frau Messner (*not waiting for him*)   I know where we can eat.

Peter   We've already been three minutes.

Exterior: Side entrance: Night:

We cut to them moving through the underground section of Frankfurt station. We see its gleaming pristine white walls as they move.

Peter (*calls after her*)   Do you know which city we're in? (*She continues walking.*) Which bloody city is this?

He glances round: the place is totally blank. He sees two fire buckets hanging on the wall, approaches one of them and tips it up. **Frau Messner** *is not waiting, she continues walking sharply through the gleaming white passages.*

Peter *stares at the bottom of the fire bucket, sees 'Frankfurt' printed on the bottom.*

Peter   We're in Frankfurt. (*He calls after her.*) This is Frankfurt.

For a second he glances opposite him to where gleaming expensive goods, cameras and watches, are staring back out of a lighted shop window, and a photostat machine, lit by a blue light, revolves on a pedestal like a piano.

Peter (*turns. A sharp smile*)   Where've you gone?

He sees **Frau Messner** *standing by a chocolate machine and moves up to her.*

Peter (*smiles*)   You've had five minutes.

Frau Messner   Have you got some money? We can get some chocolate.

Peter (*slight smile*)   No – I haven't any.

Frau Messner *drops some money into it and pulls surprisingly forcefully. The handle with the chocolate inside gets stuck half-way.*

Frau Messner   Of course it's stuck!

She starts digging at it with a key from her bag to try to dislodge it.

Can you hold this machine please?

Peter (*ironic smile*)   This is the food you promised, is it!

He holds the machine and she tries to prise it open. She manages to dislodge very little chocolate.

Frau Messner (*she eats it and hands him a piece*)   Come on, we have time.

Peter   Where on earth are you leading me?

Exterior: Outside station: Night:

They come out of the underground area, the station looms in back of shot.

Peter   Where are you going?

She moves off sharply. He watches her go for a second, then follows her, with a slight smile. A wide shot of them crossing in front of neon signs in German.

Exterior: Streets: Night:

They move down an older street. A tram rattles past them. **Frau Messner** *walks across the tram lines as* **Peter** *moves sharply up to her.*

Peter   Come on! We've already walked too far from the station.

Exterior: Opera house: Night:

We cut to them in a high shot approaching the glass doors of the Opera.

Interior: Opera house: Night:

We cut inside the plush and dramatic foyer of the new Opera building. A monumental wall and an unmistakably typical European arts complex, although from the first two shots of just foyers and cascades of metal gold clouds we could be in an airport.

Peter   What on earth are we doing here?

Frau Messner   There is no time to eat in a proper restaurant.

We move across the foyer to where the buffet food has been cleared away.

The man behind the buffet immediately says, in German, that they have finished, that it is after the second interval, but **Frau Messner** *answers in sharp German, asking to be given some food and a drink.*

She turns to **Peter**.

Frau Messner   They are trying not to give us food.

Peter (*staring out across the foyer*)   Extraordinary place to come. God, I'm so hungry.

Frau Messner   You can have a drink too. I will buy you one.

Peter   No thank you. Just some food. You're certain we have time? There can only be quarter of an hour.

Two tiny pieces of quiche lorraine are produced on large white china plates.

As this is happening **Peter** *looks across the foyer. It is deserted except for a solitary young businessman looking very similar to* **Kellner** *in his dress and demeanour, who is standing leaning against the closed bar, looking at a briefcase of papers.*

Peter (*glances across*)   He looks like that businessman in our compartment. They seem to come out at this time of night. (*He smiles.*) Crawl out into the light.

By the bar there is an incongruous tank of tropical fish underneath a poster for the opera. **Peter** *is staring into the tank with the glossy shiny fish swimming around. He smiles and turns to see* **Frau Messner** *holding two plates with the tiny portions of food on them.*

Frau Messner   Here.

She moves across the foyer, followed by **Peter**.

Peter (*crossing the foyer, looking about him*)   Euro-splendour! (*A slight smile.*) Why's it so enormous?

As they move towards the leather chairs underneath the huge plate-glass windows, two security guards begin to gesticulate and shout at them in

German. **Frau Messner** *answers them back and then turns sharply.*

Frau Messner (*explaining*)   You are not allowed to sit there unless you have tickets for the opera! And we have not. They are idiots. We will sit here then.

She sits underneath the plate-glass windows. The night lights of Frankfurt can be seen outside.

There is a close-circuit television near the stairs, mounted on the wall, showing the opera that is playing at the moment: the last act of Der Rosenkavalier *is flickering in black and white.*

A large vase of artificial flowers sprouts out near the staircase.

Peter *sits gingerly opposite her.*

Peter   I'm going to keep a close check on time. (*He takes out his watch and puts it right next to him.*) I don't think this is going to work! We can't possibly have time – we walked a long way from the station.

Frau Messner   There is time. (*Nibbling her food.*) There is no need to worry.

Peter   You better be right. (*Slight smile.*) It's important to me – not that you're the slightest bit interested. You realise it's nearly midnight.

Shot of the security guards across the foyer locking some doors and standing waiting with a large bunch of keys.

Peter (*smiles*)   It is a strange feeling being away from the train, one feels one shouldn't be. (*Laconic smile.*) Like being out of school, it's forbidden and we'll be spotted any moment. (*He stretches out his hand.*) At least the flowers on the train were real. (*He touches them.*) These are wax.

He glances at the opera on the television monitor. Music from the opera is audible.

He suddenly looks at **Frau Messner**, *sitting on the chair underneath the huge windows eating her food, sitting very still. She* *looks up and gives him a sharp stare.*

Peter   Why are you so calm suddenly?

Frau Messner   It's my birthday you know, tomorrow.

Peter   Is it?

Frau Messner   I still remember my birthday, the date,
but not the number. (*She looks at him.*) I am not very well, I
may be quite badly ill.

Peter   You look incredibly well to me.

Frau Messner   I hope my flat will be clean when I get
there – I cannot come back to a dirty flat.

Distant music starts very quietly drifting towards them.

Peter   Naturally.

Frau Messner   During the war we lived in a much
larger house of course, with its own grounds.

Peter   During the war ... if you're like this now, what
were you like then! You were probably a leading light of
the *Party*!

Frau Messner   (*stares straight at him, focusing her eyes on
him*)   We lost all our servants of course. They left us!
Except for one, he was very fat. His face was covered all in
boils. He was useless. There was dirt everywhere! Even all
over my bed. I don't know how we managed. We also had
this nice young girl – but she disappeared one day. I don't
know if she was Jewish, she may have been Jewish. (*She
looks at him to see his reaction.*) Pehaps that's where she went.
We didn't see her again.

Peter   You don't even know ...

Frau Messner   He had boils all over his face – the other
man! I haven't thought about him for years, till tonight.
My brothers were all in the Party, I think, most of them –
I took no part. I didn't care for it really. In the shops they

started to say 'Heil Hitler' instead of 'Grüss Gott' even when you just went in for a drink of coffee. Of course you don't know what it means, it is a very famous Austrian saying, 'When they came to Wien, the Germans, the Anschluss . . .'

Peter *listens quietly.*

Frau Messner   When they came, everyone threw little dried mountain flowers in bundles, tied up with bows. They were all over the street the next morning as far as you could look. It was like a lake it was so deep. They covered your feet. I have still got some somewhere I think, put away. (*Pause.*) I didn't enjoy that time though.

Peter (*watching fascinated. Smiles*)   Didn't you.

Frau Messner   It is peculiar how one talks to strangers when one is on a train.

Peter   But we're not on a train!

Frau Messner (*soothingly*)   You will be again in a minute, you don't have to worry. I have never missed a train. (*She sips her drink.*) I was young you see then, quite young. I was used to all the dances and parties. (*She nibbles her small piece of food.*) And suddenly there were not so many parties. We still had some of course. The men all in uniform, they smelt more of smoke. We still had the Viennese complexion, all of us, the girls, it was very famous, a peach complexion, not brown like everybody is today – we kept it all through the war. I was alone of course for a lot of the time in the war. So I read. I read a lot of long books. In the afternoons. It was very quiet. By myself.

Music pouring out from the auditorium.

Peter   Why are you telling me this now?

Frau Messner (*looking straight at him*)   Because it interests me to see you listen. To watch you.

Pause. **Peter** *looks back at her.*

Peter   So, what have you found out about me then?

Frau Messner (*shrewd look*)   Are you . . . from Oxford or Cambridge?

Peter (*pauses, sharp smile*)   Both.

Frau Messner (*looking at the food*)   Do you want some more? (*Indicating tiny pieces of food they have been eating.*) I think I must have some more now, bitte.

Peter (*leaning forward to restrain her*)   No. You really are trying to make me miss the train. Aren't you?

Frau Messner   Why should I do that?

Peter   Because it amuses you. Some sort of revenge.

Frau Messner   What would I want revenge for?

Peter   For not getting your own way. Everything else may wait for you – but a trans-continental express is not going to.

Frau Messner   There is plenty of time.

Peter (*loud*)   It may not matter to you if you miss the train but it matters like hell to me. I have an important appointment.

Frau Messner   Of course it's important.

She finishes sorting out her change and stands up. The singing from Der Rosenkavalier *is audible.*

But there is plenty of time. I think I will just go in there to listen to the last act. They are reaching the trio – I remember Lotte Lehmann, I won't be a moment.

Frau Messner *moves off across the foyer.*

Peter (*looks at his watch*)   Christ, I think my watch has stopped! What's the time?

He turns and rushes down the stairs. A receding shot of **Frau Messner** *climbing the stairs and opening the door into the Circle as the ushers converge on her.*

Interior: Staircase: Night:

As the music soars through the trio **Peter** *plunges down the staircase and finds that he has come out in a different part of the ground floor.*

He runs along the plate-glass windows and tries a door which is locked.

Peter Locked the audience in! (*Muttering.*) How do you get out of this bloody place! (*Muttering, half-audible.*) Why don't they tell you how to get out?

He runs back along the glass wall, past some more of the building's strange décor.

For a brief second he is trapped, unable to find his way out.

A wide shot of him moving along the great glass wall, and knocking over an ornamental ashtray, before he gets out into the street.

He smiles to himself, regaining his composure and begins to run, not a panicky run, but a fast, determined run through the night streets.

Exterior: Railway station: Night:

A shot of **Peter** *running across the tram lines with a tram rattling down them just behind him, past the giant poster, and plunging down the steps that lead to the whole underground area, where late-night music is still playing.*

He runs past the ageing hippy playing his guitar, who is still sitting against the wall, watching from the shadows, and across the concourse of the station, having to step over some kids lying on the floor by the side-entrance. A girl is lying flat on her back, her arms spread out wide, staring upwards at the roof. A whistle is blowing loudly.

Exterior: Railway station: Platform:

Peter *arrives at the platform. The train has gone. He stands still in the middle of the concourse for a moment.*

The sound of footsteps are ringing out – he turns and stares in the direction they are coming from.

Frau Messner *appears, walking briskly into view. Her footsteps are echoing out in the late-night atmosphere of the station. A look of controlled fury in* **Peter**'s *eyes as he waits for her to get within range.*

Peter (*when she reaches him, staring straight at her. Controlled fury breaking into rage*)   I have missed the train. The train has gone.

She stands some distance away from him.

It – has – gone. You have got us stuck in this bloody city. You idiot, what the hell do you think you were doing?

Frau Messner *just stares at him.*

Peter   Do you realise you have made me miss the train?

Frau Messner (*very still and calm*)   It shouldn't have gone yet.

Peter (*controlled fury*)   What do you mean it shouldn't – it has and I am stuck in this godforsaken place – with you.

They stand isolated in the centre of the platform watched by three kids.

You did this deliberately didn't you? (*He looks straight at her.*) You really are an evil old woman, do you know that.

A pause.

Frau Messner *faces him.*

A big close-up: her face impassive, just looking at him.

Peter   Did you hear what I said?

Frau Messner (*icily*)   I heard you.

Peter (*shouting*)   Well what are you going to do about it then?

Frau Messner (*staring back at him*)   There are people watching.

Peter   I don't care who's watching. (*He shouts straight at her, more dangerous.*) You have made me miss the train.

A high shot of them standing together in the concourse, with the two thirteen-year-old girls with very short hair we saw earlier, staring at them from against the wall with blank expressions.

Peter   So what am I going to do then?

Frau Messner   You could take an aeroplane.

Peter (*shouts*)   At this time of *night* – to Linz?

Frau Messner   The train *should not* have gone yet.

Peter   I told you it . . .

He is cut off by a whistle blowing.

He turns and looks back across the station. Through a gap between some advertising hoardings he catches a glimpse of a train.

A look of total surprise on **Peter***'s face.*

Frau Messner (*a slight smile*)   The train has not gone – it has moved to another platform.

He runs very fast across the station – an athletic run. We keep close to him, tracking very fast.

For an instant he falls on his stomach on the edge of the puddle – we hear the sound of a jacket ripping – but he pulls himself up instantly, and runs along the side of the train. He opens the door and climbs in.

Frau Messner *is yards and yards behind him, refusing to run.*

The whistle blows.

We hear the noise of the engine.

She does not quicken her walk.

Interior: Train compartment: Night

Peter *moves up to his compartment. His suit is torn.*

The compartment is full of strange kids he has not seen before, staring back at him. The atmosphere is smoky. There are beer cans all over the floor.

Peter   The people who were in here before. Where are they?

A shot of the kids' faces, hostile and sullen.

Dietrich   Have you had your supper?

Peter   There was a bag up here. Do you know where it is? A brown bag. What has happened to it?

Suddenly, from the shadows, **Dietrich** *stretches out a hand.*

Dietrich   And you think they've taken it! Don't panic.

He throws **Peter***'s bag at him and gives him a strange look.*

They are in the sleeping car. It's your bedtime now. That way – go on. You'll find her there. Viel Glück!

Interior: Train compartment: Night:

Cut to the steward swinging the seats over in the compartment and turning them into beds.

Frau Messner *is staring around her – and at* **Peter***. They are all standing in the corridor, lined up against the wall, except for* **Lorraine** *who is absent.*

The **Small Man** *is at the end of the row. His face is impassive, his eyes half-closed.*

The kids suddenly appear at the other end of the corridor, singing and shouting. **Dietrich** *has drunk a lot. His manner is dangerously volatile. In a sudden flurry of action during* **Preston***'s following speech, a fight breaks out in the corridor. At first it is just rowdy play, with much abuse being shouted.*

Preston   Bedtime now! Not that we'll get much sleep, mind you, I can sleep through almost everything even babies crying and burglar alarms; but not the police sirens.

(*He glances at the raucous kids.*) That's what they need now . . .

Frau Messner (*glancing at* **Peter** *and then away again*) We can't all sleep in there can we? We won't fit.

Kellner We will have to. We will fit.

Frau Messner (*glancing at* **Peter**) I think I would prefer to stand here all night.

Preston It's all right once you're in bed. They leave you a sheet sleeping bag you see, and you make up your own bed.

Frau Messner (*stops the steward loudly in English, so* **Peter** *can hear*) Can you just finish it? Make my bed for me.

The steward ignores her and slides back the door of the **Fat Man**'*s compartment. The* **Fat Man** *is surrounded by empty seats.*

Fat Man They're all in the dining car! They will be coming back soon!

Preston You make your own bed you see.

He guides her into the compartment followed by the **Small Man**.

If you don't mind me saying so, you do speak very good English.

Frau Messner I know I do. I always have done, since I was a small girl.

Suddenly the fight erupts into something much more savage. **Dietrich** *takes on one of the other kids. There is a violent fight with a broken bottle and* **Dietrich** *gets his face slashed, badly cut. It is brief and sudden.*

Peter *stares at the retreating figures of the kids, the sudden burst of manic energy has now gone and the corridor is quiet again.*

We cut to **Kellner** *staring out of the window.* **Peter** *is standing next to him.*

Kellner (*deeply agitated*) The train is going so slow. It is nearly two hours late now. (*He smiles at* **Peter**.) I have to be back in my office by seven o'clock in the morning. I should be on a plane, but we have a strike. I don't like being late. I don't know what is wrong with this train.

The train makes creaking noises.

Peter It's falling to pieces.

Kellner (*his nose up to the window, which is open to the outside blackness*) We are by a big river. There are villas down there. Huge new houses. Very, very rich people. All on top of each other, as far as you can see.

Peter (*his face to the black glass*) Out there?

Kellner (*his manner suddenly very speedy*) I haven't slept for four days, and four nights!

Peter You haven't?

Peter *turns.* **Frau Messner** *is standing right behind him in the doorway of the compartment.*

Kellner No. Been too busy, (*He smiles.*) making business. And tomorrow night I am meant to go to the opera – it's my one pleasure. We have an enormous new opera house. Yes, the stage is the size of an oil tanker. (*His hand is drumming on the window sill.*) It is going too slowly, we will never get there, what is wrong? I don't know why it is moving like this.

Kellner *retreats to his bunk.*

Lorraine *appears in the corridor.*

Peter There you are!

Lorraine (*looking at his muddy suit*) What happened to you at supper?

Peter I've been looking for you!

Lorraine I can't find anywhere here, to do my toilet. They're all occupied.

Peter Can't you? (*He glances over his shoulder at* **Frau Messner**.) Come with me – I'll show you where.

Peter takes Lorraine's hand and pulls her along the corridor, past the band of kids grouped together drinking, their aggressive drunken faces looking at them as they pass. There are cans all over the floor.

Peter (*quite aggressive*) You're going to the Gents!

He pulls open the door of the Gents, which is not locked.

Dietrich *looks up, his mouth and chin are covered in blood. He is spitting out blood into the basin.*

Dietrich Why don't you come in?

They both look startled as he bends over the basin, lifting cold water up to his cut mouth and splashing it on, seemingly oblivious to the pain.

He indicates the blood and water in the basin.

Dietrich Nice colour – don't you think? (*He smiles.*) Nice to swim in there.

He reaches out to his jacket which is on the lavatory seat and puts it on.

Did I show you my photos?

Dietrich *gives them a sharp, intelligent, piercing look, and drops the photographs one by one, into the basin, so that they are floating on the water.*

How do you say – family snaps. (*He grins.*) And photos of me doing things that aren't allowed. Verboten!

He tosses the others down the lavatory, grinning, and saying something in German.

He moves past them. He gives them a charming lewd smile.

If you go to the first class, the toilets are much bigger, much more room.

Peter Come on – go in there.

Lorraine (*surprised by his aggression*) Thank you. Aren't you going to shut the door?

Peter No. We're leaving it open. I'll stand guard. I want to talk to you.

Lorraine *washes the blood out of the basin. She lifts the photographs out of the basin and drops them on the floor.*

Peter Why the hell did you give her your dinner ticket?

Lorraine Because she wanted it.

Peter *watches* **Lorraine** *through the door.*

Lorraine *rolls up her sleeve. She is very brown, with long brown legs.*

Peter Is this a conspiracy of yours? You realise I was nearly left stranded in that station because of you?

Lorraine You're still here aren't you?

Peter For the moment.

Frau Messner *is standing in the corridor.*

Peter *can see her.*

Lorraine She doesn't mean you any harm you know.

Peter Oh really! (*A slight smile.*) I don't feel safe, I really don't.

He looks down the corridor.

Frau Messner *is standing quite close in the corridor, glancing towards him and then away.*

Peter (*a slight grin*) God, she's still watching me.

Lorraine (*looking straight at him*) You don't get much privacy on trains.

Peter No. (*Giving her a gentle tug.*) Come on this way.

Lorraine Where are we going?

Peter Where she's not watching.

He tugs her gently down the corridors of the train. They have to pick

*their way over the sleeping kids: eyes shut, young faces lying crammed
up together in the corridor.*

Interior: Train: Dining car: Night:

Peter *and* **Lorraine** *approach the dining car door.* **Peter** *opens
the door. From their point of view we see the whole dining car piled
up with sleeping kids, on tables and on chairs, or hunched up, sitting
on tables and leaning against windows. Most of them are asleep,
though occasionally they murmur or turn over. One very young girl is
sitting propped up against the window.*

Lorraine (*on seeing the crowded carriage*)   God!

Peter   Well we're sort of alone.

*With a charming smile. He looks at the kids asleep with their
belongings all around him. They sit at a table, squeezing in among
the sleeping kids.*

When I was young all I ever wanted to do was live on
trains – literally. Have my own compartment and eat and
sleep, criss-cross Europe and fall in love and write about
what I saw outside the window. And never get off when it
stopped, and become famous, of course.

While **Lorraine** *says the following lines she moves the head of the
sleeping girl on the table slightly so that there's more room.*

Lorraine   Do you really want success? (**Peter** *smiles.*) Well
maybe this is the beginning for you tonight.

Peter   Of course, in a way I want success. I'm not
obsessed about it, I don't lust after it in corners, but I'd
quite like it. I never believe anybody that says otherwise,
especially now. It's a very competitive time.

A shot of the sleeping kids.

A shot of **Lorraine** *with the night lights outside the window
passing across her face. Her long brown arms stretched out on the
table.*

Lorraine (*sharp*)   I wish you luck. I hope you manage it.

Peter *stares at her, uncertain what she means.*

As she sits by the window her body clearly visible, he moves nearer to her.

Raucous singing is still audible from down the train.

Peter   Sometimes one meets people on trains – talks to them for hours, and then they're gone and you've never even found out their names.

Lorraine   You haven't asked me. (*Straight at him.*) My name's Lorraine.

Peter (*staring at her*)   Why are you so brown? How did you manage it?

Lorraine (*looking down at her arms*)   It's coming off fast – ever since I arrived over here. (*She looks up at him. A sharp, intelligent look.*) I hated England. It gave me the creeps. (*Looks at him.*) To be crude. And Europe gives me the creeps too.

Peter   That's ridiculous. You've only just arrived.

Lorraine   That's right. It's extraordinary but I already want to go home. I can't wait to get back. I will be counting the days, I can feel it now. (*A slight smile.*) Notching them up on the hotel wall. We Americans are meant to find it so amazing over here – aren't we? (*Straight at him.*) But I don't. (*Staring at him, speaking with surprising force.*) The atmosphere here is so ugly.

Peter (*a slight smile at her*)   And that includes the people you've met does it?

Lorraine (*staring straight at him*)   Very definitely.

Peter (*startled*)   All of them?

Lorraine (*still looking at him*)   Yes, most of them. I just really don't like it. I hate it.

We feel the real darkness of her mood as the lights play across her face. **Peter** *stares at her, he too senses the darkness of her mood but* *is unable to say anything. She looks straight at him.*

Lorraine   I'd better go.

She leaves the dining car.

Interior: Train compartment: Night:

Cut to inside the compartment with all of them lying in their bunks, except for **Peter**, *who slides back the door and enters.*

Lorraine *is not there. He stands by the door. As he does so the shouting and singing wafts in from the passage. The train is creaking.*

Peter   Which is my bunk?

Frau Messner (*sharp*)   Here.

Peter (*quiet*)   Opposite you.

His is the second bunk up, level with **Frau Messner**'*s.*

Peter *taking his shirt off, moving to his bunk.*

Peter   I see you've had your bunk made for you!

Frau Messner   We must stop that noise, that terrible noise.

The noise from the passage is getting increasingly loud.

Preston (*who is in the bottom bunk*)   We can have some music.

Preston *moves to the panel above the door.*

Peter   There's a radio here?

Preston   Yes. (*Flicking the wall switch. 'Puppet On a String' bounces out.*) This won the Eurovision song contest – they always play their old winners here on this.

Peter *switches out the light and climbs into bed. He is bare-chested, still wearing mud-spattered trousers. He lies on top of the sheets, his face very close to* **Frau Messner**'*s.*

The music creaks into Beethoven's Sixth Symphony.

The only light is the blue night-light in the ceiling which is flickering badly.

Preston   We go past all the heavy industry in Germany soon. Thousands of acres of it – it makes a noise too.

Frau Messner   It is so ugly. It's no wonder some young people try to blow it up – anarchists.

Peter (*looking across to her face, which is very close*)   You're not going to talk all night – are you? Please just try to make an effort and be quiet for a bit can you?

Frau Messner (*a moment's pause. She stares back at him impassively*)   I will not be able to sleep with that light flickering like that.

Peter   Of course you can.

Frau Messner   Will you just take it out for me? Reach up and take it out.

Peter (*angry, hesitates for a second, then getting out of bed and reaching up to the blue light*)   This is probably dangerous, it may stop the whole train.

He reaches for the light. It is hot. He takes it out and puts the bulb on the end of his bed.

The compartment goes into total darkness except for a little light from the window.

Peter *glances out into the corridor. At the far end he can see* **Lorraine** *standing by herself, staring out of the window. A solitary image. He watches her for a second.*

Peter (*calls out*)   See you in the morning.

Lorraine *does not react.*

Peter *moves back into the compartment.*

For a moment we stay on **Lorraine.** *She is leaning her head against the window, staring out.*

Peter *lies down again.*

Frau Messner *is still staring at him – a hard stare.*

Preston (*flicking off the music and lying back*) My name is Preston. I live in Maidstone, and soon I'll be where no one can find me. Goodnight!

For a moment outside the window there is a noise of heavy industry. The sound of a whole plant working. Lights shine through the blinds, terribly bright and then are gone.

Outside in the corridor we hear **Dietrich** *singing an American song, half in German and half in English, really raucous and out of tune.*

Peter's *eyes half close. He opens them.* **Frau Messner** *is still staring at him.*

He closes his eyes.

A close-up of **Frau Messner**'s *eyes as kids shout in the passage.*

Dissolve on **Peter**'s *face. The soundtrack changes. He half opens his eyes.* **Frau Messner** *is still staring her impassive stare.*

Dissolve on **Peter**'s *face. He opens his eyes.*

Her bunk is empty. She is standing in the doorway, her back to the compartment. **Peter** *closes his eyes.*

Montage of vivid night-shots: of cars moving in the night, as seen from the train, and the industrial landscape, floodlit and vast.

The screen goes black for a split second and then a German voice shouts something inaudible and a torch flashes straight into **Peter**'s *eyes.*

First Guard Passport. Passport.

Two torches shine in his face. The noise of the train is deafeningly loud for a moment as he wakes up.

Peter's *point of view as two German border* **Guards** *stare down.*

First Guard Passport.

Peter *sleepily reaches for his passport. The* **Guards** *are looking down at him. They glance at the passport and look back at him. The*

First Guard's *torch wanders down his mud-spattered trousers.*

First Guard   Where did you get on the train please?

Peter   Ostend.

First Guard   Your ticket.

Peter *searches his mud-covered jacket. His eyes clogged with sleep. The torches shine on him, there is no other light.*

Peter   It must have fallen out when I fell over, but it has been clipped about ten times already. I had to run for the train.

First Guard (*shining the torch down his body*)   Could you come out in the passage please.

Peter   What now?

Peter *puts his jacket round his bare chest and goes out into the passage.*

There is no light in the passage, only the light from the torches. It is still night outside.

First Guard   Are you English?

Peter (*more awake now*)   You've seen my passport.

First Guard   And where is your ticket?

Peter   I hope I won't have to say everything four times. I dropped it.

First Guard   Why have you got mud all over your clothes?

Peter (*smiles*)   That's hardly an offence, is it?

First Guard   I asked you a question sir.

Peter (*surprised*)   Sir? (*He tries again, speaking slowly.*) I fell over – running for a train in Frankfurt.

First Guard (*sharp*)   I thought you said you got on this train at Ostend?

Peter   I did. Yes. But I was coaxed off it, against my

better judgement by another passenger, in Frankfurt.

Peter *stares back at the two* **Guards** *who have their torches trained on him.*

The **First Guard** *is a handsome man of about thirty, quite tall, with piercing eyes.*

First Guard   Why have you got mud all over your trousers?

Peter (*much sharper*)   You've just asked me that question! The answer's the same. (*Very slowly.*) I *fell* onto the ground. Into a large puddle to be precise. Splash. I had to run because she'd made me late.

They watch him.

Look, ask any of the passengers in there. They all saw me get on.

He points back into the compartment, they shine their torches. The light flicks from bunk to bunk. They are all empty.

Peter (*really surprised*)   Where have they all gone? They must have got out in Munich.

The torch lights come to rest on the top bunk. The **Small Man** *is still there asleep, his body bunched up.*

Peter   He's still here! Wake up! Come on, wake up!

The torch light is trained full on the **Small Man**'s *face but he is absolutely oblivious.*

Peter   He didn't see me get on at Ostend, but he'll do. Wake up!

He shakes the **Small Man** *who stirs very slightly, but only to start breathing heavily again.*

Peter   God he's a heavy sleeper. He's almost in a coma. WAKE UP!

First Guard   Come here.

Peter *moves towards them.*

First Guard (*his tone very sharp now*)   We are going to have to search you please.

Peter   Going to search me?

First Guard   Just turn around. No, round like that. Put your hands up there.

They search him, quite politely.

They make him face the wall.

Peter (*nervous smile*)   You've already done it once in this carriage – isn't this victimisation? No, that was in Belgium wasn't it?

He sees out of the corner of his eye the **Second Guard** *looking through a glossy catalogue with photos in it, looking at the page and then at* **Peter**.

Peter   What's he doing?

First Guard   He's looking you up.

Peter   What is it – a glossy brochure of terrorists? Do I look like a terrorist?

First Guard   We have to check. It is very easy for people to jump trains and get out of Germany, people who shouldn't be leaving.

Peter   But I'm English.

First Guard   A lot of them speak very good English. They are educated and well dressed. (*Standing close to him.*) Some person fused all the lights in this part of the train. Do you know about that?

Peter   No.

First Guard   You sure you know nothing about that?

Peter (*suddenly glances over his shoulder to his bunk where the light bulb is lying*)   No I don't. (*Loud.*) This journey is becoming a bloody assault course! And it's beginning to get beyond a joke, I'm going back to bed now, OK?

First Guard (*stops him, holding his arm*)   I'm afraid not.

The **Second Guard** *has gone into the compartment and is idly shining his torch around.* **Peter** *is watching out of the corner of his eye.*

First Guard   You're sure you can't tell us anything more about this mud? That you say you got in Frankfurt station!

Peter   God, you're really paranoid about this aren't you? (*He flicks at the mud, his voice rising, trying to smile.*) I don't want to be rude, but you are, under international law, allowed on a train wearing mud!

The **Second Guard** *walks out of the compartment. The* **First Guard** *turns. They have found the light on his bed.*

First Guard   There is the light. You fused the whole carriage. Why?

Peter (*loud*)   I took that bulb out because *she* asked me to. Because it wasn't working properly.

First Guard (*slowly*)   We are going to take you off the train now. We will check your name on our computer.

Peter (*really nervous and excited*)   Your computer! What computer, for Chrissake?

First Guard   And then we will charge you for this offence. Interfering with train property.

Peter (*disbelief*)   You're going to take me off this train? Listen I've got to be somewhere tomorrow, can't I report there . . . or . . .

First Guard   No, you must come now. With us.

The train is beginning to slow down.

Peter   Where are you taking me?

First Guard   We will have to drive you thirty kilometres.

Peter   Thirty kilometres! To some remote police station. (*Very nervous and excited.*) I'm sorry to labour the point but I *am English,* and although we are members of the

Community, I hardly think that entitles you to take me off at four in the morning, just because I have mud on my trousers and removed a faulty light bulb.

He looks at them.

First Guard   We are arresting you, come now.

Peter   For Chrissake if I was a terrorist I would have shot you five minutes ago.

The **Guard** *tenses.*

Peter   This is insane, you can't be that stupid – don't you understand – *she* asked me to remove the light bulb, the old woman, she . . . (*Suddenly the thought hits him.*) But she's still on the train of course, she was going to Vienna. (*He looks at them.*) She's on this train, we must find her.

He moves off down the corridor. The **Second Guard** *lunges for him, violently, and grabs him roughly from behind. The light of the torches is stabbing everywhere.*

They stop opposite a Ladies' lavatory. **Peter** *is looking shaken.*

He stares down at the door and sees that the lavatory is engaged.

The train has stopped.

Peter   It's probably her.

First Guard   You have to come now.

Peter (*calls at the door*)   Come on, come out. I need you out here. (*He bangs on the door.*) Come *out here!*

The door opens and a small girl emerges, blinking in the light of the torch and looking frightened.

Peter *glances up at the* **Guard**.

Peter   That's not her. (*Then he suddenly realises he has seen the girl at the beginning of the journey.*) She saw me. In Ostend. Come on, you remember, I saw you! (*Loud.*) Don't you remember?

The girl looks afraid and runs away.

First Guard (*taking him very firmly by the arm*)   Come this way please. We cannot hold up the train, it is very late as it is! We will take your luggage.

The **Second Guard** *is holding his case.*

First Guard   Put on your shoes. Do you want to wear your shoes?

Peter, *looking dazed, begins to put on his shoes and socks.*

First Guard   Quickly the train is waiting.

Exterior: Police cars: Night:

We cut to outside the train, which has stopped.

The two policemen lead him over to where a police car is waiting.

Further away a larger police van is standing, its headlights shining. The door of the police car is opened and his belongings, which have now been put in a plastic bag, are thrown inside.

There are suddenly several more police talking in German. They are near a huge industrial building which shoots into the sky.

The lighted train stands still. People peer from its windows.

The younger **Guard** *is standing a few paces away by the car, covering him, his hand on his gun.*

The **First Guard** *has leant into the car and is talking – in rapid German – on a police radio. Occasionally he smiles, chatting away on the radio, glancing over in* **Peter**'s *direction.*

First Guard   We are just checking where we have to take you.

The large police van starts up and moves off on to the road where it waits, its lights flashing.

The noise and lights from the industrial complex are harsh and loud.

Peter *is now getting more and more nervous. He looks very pale.*

Two workmen are sitting watching – listening to a transistor radio – and staring at him. A jaunty, ridiculous song is playing on the radio.

Peter *glances at the young police* **Guard** *who looks seemingly sympathetically towards him and moves up to him.*

Second Guard Cigarette?

He gives it to **Peter** *whose hand is shaking.*

Peter Listen. (*Nervous smile.*) Look, I have a letter explaining the purpose of my visit and . . .

He takes out his wallet. The young **Guard** *glances down at the wallet.* **Peter** *notices this. The* **Guard** *is looking down, seemingly interested in the money.* **Peter** *glances up at the* **Guard**'*s young face.*

Peter Would you – I mean this isn't a bribe, I mean this is probably (*He swallows.*) rather idiotic of me, but if I gave you that (*He takes out a hundred marks.*) would you just take me back on the train – just for a moment, to look for the old lady, because she'll explain, she'll . . .

The young **Guard** *looks down at the note, takes it from* **Peter**. *For a second* **Peter** *looks relieved.*

Suddenly the young **Guard** *is shouting violently, calling over another young policeman who is standing nearby. A loud sharp shout. They both suddenly pin* **Peter** *up against the car, very violently, as they frisk him quite viciously, shouting in German at him. They do not hit him, but swing him round several times, frisking him all over, violently, so that his body is pounded against the car, his head going down against the metal.*

The young **Guard** *is furious. He pulls* **Peter**'*s arm round and bundles him into the car, where he sits very badly shaken and bruised.*

The **First Guard** *moves over, calling sharply to the young* **Guard** *who starts explaining in German. They shine torches through the window at him.*

For a moment **Peter** *sits dazed on the back seat, leaning his head against the window as the police move all around. The indicator is blinking on the dashboard and the noise from the car radio is stabbing* *out.*

He glances down at the seat beside him. The light bulb he removed from the compartment is lying neatly wrapped up in a transparent bag next to him. He stares at it for a moment, then at the mud on his trousers in disbelief.

Suddenly the car is full of police. They sit close to him, holding on to him.

Peter (*very quiet*)   Where are you taking me?

The car starts off, its siren going. It reverses violently.

Peter *stares back at the train. A few people, none of whom he recognises, are staring out of the lighted windows, fascinated, craning to get a better look.*

Somebody takes a photograph with a flashlight.

The car swings round and begins to drive along the road.

Peter *glances behind him. The large police car is tracking them, its siren also on, its headlights blazing towards him.*

A police motorcyclist roars off in the opposite direction.

Peter (*very quiet*)   Please . . . could you just let me explain again . . .

His hand goes nervously up to his mouth.

None of them are looking at him. He sinks back in his seat, his face very pale.

The cars are moving along the waiting train. Suddenly in the car headlights, in the middle of the road, **Frau Messner** *is standing.*

For a moment it looks as if she is alone in the middle of the road, and then we see she is with one of the train guards.

The car brakes suddenly. **Frau Messner** *remains some distance from the car while the two policemen in the front seats get out and move over to her.*

She talks rapidly to them in German, loud, authoritative tones: 'The boy is with me', etc. They glance back towards **Peter** *after a pause.*

*The **First Guard** who arrested him on the train moves back to the car, and opens the door. He looks down at **Peter**.*

First Guard You were correct. What you told us is correct. Please rejoin the train.

*They hand him his belongings. **Frau Messner** has climbed aboard the train.*

Peter *moves towards the train, still looking very shaken. People are leaning out of the window, staring at him in fascinated silence as he gets onto the train.*

He leans exhausted against the window as the train moves off. There are bruises on his head, he flinches in pain. He is momentarily totally shattered.

Interior: Train: Corridor: Dawn:

Frau Messner *is standing in the empty corridor looking across at him. For a moment there is silence.*

Frau Messner I have sent them away now.

Peter *(still speeding with nerves)* Where the hell were you?

Frau Messner I went for a little walk.

They are standing by the join between the two carriages. Light is coming from the other carriage, through the doors, and the dawn light is coming up.

Frau Messner You were lucky I came back.

Peter I was *lucky*. You realise this is *all* your fault. I am covered in mud which is apparently a capital offence in this country, I have committed a crime with a light bulb, and I have lost my rail ticket.

Frau Messner *(rubs at the mud on his sleeve. He has his jacket draped round his bare shoulders)* The mud will come off.

Peter Don't touch me! *(Pause.)* I was taken off the train because of you. I was arrested because *you* asked me . . .

Frau Messner You should have been more careful. You shouldn't look suspicious, behave suspiciously, they are looking for that.

Peter (*furious*) Behave suspiciously?

Frau Messner You should realise these things. (*Pause.*) Now maybe we can put the beds back. It's nearly morning, it's impossible to sleep now. (*Pointedly.*) Could you come and put the beds back because they are heavy . . .

Peter (*exploding*) Christ, I've just had about *all I can take from you*. (*Really shouting.*) You realise you have ruined my journey. You have constantly pestered and provoked and jabbered at me.

He suddenly grabs hold of her arm and shakes her violently backward and forwards in the doorway as the train begins to pick up speed.

(*Shaking her, holding on to her very tightly.*) I will *not* do anything more for you. You understand? Not a single thing more. LEAVE ME ALONE. WILL YOU JUST LEAVE ME ALONE NOW. RIGHT! AND DON'T COME ANYWHERE NEAR ME AGAIN. Do you understand that. (*Screams.*) JUST LEAVE ME ALONE!

As he really shakes her body her head goes back as if expecting to be hit. **Peter** *lets go of her They are standing in the doorway. She stares back at him, her face showing no emotion.* **Peter** *looks slightly shocked at what he has done. He looks away for a second and then at her face. She turns abruptly and goes away through the doors into the other carriage.*

Interior: Train compartment: Dawn:

Peter *sits in the compartment. Dawn light is coming up.*

Cut outside into the passage with the beer cans rolling up and down the corridor as the train really begins to travel furiously fast.

Cut back to **Peter** *putting his shirt on. A close-up of him as he* *looks up, startled.*

The bottom bunk is covered in silver paper, and one chicken leg is visible.

Peter *(rather startled)*   Preston . . . ?

He stands up − his shirt still undone, but wearing his jacket − grabs his case and moves out into the corridor.

The **Fat Man** *looks up from his empty compartment. The door to his compartment is open.*

Peter *(looking at the empty bunks)*   Yes I know, they're in the dining car.

Fat Man   Sssh. They're sleeping.

He is pointing at the cases he has pushed into the bunks to make them look like sleeping bodies.

Peter *moves down the train, which is filled with early morning light.*

As he passes, he sees a bundled shape lying stretched out in an empty compartment.

He opens the door. It is **Dietrich**. *He is lying asleep on top of some magazines, looking very young.*

He looks up at **Peter** *for a second and turns towards the wall again, his cut face very noticeable in the morning light.*

Dietrich *(sounding quiet)*   I have missed my stop. I was asleep. *(A slight grin.)* Too much beer!

Peter   Where are you going then?

Dietrich   I don't know. Wherever I wake up.

The boy nestles up to the wall again.

Peter *smiles slightly and moves on.*

In the passage **Peter** *stares around him, then moves fast, looking for* **Frau Messner**.

Peter *(smiling to himself)*   Where is she?

Interior: Corridors: Dawn:

Peter *walks briskly down the train, through the other carriage which is almost empty now and through the empty bar, with its drinks locked away.*

Interior: Train: Dining car: Morning:

Peter *walks into the dining car, with the early morning light filtering into it.*

Frau Messner *is sitting alone at the same table as before, as if expecting to be served. There is nobody else in the carriage.*

The floor is covered in carnations. Vases have been knocked over and spilt, sweet papers and cigarettes are littered over the floor.

Frau Messner *looks up.* **Peter** *stands in the doorway for a second, looking at her, winding the silver paper round his fingers.*

Peter *(gazing around the carriage)*   Did *you* make all this mess?

Frau Messner *(taking him literally)*   No – it was here already.

Peter *(comes up to the table and stands over her)*   I thought I'd find you here, you look very at home, here. *(He moves the vase of flowers.)* It was Preston who took your chicken legs – the one that was nice to you. Not me.

Frau Messner   It doesn't surprise me.

Peter   I've come to say goodbye. My stop is in five minutes.

Frau Messner   You must get ready.

Peter   I am ready.

His shirt is open but he is holding his case.

Frau Messner   I am very thirsty.

Peter *(leaning up to her)*   When we arrive at my station I am *not*, I repeat not, going to fetch you a drink from the platform, and then get trapped here on this train bringing it back to you. (*Quietly.*) I can just see you fussing for your change as the train pulls out.

Pause.

Frau Messner (*sharp*)   I *am* thirsty now.

The train is rattling very fast.

There's an orange over there behind the fence, if you could . . .

Where the food was the night before a metal grid has been lowered, an orange is rolling backwards and forwards behind it. There is a gap in the wire.

Peter *hesitates and then moves up to wire. He stretches his hand through the wire which has jagged edges.*

Peter   You realise if the train jolts, I could rip my hand open.

He stretches for the orange and reaches it. He pulls it back through the hole.

There, one orange. (*He drops it in front of her.*) You're going to peel it for yourself. (*He stares down at her in the early morning light.*) You *can* peel an orange?

Frau Messner   Of course. (*She looks around.*) But I usually have a knife.

Peter (*watching her try very gingerly to peel the orange*)   You are extraordinary – like a member of a nearly extinct species. One of its last. You need a whole army of people to run around for you, before you even begin to function. A dying breed aren't you?

Frau Messner   And you? I wonder how long you'll last? You didn't manage very well last night.

Peter (*stares at her*)   I'll be OK.

Frau Messner (*looks up*)   You haven't shaved.

Peter   No, I haven't.

She looks at his shirt and bare chest. The bruises are still visible from the beating the police gave him.

Frau Messner And do your shirt up.

Peter In a moment.

Peter *fastens his cuffs.*

Frau Messner (*her tone changing*) It is my birthday today.

Peter You told me.

Frau Messner (*for his benefit*) I won't be travelling much more now. I am not very well. I most probably will be dead quite soon. In a year or so. I won't be here much longer.

Peter Now don't start getting maudlin. It doesn't suit you. You're not really at all like that.

Frau Messner (*blunt*) I was always spoilt. Always. (*She looks at him.*) We're rather alike in many ways, you know.

Peter (*looks at her*) You're taking ages over that orange.

Frau Messner (*pushing it across to him*) You can finish it for me now.

The train is beginning to brake. **Frau Messner** *watches* **Peter** *standing in front of her, peeling the orange. He smiles at her.*

Frau Messner Have you ever been to Vienna?

Peter No.

Frau Messner You should have. You really must. You should see the Spanish Riding School, it is very famous, and the Grinzing, very famous Austrian wine gardens.

Peter Yes.

Frau Messner (*a shrewd look at him and then away*) Of course you could come today if you wished. I don't mind. I have a large flat. There are many rooms.

Peter (*involuntary smile*) I don't think I heard you.

Frau Messner Yes you heard me.

Peter Come to Vienna with you!

Frau Messner If you wished.

Peter (*unable to resist*) Why?

Frau Messner (*looking back into his blue eyes – a strong look*) Because I wish it.

Peter *smiles. There is a moment's pause as their eyes meet.*

Peter (*quietly*) Do you often ask men on trains home with you?

Frau Messner (*looking past him*) I didn't hear what you said.

The train brakes.

I don't mind if you come or not.

He is looking down at her. The light is on his hair.

You should see Vienna.

Peter It's very kind of you ... but I can't, I'm afraid, my work. I have to go and ...

Frau Messner Of course. Your important work.

She looks away. He smiles to himself.

Why are you smiling at me?

Peter I wasn't.

Frau Messner You're lying. You were smiling in that way you have. I know what it means. I don't like your smile very much.

A pause.

She looks directly at him, the train is really braking.

Peter I must say goodbye now.

Frau Messner Yes, go on then.

Peter Maybe – (*A nervous smile as she looks at him.*) we'll catch the same train again sometime.

He moves slightly towards the door. She turns away, but then looks up as he nears the door.

Frau Messner (*her tone is very precise*) You're a nice boy in many ways.   '

Peter *stops.*

Frau Messner You're good-looking. You're quite clever. You notice things. And you're not at all cruel. (*She suddenly looks directly at him, then louder.*) But you *don't care.*

The train has stopped.

You pretend to of course, you pretend. (*She is staring straight at him.*) But you don't really care about anything do you? (*She stares at his pale young face, as he stands holding his case.*) Except maybe success in your work. Becoming very successful. It's all you have. You don't <u>feel</u> anything else. <u>Nothing. You just cannot feel anything else.</u> (*She looks at him.*) Can you?

Silence.

I wonder what will happen to you?

Peter *is staring at the train door, looking bewildered.*

Frau Messner (*matter-of-fact*) You can go now. The train has stopped.

She turns away. She is quite calm, she does not look at him.

Silence.

A noise of train doors banging.

Peter Frau Messner?

She does not react.

He goes up to her. As he gets up to her she closes her eyes.

Peter Frau Messner?

Silence.

She does not look up. Her eyes are shut. **Peter**, *staring down at her, moves as if to touch her face. Her eyes open.*

He immediately moves back.

She closes her eyes again.

He stands for a moment, unsure of what to do.

She is sitting back, her eyes closed, her face expressionless.

Peter Goodbye then. (*He moves towards the door.*) This is my station.

He is by the door. Her eyes are closed. She does not look at him.

Peter (*sharp*) Aren't you going to say goodbye?

She does not look at him.

(*Sharper.*) Aren't you going to say goodbye then?

Silence.

He half moves.

Do you want to know my name?

Silence.

She is looking out of the window.

(*Louder, more urgent, angry.*) Don't you want to know my name?

Exterior: Station: Morning:

Cut to **Peter** *walking along by blank, white walls. We stay close to his face. He looks shaken, dazed, a little lost for a moment. We stay on him as he passes more white walls and puts his case on a luggage and passenger moving pavement. His case moves away from him, down the pavement.*

He watches it go for a second and then climbs on the moving pavement, and with his back away from the camera, he slowly recedes along it, out of view.

Coming in to Land

Coming in to Land was first presented at the National Theatre, London, on 18 December 1986 with the following cast:

Halina	Maggie Smith
Neville	Anthony Andrews
Andrew	Andrew C. Wadsworth
Peirce	Tim Pigott-Smith
Booth	Michael Carter
Waveney	Ella Wilder
Turkish Woman	Nezahat Hasan

Directed by Peter Hall
Designed by Alison Chitty
Lighting by Stephen Wentworth

Place: London

Time: 1986

Act One

Scene One

Blue light, very early morning, the pastel-shaded walls of **Neville***'s flat.*

The room is composed entirely of clean, soft colours. There is a large window, a plain expanse of glass, overlooking the cyclorama.

There is hardly any furniture at all, bare walls with no marks on them, and almost invisible cupboards, the doors and handles of which blend imperceptibly into the pastel walls. There is a low glass table, a black desk against the far wall with an electric typewriter on it. The effect is of pale effortless spaciousness.

None of this is visible yet, there is dark blue light outside, dawn coming up, an almost totally dark stage. The light continues to change outside the window through the scene, sliding into a crisp morning light.

News, jingles, and advertisements are coming out of a radio, in the blue light, onto an empty stage. The news is about sterling dropping, Russian arms control initiatives being greeted with suspicion by the Foreign Office and local London traffic news, all muddled in together.

Neville *comes onto the darkened stage, closely followed by* **Andrew**. **Neville** *is in his mid thirties, and has an incisive manner, authoritative and quick, but he also shows a sudden charm. He is immaculately dressed in a grey suit.* **Andrew** *is the same age, ruffled worn appearance, an extraordinarily pale, almost dead-white face.*

Neville I didn't realise you meant a *dawn* meeting. (*He smiles.*) I'm not really at my best this early.

Andrew Only time I could do it, I'm afraid.

The news continues in the background.

Neville It seems very appropriate somehow.

Neville *moves around the stage switching on all the lights.*

Jesus it's cold! The heat wasn't even scheduled to come on. (*Glancing across at him.*) You look even paler than usual Andrew – it's all these odd hours you keep. Scurrying around London.

Andrew (*switching off radio*)   You are sure you're genuinely interested?

Neville (*flicking on last light*)   Interested in what?

Andrew   In going through with this.

Neville (*charming, authoritative*)   Of course. I told you next time you needed someone I'd be willing (*Very slight pause.*) and I am. Now's the moment, it's easy for me.

Andrew   She may not exactly be what you expected.

Neville   This is the Polish woman – the one who came over with this Polish student group?

Andrew   Yes, fifteen of them. *Mature* students on an exchange course, interior design at a college of art.

Neville (*smiles*)   You haven't I hope brought fifteen of them round now have you!

Andrew (*seriously*)   No, just the one. If you change your mind at this meeting and decide you can't do it, please let me know at *once*, that means during it, because every day wasted makes it more difficult.

Neville   I will. (*He smiles.*) I assure you.

Halina *is standing in the doorway, behind them, half in darkness. She is wearing a very large bulky old grey coat, and carrying two huge plastic carrier bags which are stuffed to the brim, one of them is splashed with mud.*

She is in her late forties or early fifties, she stands in the doorway behind them, having put one bag down, puffing on a Polish cigarette, staring through a cloud of smoke.

Neville   She does speak English?

Halina (*from behind them*)   Yes, I think so.

They turn and look at her.

Am I coming in too soon? Should I be outside still? (*She stands in doorway with bags.*) I was not completely sure what I was meant to do – whether I was waiting for a signal or not.

Andrew   No, you can come in Halina.

Halina (*moving with the large bags*)   It is very good of you to make the time to see me, and maybe . . . (*Clouds of smoke pour round her.*) Excuse me, I have been smoking all night, waiting for this meeting.

Andrew   This is Halina – Halina Sonya Rodziewizowna, that's right, isn't it?

Halina   Yes. (*To* **Neville:**) How do you do?

Neville (*shaking her hand*)   Neville. (*Pronouncing her name differently:*) Shouldn't it be Rodziewizowna?

Halina   Yes, I think so. That's even better.

Halina *takes off her coat.*

It's very heavy I'm afraid, (**Neville** *takes it.*) the pockets are full of menus and theatre programmes, stuck together with chocolate – and peanut butter sandwiches – (*Her voice trails off.*) there are all sorts of things in there.

She is wearing a strangely shaped grey dress underneath.

Neville   I'm sorry about the temperature here – it won't be so freezing in a minute.

Halina   It's not cold at all. (*Waving her arms.*) I'm very warm in fact.

Neville *watches her with apprehension.*

Andrew   Because of the strictly limited time for this meeting – (*To* **Halina:**) I always have to fit these in before my normal work, my conventional job – we must get down to the business at hand immediately.

Indicates **Halina** *to sit in one of the very few chairs. She sits in her grey dress surrounded by her bags.*

Halina I must say before you begin, the absolutely, the completely last thing I want to do is cause any more trouble.

Andrew (*businesslike*) Of course. I usually ask at this stage (*Glancing at* **Neville**.) when people aren't certain what to do, (*Slight pause.*) is there any alternative?

Halina *blows smoke, sitting in the centre of the stage.*

Neville Any other possible way of getting Halina in – other than marriage.

Pause.

(*Lightly, looking across at* **Halina**.) Yes, it's essential to ask that I think.

Andrew LANDING Halina – to use the language of immigration officers . . . we have to be brutally honest about the position.

Halina (*staring about through smoke*) Please be brutal, yes.

Andrew It has to be a bald selection of pros and cons.

Neville (*sitting at typewriter, deciding to take notes, beating out her name*) R-O-D-Z-I-E-W-I-Z-O-W-N-A.

He pronounces it perfectly.

Halina (*startled*) That's right, yes.

Andrew Neville is infuriatingly good – at a surprising number of things. (*Moving across room, up and down, flicking out red and blue notebook.*) To start with the *cons* – with the negative factors.

Firstly, Halina has waited, which is usually fatal. There is a detestation of casual applications – unless you arrive screaming at the airport, I can't stand it back home and I'm not safe there, demanding immediate asylum, they are intensely suspicious, they are paranoid about all sorts of

odds and sods being dumped on them from Eastern
Europe.

Halina (*blowing smoke*)   I have waited far too long, yes.

Neville (*typing*)   Too late.

Andrew   Secondly, every attempt to land is made in
context – the context of world events, and that isn't too
good at the moment, is it? The recent sudden squall of
East–West tension, the expulsion of five Polish students in
the US for industrial and military espionage, and three
Russians from here.

Halina   It is quite a bad time, yes.

Neville (*types*)   Wrong timing.

Andrew   Moreover Halina does not wish to get involved
in ritual 'hate' propaganda about her homeland,
understandably.

(*Sharply.*) Lastly – Halina is not unfortunately a famous
dissident, or even a member of Solidarity, no fashionable
reason here, nor obviously is she something nationally
desirable, like a ballerina, Olympic athlete, boxer, squash
player, or even a film director!

Halina (*sitting with her bags, staring ahead*)   No, I think that
probably is right. (*Slight pause.*) I'm not.

Neville (*typing*)   Professional status – absent.

Andrew   And that brings us to the personal history of the
case, and the chances of media or parliamentary
exploitation of Halina.

Neville   Which can be vital of course.

Andrew   Is there any possible angle her story suggests?

Neville (*lightly, looking across at* **Halina**, *clasping her
bags*)   There must be something isn't there?

Andrew (*briskly*)   See if you can spot anything. As a child
she is separated from her family for a few months during

the war, and had to fend for herself on the streets of Warsaw, amongst the German troops. But that had a happy outcome, they are reunited – nothing there. Next –

Neville   Maybe Halina would like to tell us.

Halina   Me? (*Pouring smoke.*) The big event, the one that is interesting, every *angle* leads back to my father . . . and the large event is – he was found guilty of corruption, deceit, and incompetence. He was a member of the government, this is many years ago of course. He lived for ages afterwards, on and on, and on, I think you should tell it, it sounds much better when you do it.

Andrew (*confident*)   Her family plunged into semi-disgrace.

Halina   Yes.

Andrew   Her father, a minister, involved in the internecine party warfare of the Stalinist fifties, he loses, made to retire early from a government department to do with *fish.* He isn't even thrown in prison!

Neville   Really. He doesn't go to prison, at all?

Andrew   No . . . His teenage daughter writes vigorous letters in his defence, he dies twenty-nine years later having been cared for by said daughter, and drunk himself into oblivion.

Neville   That *is* a long time.

Andrew   Halina finds normal avenues to her all closed, she couldn't join the film school she very much wanted to, couldn't get into design college, (**Halina** *staring ahead, blowing smoke.*) works occasionally as a part-time assistant for an elderly optician, and goes to design evening classes. *Finally* resulting in her being allowed to come over here on this course – reaching England.

Pause, **Halina** *moves on chair holding one of her bags.*

Andrew   But unfortunately this story is very mild, they've heard it a thousand times before.

Halina   Yes, I know.

Andrew   Even worse it's thirty-two years ago, there's no room now for subtle grey areas, mournful little tales from way back, only for something very strong, black and white.

He moves.

Halina is a victim of a tiny speck of history, no more than a pimple, so small the story wouldn't even show up on their screens, so to speak.

Pause.

She is too small to register.

Silence, **Halina** *staring ahead.*

Halina (*blowing smoke*)   Absolutely.

Neville (*watching* **Halina**)   And there is nothing else that is usable at all?

Andrew   There is no real story, no.

Neville (*laconic smile*)   Maybe we ought to move on to the plus side now.

Andrew   Of the plus side, the pluses – Halina is a woman. It is generally considered easier for women to land than men, because of the employment situation.

He stops, silence.

Neville   That's it? That's all?

Andrew   Yes – on a scale from A to G, I would put the chances of a straight application succeeding hovering between F and G.

Slight pause.

This analysis is devastating I know – and it is intended to be.

Halina   Of course.

Halina *moves with her heavy cluster of bags towards the window.*

Neville   I think he may be suggesting there is no alternative.

Andrew   I am. (*He smiles.*) That is why she was put in touch with me.

Neville (*watching her, sharp*)   Halina – you can leave your bags, you don't have to take them everywhere with you.

Halina   Yes.

Halina *with her back to them by the window, sunlight and artificial light now mixing in the room.*

Andrew (*pointedly*)   Neville may need more time to decide if he's not too busy to do this.

Neville   Yes. (*Staring at* **Halina**.) I just have to weigh up a couple of things on my schedule.

Halina (*by window*)   You can see out now – what leafy, beautiful streets. (*Lightly.*) This is how I always imagined London to be, when I was small. Lush, tidy squares just like this one. How marvellous to have such a view out of the window.

They both look at her.

Andrew   Of course the secret of a successful landing with no media potential is picking the exact moment to move and where to do it.

Neville   And how on earth do you decide that?

Andrew   Everything has got more difficult – but there are still some very sleepy registrars left, who will merely mumble a few easy questions before they marry you.

Halina   And you will find one of those?

Andrew   Yes. (*To* **Neville**.) As in every case, a sudden international crisis can blow one out of the water on a single afternoon. (*He moves.*) We're between crises at the moment, but if East–West relations suddenly inflame further, a Warsaw Pact passport wanting to get married in the middle of that, they'll put it under the microscope. I often find myself racing against events, as they begin to brew, (*Sharp smile.*) so always listen to the news.

Halina (*holding bags, facing them from the window*) There is a wonderful smell of coffee, I wonder where it's coming from?

Neville (*not moving*) It's nearly ready, I'll get it in a minute.

Andrew I usually feel while things are at this stage – the *passenger*, that's Halina naturally, is entitled to a word about the current marital status of the prospective 'husband'.

Neville (*effortlessly*) Of course. Neville is single, and unlikely for recent personal reasons to wish to get genuinely married for the immediate future. (*Laconic smile.*) It suits me to be unavailable, for a certain time.

Andrew One of the reasons he's doing this I expect – thinking of helping us.

Neville Yes.

Andrew (*telling* **Halina**) And Neville is a reasonable and reliable person.

Halina Of course. (*Moving across the room with bags.*) I can tell that.

Andrew It is only fair to remind you this is an illegal act, there is a risk attached, it is very small, but it is there, and for Neville too, if he agrees to help us, as a member of the legal profession, he could face . . .

Neville (*sharp*) We know this. (*Watching* **Halina**.)

Andrew To lighten the atmosphere, (*He smiles.*) this usually goes down well, I have a selection of rings here. (*He pulls out a transparent plastic bag full of wedding rings.*) Different sizes, they've all been used countless times of course, one or two are even gold, choose the one that fits and keep it.

Halina (*spilling out rings to look at them*) What a lot of rings

– you almost expect them all to have fingers still stuck in them.

Neville (*watching* **Halina,** *then pointing at rings*)   I take it these were all *successes.*

Andrew   Of course. If you decide to go ahead Neville, there is the question of accommodation – since landing Halina is going to be tough – a shared address for a few weeks *before* the marriage, in case of official investigation, even just for the post office would be desirable. It will cease immediately afterwards.

Bright early morning sunlight.

Neville   Naturally, if I . . . Halina can stay here.

Halina (*turning*)   No, that will not be necessary, I'm causing too much bother already.

Neville   It's no problem, there's a lot of space here.

Halina *moving agitated with her bags.*

Halina   Please – I don't want to be such a nuisance. I don't want to disrupt everything! Please do not let me, I needn't come here!

Neville (*sharp*)   It's *OK* – I told you.

Pause.

Andrew (*steering him across room*)   Neville – are you sure you want to do this, this is the time to say no.

Neville   I realise that.

Halina (*one of her bags has split open, pouring out its contents*)   I'm sorry, I've already made a mess.

Andrew (*with* **Neville**)   Obviously it will make a hell of a difference to Halina.

Neville (*watching her*)   I know. I don't need more time, I don't think, (*Pause.*) I'm willing – I think . . .

Halina (*by window*)   I do not want to look as if I'm

begging.

Pause.

Neville (*firm*)   Yes . . . I've decided.

Pause.

I'll do it.

Blackout.

Burst of classical music.

Scene Two

Peirce's *office.*

Peirce *and* **Booth**, *at a very small crowded desk, at the far side of the stage.*

One of the pastel squares in the main wall has been removed, revealing a peeling, flaking wall behind them; in the side wall there is a tiny yellow blind covering a window. There is just one chair, a very small desk, smothered in paper and files, and a clothes stand.

Peirce *is a short man in his forties. He is in shirtsleeves, just beginning to tie his tie. He is wearing running shoes.* **Booth** *is a tall dark-suited man, a little younger, with a large expressionless face.*

Peirce   Pass me my jacket and my tea in that order.

Booth *doesn't move.*

Peirce   If you could be so kind. I don't mind drinking cold tea, but I have to be properly dressed for them. Otherwise I don't function.

Booth *helps him on with his jacket.*

Peirce   This is the worst part of the day – the beginning.

Booth *does not react.*

Peirce   I expect you look forward to it.

Booth *passes tea.*

Peirce (*glancing through the yellow blind*) My God, the queue grows larger every morning, it's seething around down there. (*He stands by the blind, noises coming from below.*) You know something interesting about this queue, it is not nearly as orderly and neatly shaped as when I first came here. They lined up as straight as an arrow then. (*Sipping tea by yellow blind.*) It looks an amazingly mixed bag today.

He turns.

Right! Applications not processed from yesterday.

Booth, *totally expressionless, hands him large pile of files.* **Peirce** *glances in an instant at the name and date of each one.*

Peirce *Abbas* – too late, by three days, no need to consider. Yilmaz too late, no need to consider ... Shanatram too late, Tomasial – owicz – too late. (*Tossing files to the side.*) Smith, on time – but filled up the wrong form. (*Tosses it aside.*)

Booth, *expressionless, collects them, and puts them in out-tray.*

Peirce The rest will have to wait – we'll do the same at lunchtime. (*He glances down at one of the files.*) It's amazing the number of different ways they find to spell *Lunar* House, Lunar as in Looney, or Lunar as in Lewd.

Peirce *moves up to desk.*

I should have *three* sharpened AB pencils ready waiting here.

Booth *doesn't move.*

Peirce You couln't be so kind.

Booth *starts sharpening pencils, a loud bell rings.*

Peirce Not yet! Can't let them in yet. I have not got my shoes on.

He starts changing his running shoes.

Once the door opens, this floor actually shakes, as they fight to get the best positions. Have you noticed that yet?

The whole building seems to sway from side to side for just those first few moments as they stampede in.

Booth *deadpan sharpening pencils.*

Peirce   Even the lavatories are full within the first few seconds, they'll flatten anything in their path, as they go up those stairs. (*Glancing at* **Booth**.) You will learn to avoid being out there for those opening minutes – it can be a very risky business. (*Doing up shoelaces.*) God knows, their patience *after* that is incredible, phenomenal! They'll go without food for an entire day, and when you go out there, they stare at you with such longing.

Pause, noises from below.

Is there a clean handkerchief in that drawer?

Booth *doesn't move.*

Peirce   If I could trouble you.

Booth *moves silently.*

Peirce   I had an American girl in here yesterday, she *whispered* everything, this soft little voice. I couldn't hear her. Each time I leant forward to listen she got even quieter, fading a bit more with each question – until I was right· up close to her mouth. Then suddenly she screams 'You bastard, just let me stay in this fucking country can't you!' Her saliva shot straight into me – a direct hit.

Booth *hands him a pristine white handkerchief.*

Peirce   And two fake marriages last week. Haven't had one for a while, (*Sharp smile.*) maybe they're coming back into fashion. A particularly ludicrous couple, a young Chilean woman and this huge Glaswegian, covered in boils, they'd found for her from somewhere.

(*He stands up sharply.*) I see you are your usual talkative self. I'm beginning to enjoy our little chats more and more.

Bells clamouring much louder.

Not yet!

He moves into position behind his desk. There is a loud clang, and a shadow of light across the back wall suggests the main doors opening.

Let us survive another day.

Blackout.

Scene Three

Neville's *room: a few days later.*

News items, as if radio channels are being changed: late-night music, and then domestic news settling on an item about whether the Russians are going to retaliate over the expulsion of three members of their embassy staff in London – so far threats have been issued, the report runs, but no action has been taken.

The news mixes into the sound of torrential rain. Warm evening light in room. **Neville** *and* **Halina** *enter with gleaming umbrellas and wet coats, muddy water pouring out of* **Halina**'s *umbrella, she has also one of her large plastic bags with her which is very wet, its contents sodden at the top.*

Neville   My God, what violent rain. (*He moves across the stage.*) It's probably the Fön.

Halina   The what?

Neville   The Fön, (*Putting his umbrella sharply in the stand.*) a warm wind they often get in Munich, it comes up from Africa, very occasionally it pierces as far as here, causing thunderstorms. (*He taps the thick glass of the window.*) It can't get in.

Halina, *dropping her umbrella on chair, begins to unwind long sodden scarf.*

Halina   I didn't realise you knew so much about the weather.

Neville (*moving her umbrella and switching on his answering machine*)   Did you enjoy the film?

Halina (*unwinding her long scarf*)   Yes – I liked it.

Neville (*very surprised*) Really? The sort of film you feel evaporating before you're half way across the foyer.

A woman's voice comes out of the answering machine during **Neville***'s speech, 'Where on earth have you been . . . where've you been hiding yourself . . . are you free on Friday?' etc.*

Neville (*charming but firm*) The attempt to make England a wild dark place was a little elephantine wasn't it, everybody popping up seething with trapped energy. (*He smiles.*) The English can't really make films. What about the play? This afternoon?

Halina Yes – I hated it.

Neville (*sharp surprise*) Really? It did rather more than the usual boulevard comedy.

Another woman's voice curls out of the answering machine: 'What have you been up to . . . I thought you were going to call me . . . there's a party on Saturday, fancy dress, "fin de siècle", whatever that means.'

Halina (*rolls up her scarf into big wet ball and sticks it unceremoniously into plastic bag*) Maybe there is a night film I could go and see. An *all* night showing, four movies together.

Neville Don't you think you've had enough Halina?

Halina Enough of what?

Neville (*watching her*) Such an incessant diet of films and plays, you must have sampled nearly everything on offer, you're beginning to gorge yourself.

Halina (*looks at him*) Certainly I'm gorging myself. (*Pause.*) You don't have to come with me to the things I . . .

Neville (*cutting her off, very detached*) No, it helps, to make the story plausible, if anybody attempts to check before this marriage.

Halina *takes off her heavy grey coat. She's wearing a new dress, in vivid, garishly-coloured squares. It doesn't fit her.*

Halina It's the only thing I've bought for myself yet, do

you like the colour? It was a bargain of the week,
tremendous value.

Neville (*watching her, in the baggy dress*)   So I can see.

Halina   I like it.

Neville (*very detached*)   It's certainly a change of style, yes.

*Old woman's hoarse voice comes out of answering machine saying 'I
still need to talk to you. I do . . . I do.'* **Neville** *switches it off.*

Neville   Not again! She's always on the tape, completely
mad.

Halina *is moving around, touching the sides, the walls, all the
smooth unbroken surfaces, moving around his territory.*

Halina   If you don't mind me saying so . . . everything is
so clean here.

Neville   Is it? (*Immediately picks up her wet coat.*) Nothing out
of the ordinary.

Halina (*beginning to touch every object in the room*)   There's no
trace of *anything*. There are no stains, no chipped paint, no
spilt coffee, no dust even. You don't mind me touching, do
you?

Neville (*very warily, watching her*)   No.

Halina   And no sign of your work, if I had to say what
does this person do?

Neville (*sharp*)   So you want to know more about my job?
I told you I'm a solicitor.

Halina   And?

Neville (*sharp look*)   It's a large firm, which has been
moving more and more into the entertainment field,
constant fights over clients' copyright, their royalties, their
inalienable rights, it's a real growth area. So much product
is being spewed across the world, across frontiers, via
satellites, there's all this money escaping into the ether,
uncollected.

Halina *moving through cupboard, finding the new invisible blending doors.*

Halina   A successful young lawyer. And? . . . There's no sign of your friends, is Andrew a close friend?

Neville *(warily)*   Reasonably close. There were five of us, 'friends' at college in the late sixties, one's dead, one's in America, one writes successful books, and Andrew works for Shell and does his good works on the side, a peculiarly English arrangement, impossible to fully explain.

Halina *looks at him.*

Neville   He started on Sunday afternoons, going to a charity in Peckham and helping out, and gradually he got involved in all of this. – And then there's me. *(Watching her closely.)* Who do you want to tell this to anyway?

Halina *(ignoring him)*   And?

Incessant sound of the torrential rain, **Halina** *looking in every nook and cranny.*

Neville   What do you mean, and?

Halina   And there's no trace I can find of women. Girlfriends. Not even shoes in the cupboard, nothing squashed into the corners, not even anything in the bathroom.

Neville   Really? You obviously haven't looked hard enough.

Halina *(touching a chair)*   No hair even. You must like them to totally remove themselves every night.

Neville   Maybe. *(Laconic smile.)* I have just concluded a relationship in fact, rather messily, with a woman I've been seeing for several years. *(Sharp smile.)* One and a half relationships to be more accurate. There was another girl, a little younger. It was time for a change, all round.

Halina   You prefer to be really independent obviously. *(At last cupboard door.)* Who were those people gauling at us outside the cinema?

Neville   Gawping. I didn't see.

Halina   I thought they were friends of yours, they were pointing at you and me, you didn't seem to want to be recognised with me, standing in the rain . . .

Neville   I didn't notice, any of this.

Halina   Gawping – I'm still collecting a few new words. (*Sliding back cupboard door.*) It took me a long time to even find the drinks here. (*Pouring herself a large whisky.*) I can have some more, can't I?

Neville   If you want.

Halina   (*watching him*)   Gawping – I started reading English literature when I was very young, I learnt from all these large ripe books, that's when I started thinking about England, while I was nursing my father. (*She throws back her head, downs the whisky, like vodka.*) I had the time.

Neville   Yes, I wondered where you'd got your English from.

Halina   (*lightly, immediately pouring herself another glass*)   I was a young girl watching the manoeuvring and silent fighting and party purges. These monstrous old men. I was near it all, I even saw my father lose his job, through a half-opened door. I was waiting in the passage for him, holding his galoshes. He smashed two busts and two oil paintings and tried to set light to his desk. He wouldn't let go of his official car for a whole week, their cars meant a lot to them I assure you! He personally drove it round and round Warsaw so nobody could collect it. For the next thirty years he shouted at the wireless, and then at the television, whenever any of his old colleagues appeared, wallowing in rage and envy for being out man –

Neville   (*briskly, cutting her off*)   Yes, you told us the story, Halina I know that's why you're here. (*He moves to switch off a couple of lights.*) By the way have any of the other Poles, Polish people, on your course, wondered about you moving in here?

Halina   No.

Neville *moves to exit,* **Halina** *turns.*

Halina   Somebody rang up on the telephone about me, wanted to talk to me.

Neville *stops.*

Neville   Rang you here. Who?

Halina   Somebody from a newspaper or maybe it was a television station.

Neville   The way they smell out even the smallest fragment of a story! How on earth did they get onto you?

Halina (*facing him*)   They may have heard about the group of us at the college – in the present climate they were interested.

Neville   What did they want from you?

Halina   He yattered very fast – what did I think of England compared to Poland? I told him I didn't believe in facile comparisons, which I don't, that I'd resolved not to talk about this country till I knew it – and then he said is there anything else of interest about you?

Neville (*watching her*)   But he wasn't interested presumably because you had absolutely nothing to tell him.

Slight pause.

Halina   That's correct.

Neville   No small secrets swimming about anywhere Halina?

Halina (*very slight pause*)   No.

Sound of the torrential rain.

Neville   Good. The arrangements are being made. You're safe here. (*He moves breezily.*) Turn out the lights please, and perhaps you could get rid of your plastic bags.

Halina (*calls*) Neville!

Neville *stops at exit.*

Halina I can call you that – I am a little unsure about using your first name.

Neville Of course. Since we are getting married, it seems appropriate.

Halina Neville seems the wrong name for you for some reason.

Neville Why? (*He begins to move again.*)

Halina (*louder*) Neville. I have made a decision – I have to ask you something urgently.

He turns facing her, in her garish baggy dress.

Find me a job.

Neville (*immediately*) It's out of the question, you haven't got a work permit.

Halina I *must* earn some money. I have lots of spare time on this course. I'll do anything for it, almost. I can do something for you?

Neville Like what?

Halina Cleaning is obviously not necessary, (*Looking round.*) maybe a little typing, some sewing.

Neville Not required.

Halina (*forcefully*) I'll do anything Neville – I can work in a shop, a back-street hotel, a spaghetti restaurant, you must have clients who – you must know somebody who'll need me.

Neville It's illegal Halina.

Halina People manage it all the time, you know they do.

Neville It's a totally unwarranted risk. Why . . .

Halina So many people have spent money on me over

here, I must be able to pay it back, especially if something goes wrong.

Neville   It can wait.

Halina   (*loud, facing him*)   *Please* – I need to do this Neville.

Neville   (*very slight pause*)   I'll sound out one of my clients, a hi-fi mogul, he owes me a favour, he's doing sensationally, always expanding, he may be able to fit you in sorting stock for Christmas somewhere.

Halina   You will! You'll do it! (*Touching him.*) You don't know how pleased that makes me.

She kisses him, **Neville** *flinches, embarrassed.*

Halina   Don't worry. I am not going to sample *everything* that's on offer around here.

Blackout.

Scene Four

The hi-fi and video emporium.

News and music mixed together. The radio news concerning a clash between Russia and Britain over the expulsion of Soviet personnel from Britain, the Russians in retaliation have thrown out three Britons from Moscow; the channels change, end of an item about American statements on arms control . . . the world news changes into a blast of local traffic news and then into the mild hum of muzak.

The hi-fi and video emporium suggested by three hi-fi towers about eight feet high, two of them crowned by televisions, sliding into place. They are spaced across the stage on the main pastel set. Two revolving stacks of cassettes are front stage, and a large blank video screen moves across the window upstage.

Behind the screen the cyclorama gradually turning during scene from bright hard winter blue to a very sharp white.

Waveney, *a black woman of thirty-one, stands alone in the shop among the machines. She is beautifully dressed in very carefully chosen* *stylish clothes.*

She is holding a very bulky glossy catalogue in front of her.

Waveney (*reading off catalogue*)   The Pioneer 5770 EX, price £780. Not in stock, unavailable at this store! (*Smiles to herself.*) So don't ask for it. (*She moves among the machines.*)

The AIWA V1100 and V1200, price eleven hundred quid – never been in stock, never will be, unavailable at this store.

Looks through catalogue.

Jesus there are so many new machines in here; loudspeakers – the Wharfdale 708, price £450, haven't seen them round here, not delivered to this shop, *never likely to be.*

She turns the page and smiles.

We must never forget the Panasonic NV870 – piles of them for sale, they are dangling out of the window. Right!

She puts down catalogue and picks up a pile of large 'REDUCED' labels.

The bargains start here! (*Standing over machine.*) Hitachi MD50 – reduced from £699.99 pence to a wonderful seasonal (*Slaps on label.*) £589.95.

Moving to another machine.

The AIWA 0800 with fully automatic DC Servo turntable and linear tracking tone arm reduced to a sensational £749.99. *NO.* (*Suddenly choosing another label.*) Why not an unbelievable bargain of the year £599. (*Slaps the second label on machine instead.*)

She moves.

The video screen – an ideal gift for the kids' Christmas stocking at a knockdown £1800 (*Slaps label on base of screen. Then decides on second label.*) or why not an even better £45.90! (*Slaps label on.*) Everything as far as you can see reduced beyond your wildest dreams.

She spins on her heel and slaps a £500 reduced sign on one of the ordinary shop chairs and another on a stand-up ashtray.

Halina *enters wearing a different stylish sweater over her new dress, her grey coat hanging open.*

Waveney *(watching her approach)* You're late.

Halina I'm so very sorry. It's the first time I think.

Waveney Maybe.

Halina It won't happen again.

Waveney Maybe not.

Halina *(looking about her at the machines)* What should I do? What needs doing first – is this the most important? *(Moving over to the revolving cassette stacks.)*

Waveney *NO. (Mock anger.)* You haven't learnt all the stock yet – two weeks and you haven't mastered it! You must know the names of all the styluses.

Halina Styli.

Waveney Styluses – what's this? *(She holds out a small plastic box.)*

Halina *holds up box to light.*

Halina That's a Lingtons Sonatone STA.

Waveney And this? *(Holding up another one.)*

Halina It's a stereo cartridge – a Nagouki.

Waveney Wrong. A Nagoaka moving *permalloy* stereo cartridge MP30.

Halina Moving PERMALLOY. Nagoaka. I think that's fixed in my memory now, I hope. I'll take a few examples home, if I may, and study them – so I can get all their names.

Waveney Yes, you'd better.

Halina *(looking across the stage)* Does the Supervisor know

I'm late?

Waveney　I have no idea where he is, probably staring longingly at some new stock somewhere, which he knows he'll never be able to order, never be able to touch! You should see how fantastically excited he gets by new equipment, new models. (*She waves the catalogue.*) The trade magazines are really erotic for him.

Halina　That's how he gets his pleasure – I wondered why he was so pale.

Waveney　But I don't think he can keep this pretence up much longer. And we shouldn't either. It'll drive me crazy if we do.

Halina　What pretence?

Waveney　*standing among the gleaming machines.*

Waveney　What do you think? Where are the PEOPLE? Where are they? (*She turns, loud.*) Didn't you wonder about it.

Halina　A little.

Waveney　You thought this was how we did business in this country! – somehow people shuffle in here when we're not looking, buy things silently, leave their money in a collecting box, and vanish!

We have to admit it, somebody has finally got to say it. There are NO FUCKING CUSTOMERS. None.

She pushes one of the hi-fi towers, it rolls gently on its wheels across the stage. Pauses.

Halina　I think I may have seen one yesterday.

Waveney　That was my daughter. The little girl that came in? That was my little eight-year-old daughter – she bought some record cleaners. Four weeks before Christmas I think we should be doing a little better than that.

Halina　Maybe someone will come in *today*. You never know.

Waveney   You want to bet! (*She muses.*) It's been getting worse every month, creeping downward, first to a trickle, and then to a complete full stop. *Dead.* There are too many shops selling stuff like this.

Halina   Yes. I'd noticed . . .

Waveney   Nine in this street alone. Soon be eating each other, you can already see the teeth marks on the door of this one. This was meant to be the start of a new chain too, of high-tech elegant shops, buy your video machines as if you're buying clothes at the most fashionable store, it obviously isn't catching on, is it! People just want to grab, buy it, and run . . .

Halina   Why should they want to employ *me* here then?

Waveney   That's an interesting question. *Why?* Perhaps the owner of this joint didn't want to admit to your friend how badly things are going. (*She stops.*) I thought we'd got one for a moment – a customer.

Halina (*watching*)   Hovering . . . Gone! A near miss.

Waveney *leaning back against one of the hi-fi towers, pushing it gently across stage.*

Waveney   Haven't you got something you want to ask me, Halina?

Halina (*innocently*)   You mean where to find the audio-technica dual magnet phono cartidge?

Waveney   *NO.* (*She looks at* **Halina**.) Don't you want to find out if I know what you did? You must want to tell someone about it, I think you may have to make do with me, (*She smiles.*) you have to trust me . . .

Pause.

I saw what you did, Halina.

Halina (*loud*)   Really? (*She moves away apprehensively.*) When it happened?

Waveney   Yes. I turned round, suddenly there were

thirteen of you – thirteen heads dotted all over the shop. (*Indicating televisions.*)

Halina   Thirteen! (*She moves.*) They approached me, and then I was telling them, telling them my story. That's why I left early yesterday.

Waveney (*cutting her off*)   How do you want to see it, big or small?

Halina   See what?

Waveney   You – yourself of course. I recorded it, the early evening news. (*She moves among the machines.*) Let us use the widescreen, why not? The bigger the better.

Halina (*moving away*)   I don't know if that's a very good idea Waveney, please don't.

Waveney   You have to see yourself – what is the point of having done it otherwise. You've got to use it, improve your technique.

Halina (*moving to leave the room*)   I think . . . I must look at the catalogue now – I have to memorise the new range of Panasonic video recorders by the end of the day . . .

Waveney (*as she starts VHS machine*)   I'll put it in black and white – because I prefer black and white.

Halina *is right at the side of the stage when the enormous silent image of herself, her head in close-up, appears on the video screen, mouth opening and closing, no volume as yet, clouds of smoke blowing out of her mouth as on screen she tugs at a cigarette.* **Halina** *stops at edge of stage, dwarfed by her own image staring down at her, she turns away abruptly with her back to the screen.*

Halina   I will not watch this.

The silent face moves for a moment on the screen, above them.

Waveney   Doesn't it look great! Now for your voice Halina.

She brings in the sound, booming sound, **Halina**'s *voice coming out of the screen, harshly and authoritatively.*

Halina on screen (*sound comes in mid-sentence*)   Yes, it was obviously a very frightening experience and without any warning, because one minute we were driving along, just an ordinary group of people, late one night after a party, in this old car, and the next we were bundled out, made to lie on the road – and then what I can only call this nightmare began, without any reason, any cause.

Halina *has turned during this to see herself speaking down from the screen, staring down from up there.*

Halina   Oh my God! (*Looking up at herself.*) Stop it, please stop the machine.

Waveney *freezes her image,* **Halina**'*s head caught staring ahead, her hat a little askew.*

Halina   What have I done – oh what have I done!

She waves her arms.

How could anybody believe a thing that looks like that – I look monstrous, like a creation from another planet.

Waveney (*smiles staring up*)   The hat was a mistake I agree.

Halina   Yes, I have never seen myself on television before – it seems to have photographed somebody else.

Waveney (*pointing at the frozen image of her with a broom handle like a lecturer*)   But the stare is good, fastening the audience with that gaze, trapping them in their seats, makes them think 'We have to listen to this woman' – it shows a natural instinct.

Halina   I look like somebody who talks to themselves on trains.

Waveney (*sharp smile*)   You look foreign, yes. A little odd – but that's no bad thing. If it happens again, the hands are far too busy, keep still, no twitching.

Halina'*s voice less loud as she moves again on screen.*

Halina on screen   There were about five of them, police. 'You are under arrest,' they said. (*In reply to unseen* *questions:*) No, there was no charge made at all, they didn't even bother to look at our papers. Then they drove us at very high speed through the streets of Warsaw to the police station, and *that's* where everything happened . . .

Halina (*facing her image on the screen as it talks*)   I've done it now! I can't take it back. (*Points to herself.*) That weird-looking object has gone out across the airways.

Waveney *suddenly stops the tape,* **Halina***'s face caught staring down, her cigarette half raised,* **Neville** *has entered.*

Waveney   A customer?

Halina   No. I'm afraid not.

Neville   There you are Halina. (*He looks up at the screen.*) And there.

Halina   Yes . . . (*Pause.*) I think I can explain.

Neville *dwarfed by her massive image on screen, he looks from one to the other.*

Neville   Clearly something has happened, how did you manage to get up there?

Halina   There has been a little publicity about me.

Neville (*staring at the huge head*)   Little is not the word that immediately springs to mind.

Waveney (*watching him*)   So *this* is your friend.

Neville (*waving newspaper*)   It's in here, too, the evening paper, your face staring out of page 5, above a story about an escaped python from Chessington Zoo. (*He holds it up.*) Somebody catch you unawares did they – coax you into talking?

Halina (*cutting him off*)   No – I decided I had better tell my story.

Neville   It's an extraordinary story Halina – we had no idea. You didn't tell me, you said there was nothing else.

Halina   No I know, I thought I wasn't going to tell

anyone. (*Looking at him.*) But I changed my mind.

Neville (*reading off newspaper*)   Polish housewife tells dramatic story, breaks ranks with visiting party . . . her story throws disturbing light on what's still going on there, innocent citizens plucked out of their cars . . . arrested on New Year's Eve with friends . . . subjected to a startling and terrifying ordeal . . . prison guards . . .

Halina (*staring at him*)   Yes, the language is a little lurid in your newspapers, but that's what happened.

Neville (*waving paper at screen*)   This has implications Halina . . . have to calculate the life expectancy of the story, (*He smiles.*) we'll have some photographers at the wedding almost certainly, 'Solicitor marries Polish prison drama person' – a few lines –

Halina   I have something to tell you which may have some relevance to the calculations.

Pause.

I don't want to marry you.

Pause.

Neville (*slight smile, patient, slowly*)   Halina – I am not sure you fully understand, this is only an arrangement, to help you . . .

Halina (*facing him across the breadth of the stage*)   I know it's only an arrangement.

Neville   This is a plan, a scheme to get you into the country, to land you, to outwit the immigration authorities.

Halina   I don't think I can marry you – even as an arrangement.

Silence. **Halina**'*s face staring down at him from the screen.* **Neville** *stares from the screen to her.*

Neville (*sharp smile*)   Is this some sort of Polish joke?

Halina   No, no it's not.

Neville (*moving up and down*) You must have moral scruples then? Are there religious reasons why . . .

Halina No, definitely not. I just don't want to marry you.

Waveney That's clear enough isn't it.

Halina (*staring at him*) Don't take it personally, please.

Neville (*sharp smile*) I am not taking it personally I assure you, I'm merely curious.

Halina'*s face moving on the screen without volume,* **Waveney** *has started the tape again, and is looking at* **Halina** *on screen, at her giant face, as* **Neville** *talks.*

Neville (*his manner very effortless, sharp smile*) This must be one of the quickest rides from meeting – to engagement – to break-up ever recorded. (*He glances between* **Waveney** *and* **Halina**.) Has somebody else been advising you?

Halina No.

Waveney Of course not.

Neville (*appearing nonchalant*) It's all right, there's absolutely no need for me to know any more, no explanation is necessary . . . (*Suddenly.*) Has pressure been brought to bear on you?

Halina Absolutely not.

Neville (*sharp*) Fine – I don't need to know. (*Staring at her.*) And – would you like to be found another candidate?

Halina As an arranged husband.

Momentary pause.

No, I don't think so.

Neville You don't sound absolutely sure.

Halina No, (*Slight pause.*) I am. I've decided to get into this country by a different route, to tell my story.

Neville (*swinging round sharp to* **Waveney**) Can you stop that machine please, I'm finding being dwarfed by her enormous head a little distracting.

Waveney (*suspicious, hostile*) You do, do you? I think she looks rather good up there, very powerful. I wouldn't mind having a spell up there myself. (*Defiant smile, to* **Halina**.) I think I want to see you now in slow motion.

She puts the tape into slow motion, **Halina**'s *head moving on the screen, her mouth opening slowly, her head lifting up, the smoke coming out.*

Neville (*cool smile*) This is what you get up to together here. How come you can splash yourself all over the equipment?

Waveney Nobody minds.

Neville Why not.

Waveney Because there are no customers, as you can see.

Neville Don't be stupid – it's Christmas, the pre-Christmas boom time, locust time, people stripping whole shops bare.

Halina Where are they?

Waveney Not here, they're not, nobody's stripping this place bare.

Neville A momentary lull, that's all, the stampede will start any moment.

Waveney If *you* see a customer, it's such a rare sight – we may just photograph it and exhibit them in the window.

Neville (*sharp*) I don't want to hear any more of that – this store is owned by a client and friend of mine. I would know if there were any difficulties.

Waveney (*loud*) I ought to know oughtn't I! I'm alone with these machines – I lock them up at night. (*She jangles a bunch of keys.*) And dust them down in the morning. (*Defiant* *smile.*) I'm the one that has to talk to them! (*She moves.*) And I tell you this place is finished.

Neville (*turning back to* **Halina**)   Maybe *you* could tell yourself to stop moving up there.

Halina*'s face moving very slowly above their heads.*

Neville   I don't know which Halina to talk to.

Halina (*to* **Waveney**)   *Yes.*

Waveney *stops the picture, freezes* **Halina** *on the screen staring ahead.*

Neville (*sharp smile*)   This is extraordinary Halina. You peering down from that screen. (*He looks across at her.*) I leave you unsupervised for forty-eight hours and you pop up all over the media, handling it with alarming efficiency.

Halina   Thank you.

Neville (*detached smile*)   You've only been in the country a few weeks – and you've already had your fifteen minutes of fame.

Halina (*immediately understanding the reference*)   You mean like the American painter Andy Warhol said, everyone famous for fifteen minutes. (*Slight smile.*) I hope to do better than that.

Neville (*glancing at screen*)   You want it to continue do you.

Halina   Until I'm safely, completely inside this country, yes.

Halina *moves, turns.*

I'll move out of course, you must want me to leave.

Neville   Leave where?

Halina   Your rooms – I'll put everything in a few bags, (*Indicates her plastic bag.*) I must be able to find a few more of these, and move out tonight.

Neville   Move out? Don't be stupid, why should I want

you to do that?

Halina   You can't want me to stay, blocking up your apartment.

Waveney   If you're worried about where to go – I can find you a place.

Neville   *No* I don't want to hear any more about that. (*Louder.*) That will not be necessary.

Halina   If that's what you want.

Neville (*sharp smile*)   So that's why you were so desperate for me to find you a job? You thought you'd need the money when I threw you out on the street.

Halina   Perhaps.

Neville   I'm right. You planned that. (*He smiles, moves up and down.*) You will have to be very careful from now on . . . each move you make will have to be considered, if you're going to get in because of what happened to you, applying in the normal way. (*He glances up at the screen.*) Because of the publicity you have to leave here at once of course. It's illegal for you to be here. (*Points to the image on screen.*) This must be erased at once, there must be no trace left here.

Halina   Yes.

Waveney   *I'll* see to that – this is my equipment.

Neville (*to* **Halina**)   And you'll need legal advice of course – timing of interviews, deadlines for application, somebody to check out the opposition, the immigration authorities.

Halina (*interrupting*)   I don't want a lawyer.

Neville (*stops*)   What on earth's got into you Halina . . . you need professional advice.

Halina   I will *not* use a lawyer. I don't have to do I – I don't want to do it that way.

Neville But you need.

Halina *is standing under her picture on the screen, two of them facing him.*

Halina (*forceful*) I don't want a lawyer.

Pause.

Neville Right.

He moves.

Then I will have to act for you, unofficially, advise you. It's not my area of course, but I'll do it.

Pause. He looks at her.

That is – if it's acceptable to you Halina?

Halina If you want to do that. (*Slight pause.*) I'd be grateful.

Halina's *face moving on screen again.*

Neville (*smiles*) Thank God for that. One thing is settled. (*He moves towards* **Waveney**.) And now, if there's the possiblity of any service round here.

Waveney There might be . . .

Neville I think I'd better buy something (*Sharp disbelieving smile.*) – make sure this place lasts until Christmas at least!

Blackout.

Scene Five

Peirce's *office.*

The machines glide back off-stage, leaving for a moment **Halina**'s *picture on the screen lit by a spot, she is staring straight at us.*

Music, then a news item – **Halina**'s *story moving through the radio channels: 'Polish housewife tells astonishing story . . . unprovoked ordeal . . . out of nowhere . . . out of the night of Warsaw . . .*

dramatic nightmare happenings in Polish police station . . . to ordinary citizens', etc.

Neville *standing in* **Peirce**'s *office. Another panel of the pastel-coloured walls comes away and stays away, making the office slightly bigger than before. The desk has also grown bigger; it is still covered in mounds of paper, and files, and a paper spike. Voices shouting in the distance, bells, a paper-chain dangling incongruously on wall.*

Neville *picks up metal spike on desk,* **Peirce** *enters rapidly, shouting as he comes.*

Peirce   No, no more today. I can see no more. It is out of the question, I have finished.

Seeing **Neville**, *he stops.*

Peirce   Been waiting long?

Neville   No.

Peirce (*sounding disappointed*)   You haven't? (*Moves.*) You won't object then if I do certain things while we talk – it being Friday there are various urgent tasks to perform.

Neville   Please feel free.

Peirce *takes his sweater off with a sharp movement. On the hat stand there is a complete change of clothes.*

Peirce   These off-the-cuff chats are becoming the fashion – people say they save time, I don't like them.

During following dialogue, he removes tie, changes shirt, slips tracksuit bottom over his trousers, puts on casual shoes.

One doesn't want to take any of the place home with one, does one.

Neville   I imagine not.

Peirce (*matter of fact*)   One never knows what's been brought in here. (*As he begins to change.*) I have been interviewing all day, fifteen, maybe eighteen different cases . . . a brother and sister from Ecuador looking enormously alike, (*He looks up.*) suddenly I realised they were not brother and sister at all.

Neville (*charming smile, one professional to another*)   Obviously a full day . . . (*He picks up metal paper spike.*) I see you're allowed one of these.

Peirce   Allowed?

Neville   Yes, when I was a solicitor in North London, a slightly decaying inner-city practice, *all* spikes were banned from all desks.

Peirce   What on earth for?

Neville (*breezy smile*)   Because as you sat there facing this succession of odd, often crazy clients, every now and then a particularly frustrated person would leap up and turn one of these (*He moves paper spike.*) into a deadly weapon – a lunge straight for the eye. (*Charming smile.*) I imagined it might be the same here.

Peirce (*sharp*)   It is not. (*Finishing doing up a shoe.*) So what do you want to know?

Neville   I have an acquaintance – a woman who I'm advising on a consultative, unofficial basis, I think you are aware of the case I am referring to.

Peirce   Yes.

Neville   You are?

Peirce   I didn't say that.

Neville   Halina Rodziewizowna, the Polish woman who was arrested on New Year's Eve in Warsaw. She's applied for residency – I wanted to know what you think her chances are?

Peirce (*looking up*)   Her chances?

Neville   Yes.

Peirce   Chances of success?

Neville   Yes!

Peirce   You wouldn't want me to give you a straight answer about that.

Neville   Wouldn't I?

Peirce   But unofficially, which is not necessarily worth having ... I'd say have a go, should be, *almost* certainly, worth a try.

Neville   You would advise that?

Peirce   I'm not advising anything.

Neville   Of course not.

Peirce   Nor am I giving an opinion, I'm merely saying why not?

Neville   Good. That seems clear.

Peirce   (*beady, suspicious*)   Does it? (*He moves.*) There are minus points of course – no request for asylum, application delayed until it's far too late, a Polish passport – always a major liability, near Christmas, the worst time possible, delays often prolonged, could easily prevent even a short extension to her visa.

Neville   On a scale from one to ten, where would you ...

Peirce   No! Not the scale of one to ten please – that always comes up, I never respond to it.

Neville   Below five?

Peirce   Below six.

Pause.

Neville   I see.

Peirce   (*surprised, sharp*)   Do you? (*Stands by yellowing blind, glancing out.*) the patterns people make in the snow, extraordinary neurotic shapes as they have a last cigarette before they drag themselves away from the building. You're suddenly able to see all sorts of things in this weather ... that weren't visible before.

Neville (*puzzled by this, breezy smile*) The snow won't last – it never does.

Peirce (*beady, turning*) Of course it depends slightly on who she comes up in front of – your acquaintance – which officer does the interviewing.

Neville Naturally. Have you any idea who that might be?

Peirce Some officers are more taxing than others – *I* can usually tell in ten minutes, the average hovers between ten and fifteen minutes; it's normally blindingly obvious if there are any discrepancies in what they say, in the passenger's version.

Neville So she'll be seeing you will she?

Peirce I don't think you'd want me to answer that question.

Neville (*slight smile*) No . . . of course not.

Peirce *takes a handful of papers, with brisk movements he tears them up.*

Peirce PUBLICITY – is another matter isn't it? If there has been some, and I'm not saying if I'm aware of any or not, generally we take a very dim view of people that have gone public before coming to us.

Neville I'll make absolutely sure there's no more of that – it will be stopped as from now. If you'd like I'll fill you . . .

Peirce (*holding up his hand*) No, no, save it, no facts please – we want it fresh. Absolutely fresh.

Peirce *stares down at the tape recorder on desk.*

I have one small task to perform before I go. (*Looks up.*) To rewind the tape and see what we've netted during last night.

Neville What's been netted?

Peirce   Yes, information that has come in ... People informing about cases under consideration.

Peirce *zips up tracksuit with a sudden single movement.*

Neville (*surprised*)   *Informing?* Really? (*Then more urbane.*) I knew some of this must go on of course – but I've never seen the results before.

Both staring down into the tape.

Peirce   Yes, it's a consistent source of intelligence, a constant and valuable flow.

Peirce *switching the tape volume up, we hear the loud blank hiss of the empty tape, interrupted several times by a click of people ringing in but not leaving a message.* **Neville** *moves, assuming he has to leave.*

Peirce   No Mr Gregory, you don't have to go yet. If there's anything on here, I will stop it when we reach it.

Neville (*surprised but pleased, moving back to the tape*)   So you get all these informers on tape, it must make interesting listening.

Peirce   Yes, it's a twenty-four-hour service – when there isn't a duty office available, we resort to just the machine.

Loud click on the machine, noise of somebody breathing into the receiver nervously, then ringing off. **Peirce** *looks down.*

People get to the water, but they don't always drink. Their nerve fails and they slip away. It's a very poor catch today, I'm afraid. On a good night sometimes the tape is jam-packed from end to end, with a whole cross-section of nationalities.

There's a wild soft jabber suddenly on the tape in a difficult-to-recognise language, and then the speaker disappears.

Neville   I think that was probably Persian. Yes, Iranian Arabic.

Peirce   Really? Is that what it was. He slid off the hook anyway. (*Glancing at tape.*) They often tend to come in a rush, squashed together on the same part of the tape, about 2 a.m. at night, that's their favourite time – suddenly there they are.

Neville (*moving close, fascinated*) All moved to call at the same witching hour. (*He looks at* **Peirce**.) Why do they do it, inform? It can't be greed, you don't pay them?

Peirce Absolutely not. They do it to get rid of 'friends' and relatives they don't like – or detest. Or because they're not doing as well over here as they hoped and are very resentful. (*Turning to look at him.*) It's safe to say their motives vary.

Neville (*intrigued smile, staring down at machine*) There're a lot of curious people out there, swimming about at two o'clock in the morning.

Suddenly a voice, urgent, stabbing out of the tape. 'Are you there, are you listening, I want to tell you about, I have to tell you everything I know about Marie, about how she's really not, not, NOT . . .'
Peirce *clicks off tape before it goes further.*

Peirce Some people shout, I'm afraid . . . You must leave me to my listening now.

Neville *moves.*

Peirce You wouldn't want me to wish you good luck – so I'm not going to.

Blackout.

Scene Six

Neville*'s flat.*

The last seconds of a radio commercial, followed by a mention of **Halina***'s experience on a late-night radio phone-in, which blends into the sound of carols being sung outside the window, in the square, in the distance at first.*

Snow pouring down the cyclorama, heavy incessant snow, for a moment back-lit, forming a white Dickensian Christmas-scene outside.

Inside, a small Christmas tree stands at the far end of the room with coloured lights and decorations on it, among the clean pastel walls. The lights in room come up only half way leaving a late-night feel.

As the angelic sound of the high voices singing the carol, 'Good King Wenceslas', gets nearer and passes right below the window we hear the lyrics to the familiar tune are darker, obscene, unsettling, still sung by the high voices. A hooligan version. The voices take some time to recede during the following dialogue.

Andrew *standing with his back to the audience watching the snow drive down.* **Halina** *in her long heavy coat,* **Neville** *is opening a bottle of champagne.*

Andrew   My God has it ever snowed like this. This is *London* doesn't it realise that! It's far too deep, it's lying there like it's never going to leave.

Carol singers approaching.

Neville (*opening champagne*)   I see no reason why we shouldn't have the champagne – even though there is nothing to celebrate. No date for Halina's interview.

Halina   Yet. (*She takes her glass of champagne, moves round the room by herself.*)

Neville   What an extraordinary noise!

Carol singers right underneath.

It's nearly three o'clock in the morning, what are they doing.

Andrew   Yes. X certificate carol singers moving down below. They look a fairly grisly terrifying collection to me.

Neville   I've never heard that sound in the square before.

Andrew   Maybe they only come out when we have a really bad winter.

Andrew *takes his champagne from* **Neville,** *boyish manner together.*

Andrew   I see you still haven't read the book –

Christopher's new book I lent you.

Neville (*clicking on his answering machine*)   I read half a page.

Andrew (*sharp smile*)   As much as that!

Neville (*picking up book*)   It was precisely how I'd imagined it'd be, very bland – and extremely short.

Andrew   You pick it up like it's going to scald you! (*He smiles.*) I think you may be a little jealous.

Soft woman's voice leaking out of the answering machine.

Neville (*charming smile*)   Jealous? Slightly, I admit. It's not exactly gnawing inside though, more a very mild hum. It occasionally spurts out when I catch sight of him in one of the Sunday papers.

Voice urgent, stabbing out of the answering machine, the hoarse old woman's voice we heard in Scene Three, asking when she can see **Neville**.

Old Woman's voice   I have to see you about my house, they're trying to get me out of my house. I have to stay in all day, I know they are coming . . .

Neville (*clicking machine off*)   Just one of my old ex-clients – she still pursues me, obsessed with a problem she'll never let go of, about her house! (*Looking at machine.*) No news for Halina though.

Halina *moves offstage in her long coat, carol singers in distance.*

Neville (*watching her, as soon as she's left*)   It's been a peculiar few weeks, I can tell you. She's a slightly batty character of course . . .

Andrew   Is she?

Neville   Oh yes – but curiously interesting. I like the thought of her being a witness to these bits of recent history, rather vivid slices, the German occupation, the Stalinist struggles –

Andrew (*smile*)   And having all that right here in your room.

Neville   But what's really intriguing about Halina is . . .
(*He smiles.*) she's a long way from being a wholly admirable
person.

Andrew (*indicating flat*)   She's probably a little shy – a little
nervous of all this.

Neville (*suddenly*)   They have to at least *see* her here don't
they, give her an interview.

Andrew   I'd say yes, normally they would.

Neville (*cutting him off*)   The immigration officer I saw was
a real shifty little creep, just like one'd imagine them to be
– he even seemed to be showing off his intelligence
operation to me.

Halina *enters behind them. They don't notice.*

Andrew   They will delay as long as they can of course.

Neville   And then say it's too late.

Andrew   It's possible they may never see her, but of
course the publicity is good, and what happened to her in
Poland is very strong . . .

Halina *topples sideways, brushing the side wall, she breaks her fall,
steadying herself.*

Neville   Halina?

Andrew   Are you all right?

Halina (*calmly refilling her glass*)   I'm very well. (*Her manner
and voice are not drunk at all.*)

Neville (*watching her with glass*)   She must eat something.
She hardly hate anything in the restaurant did you Halina?

Halina   No, but I can assure you I didn't waste it, when
you weren't looking, old habits die very slowly, I managed
to bring it back home.

Halina *is kneeling unselfconsciously in her heavy coat in the middle* *of the stage, she reaches into the pockets.*

Neville   No wonder you were walking so far behind.

Halina   These deep pockets are very useful, this is a coat for gourmets. (*Slight smile.*) Now I've been deprived of my bags, it has become even more valuable. There're a lot of recent meals down there, the sauces running together, (*Indicates left pocket.*) fish and seafood are on this side . . .

Halina *bends her head, kneeling in middle of room, eating small piece of bread from her pocket.* **Neville** *watching her.*

Neville   Halina.

She looks up.

It's not true, is it?

Halina   What's not true?

Neville   Your story, the armed guards, the prison yard, the whole dramatic ordeal – you made it all up.

Halina   (*giving nothing away*)   What makes you say that?

Andrew   (*louder*)   Is your story *true* Halina?

Slight pause.

Halina   Not exactly.

Neville   Not exactly? (*Sharp.*) Is it true or not?

Halina   We were arrested on New Year's Eve . . .

Neville   You *were.*

Halina   A group of us were driving in a car which wasn't properly licensed, there was a little confusion about our papers as well, they were being lazy, the police, because it was a holiday, so we were held for about forty-eight hours in the station playing cards and drinking a little and smoking a lot. Then they let us go.

Neville   That's all! No drama, no nightmare?

Halina   That is everything – that's what happened.

Snow outside.

Andrew Jesus! I believed it. I believed her story.

Neville (*very quick*) *That's* why you didn't want a lawyer, because it isn't true!

Halina (*correcting him*) I had to improve on the truth, a little. It was obvious from everything you said I needed something stronger, darker. (*Lightly.*) Something more than just being the victim of a tiny pimple of history. So I did.

Carol singers beginning to cross square again in distance.

Andrew My God! (*Moving rapidly.*) I have to make some quick calculations – the risk factor?

Neville Which is what?

Andrew Of course people trying to land often lie, sometimes very elaborately and on rare occasions a few get in that way.

Neville (*sharp, sceptical*) Really? People do?

Andrew I personally know of at least two cases. It's incredibly difficult not to get tripped in the interrogation – but it can be done.

Neville But will they believe she was allowed out of Poland, if this is *meant* to have happened?

Andrew (*precise*) That's not a problem. Either the Polish authorities didn't know – Halina too frightened to tell etc – or they let her go because they wanted to get rid of her, dump her out of the country.

Halina can choose which she goes with – the British will buy either – *if* they believe her story.

Neville And will they?

Andrew (*pacing, calculating*) She *was* in prison, they can check that if they like. They will never be able to confirm or deny what went on there. The Poles will say it's all lies, the British won't believe a single bloody thing they say –

now it's a tremendous advantage it's Christmas time, everything moving so sluggishly here, they may not look too hard. It will all depend on the interview, it's a strong story, they may like its melodrama, it's what they expect . . .

Neville   What are the chances, Andrew?

Andrew (*stops pacing*)   If you want a first estimate . . . and this is very much a first estimate . . . 75/25.

Halina   In my favour?

Andrew   No, in their favour of course.

Halina *turns.*

Andrew   The odds always favour them.

Neville   She hasn't a hope, I've seen the opposition. She hasn't a chance!

Andrew   Of course there is still the possibility if she failed, even if they were told her story was false and proved it, of reverting to the original plan.

Neville   There is? Going ahead with the original scheme?

Andrew   Yes, obviously the longer we delay on that, the more difficult it becomes.

Neville   Obviously.

Andrew   It would need to be exceptionally convincing. (*Pacing.*) I should say the same odds apply. Of course, if outside events suddenly change, a quick extra freeze of East–West relations, if it suits them to let . . .

Neville (*staring at* **Halina**)   I think you better leave us Andrew.

Halina (*sharp*)   Why?

Andrew (*suddenly stops pacing*)   Yes, I have an appointment.

Halina   What? At 3.30 in the morning?

Andrew (*moving to exit*)   Yes, it never seems to stop, I have

to fit some of my cases in at strange hours. People hanging
on by their fingertips, about to be thrown out of the
country – and getting around in this snow takes twice as
long as usual. I'll be in touch.

He's gone.

Pause, **Neville** *looking across at* **Halina.**

Neville (*very icy*)   So Halina – what are you *really* up to?

Halina   Just what you see.

Neville   What sort of answer is that?

The snow increasing all the time.

Halina   It's the only one I can give you.

Neville (*moving towards her, sharp, legal*)   But that is simply
not the case is it. Why all these lies?

Halina   What lies?

Neville   Come on Halina, the psychotic guards, the
prison drama, you've taken a ridiculous risk.

Halina   I do not agree.

Neville   They'll crack your story in a few minutes. (*Sharp
smile.*) Between ten and fifteen minutes to be precise. We
had a perfectly simple arrangement.

Halina *facing him, very still.*

Halina   I know. It was a choice between the devil and
the deep black sea.

Neville   Is that deliberate?

Halina *doesn't move.*

Neville (*crisp*)   Halina, I am a rational man – and I want
some reasons now.

Halina (*surprised*)   For what?

Neville (*louder*)   What are you trying to do?

Halina *moving, taking her heavy coat off, underneath the fashionable sweater and a new skirt.*

Halina   I am just trying to get into the country – your country.

Neville   I don't believe that's all that's going on, why did you come over to England *now*, at this precise moment.

Halina (*facing him*)   I've told you, why can't you accept it. I was taking care of my father, I had years of sitting at the end of his bed, his voice still goes round and round my head every night. And then he died.

I had to make up for lost time. And I couldn't do it in Poland.

Snowing increasing outside. Carol singers in distance.

Neville (*moving up to her*)   From what I've seen of you Halina, I can believe in you as a little girl scuttling around Warsaw by yourself, dodging between the German tanks, but I don't believe for one moment in you sitting quietly at your father's bedside for the rest of your life.

Halina   It doesn't make any difference what you believe. That's what I had to do. (*Lightly.*) I'm not expecting you to shed tears over it.

Neville   Who sent you here?

Halina   What do you mean who sent me? That's so predictable Neville, you must stop thinking that I have some spy contact, feeding squirrels in the park by the litter bins, forever waiting for me to show up.

Neville (*watching*)   Are you a communist Halina?

Halina   That's not really your business is it? I lost all my politics in my twenties, while I was on this island, so to speak, with my father. (*Facing him.*) I'm only just re-emerging to look around.

Neville (*bearing down on her*)   Really? So how on earth did you know enough to use the media the way you did? Pitch your story so right?

Halina (*slight smile*)   Oh that's simple, that's easy, all the repeat programmes on the BBC we have, like *The Forsyte Saga*.

Pause.

Neville   Why don't you surprise me Halina? Give me a straight answer for once.

Halina   That was. I think I watched every English television programme ever shown in Poland. I'm full of English trivia.

Neville (*sharp*)   I thought you were meant to be a harmless Polish 'housewife' interested in wallpaper design! Who didn't want to get involved in East–West propaganda. (*Flaps newspaper.*) And now look what you've achieved with your story.

Halina (*cutting him off*)   I didn't want to get involved in painting an even worse picture of the East than already exists, going before some tiny official and debasing myself with Cold War platitudes, but the police are different – a story about them. They can look after themselves.

Neville   The distinction seems far from obvious to me.

Halina (*facing him*)   It's the price of admission – isn't that right? (*Pause.*) Of getting in here.

Silence. Snow even harder.

Neville (*suspicious*)   You keep changing Halina.

Halina   Do I?

Neville   Yes, one moment you're this comic character emerging with a heap of scabby plastic bags that you won't let out of your sight. And now you look like this. You seem to have gone through the voracious buying-the-first-thing-you-see stage to something else amazingly quickly.

Halina (*watching him*)   You mean from bad taste to style in two easy leaps. (*Indicating clothes.*) I just borrowed these.

Neville (*pointing out*) And outside here – outside this window, odd things keep happening. There's this violent vivid un-English weather.

Halina   So I am to blame for the weather as well!

Neville   And then across this snow-covered scene these weird psychopathic carol singers wander singing sweet murderous songs – unlike anything I've ever heard before! I come into a friend's video shop and you immediately claim it is about to go bust ... which is rubbish of course.

Halina   Why should I make something like that up!

Neville   I feel I'm inhabiting one of those infuriating East European cartoons they show before the main feature in art houses where everything keeps changing shape, while a little blob-like man travels through it all making squeaking noises!

Halina (*watching him*)   Yes.

Pause.

Your room's a little different too, Neville.

Neville (*looking around*)   What do you mean?

Halina   It's been searched.

Neville   Searched? Rubbish.

Halina *indicates low soft white chair.*

Halina   This chair has been moved several inches from where it was before.

Neville   I see no difference.

Halina   He's left a rather more obvious sign I'm afraid, I have a nose for these things.

She lifts cushions on chair. The inside of pale white armchair is smeared with oil stains, heavy black stains.

Neville (*suspicious*)   What's that?

Halina   He seems to have been bleeding oil, (*She smiles.*)

his motorcycle must have been leaking and he brought a
lot in with him.

*She moves one of the few decorations on the wall, underneath it black
oil fingermarks smeared.*

Probably a little bit of it under most things, smeared his
little fingers everywhere. Rather an amateur effort by our
standards back home.

Neville (*sharp*) They've been inside here! In my flat –
what on earth for?

Halina They decided to run a check on me, (*Looks up.*)
maybe they think like you.

Neville My God. Halina (*He moves.*) it is clear what
should happen now. It would be so simple – you ought to
revert to the original plan. You can marry me.

Halina No.

Pause.

Neville (*calmly*) You need never see me again.

Halina No.

Neville (*staring at her*) You would rather take on the
strength of the Immigration Service, telling fantastic lies,
than go through with this marriage.

Halina Yes. (*Pause.*) Don't take it personally again.
(*Calmly.*) Please do not let it scrape your ego.

Silence.

You do want me to leave now, don't you?

Watching him.

You must, don't you? If you want me to, please tell me
now.

Silence. They look at each other.

Neville (*very precise tone*) You can stay on one condition.

Halina (*turning*) And what is that?

Neville You let this mask drop.

Halina Mask? What do you mean?

Neville You've spent the whole time appearing confident, forcing yourself to be polite to people, being calm and enigmatic, spreading all this Slavic mist – you can't keep it up for ever. (*He looks at her.*) It's driving me totally crazy.

Pause.

You have to let it out Halina – and this is the time to do it.

Halina (*calmly*) You're giving me permission are you?

Neville Yes.

Halina To 'let it out'.

Neville Yes.

Halina You mean it?

Neville (*very slight pause*) Yes.

Halina *moving towards Christmas tree.*

Halina And you won't retract the permission, if I . . .

Neville No.

Halina I know, I'm sure. (*Loud.*) I KNOW I CAN BEAT THEM.

Taking ball off Christmas tree.

If only giants are allowed in, then from the ordinary material that is my life I had to make at least one gigantic episode. And I *can* do it, use my brain for once. It's rusting from lack of use. When I'm at the interview I can't lose.

But – if they don't see me.

She breaks Christmas ball.

This incredible wait, every day passing and there's no

news, the slowness of this country makes Poland seem a place of supersonic speed. (*She takes second ball off tree.*) They won't tell me when they'll see me.

Neville (*nervously*) Careful Halina.

Halina Every time I call them. They are so polite, it is almost like they are caressing me with their apologies – and each time they delay just a little longer, just one more week closer to the deadline when I have to leave. It's like they are tearing your arm off, but one centimetre at a time.

Suddenly breaks the decorative balls on the tree, an assault on the Christmas tree, golden balls popping, as her frustration explodes.

It is the only way they can win – not letting me fight the first round.

Neville Leave something on the Christmas tree, if you possibly can.

Halina You did ask me. (*She turns.*) I thought the permission covered everything.

The fury, the temper gives way to something very quiet and still. Outside the snow pouring down.

I was determined not to feel the usual conventional guilt on leaving one's country, leaving everyone behind, because if I did I was finished, and so far I've done very well. I *don't*.

Kneeling on floor, quiet.

But there is something else. I am a little afraid, I have a slight terror of being passed from country to country if I fail, being made stateless. A rotting package shovelled from one border to another, getting a little smaller each time, a piece coming off with every frontier, have you ever thought what that might be like – I haven't – with absolutely nowhere to go. Like falling into space, into the crack between land and sea.

She moves rhythmically backwards and forwards, **Neville** *watching,* *not knowing what to do.*

Not just without a home, but with nowhere to *be*. Ending up in the last possible airport, surrounded by plastic bags.

Moving rhythmically.

Don't get alarmed, I'm sorry, it'll pass quickly.

Neville *staring across at her.*

Neville   Halina.

Halina (*quiet, calm*)   It's going . . . bit by bit.

Neville (*staring at her*)   All this darkness coming out of you.

Halina   I told you, don't worry.

Neville (*moving cautiously up to her*)   Halina, I don't know you very well, in fact I hardly know you at all . . . I'd like to *help* you – but how? (*Pause.*) I'm not sure what to say next, (*Slight smile.*) very rare for me . . . because you're so determined, set on the wrong course of action.

You won't listen to reason. You don't know this country, you don't know your way around. ·

Halina (*crunches final Christmas ball, lightly*)   It's over, no problem now, it's all come out. No more to come.

Neville (*watching her, intrigued*)   Halina Rodziewizowna.

Halina (*looking up*)   Yes, (*Slight smile.*) you still pronounce it right.

Halina *is smoking.*

Neville   You're burning holes in the carpet.

Halina   I didn't have permission for that?

Neville   If you knew you were going to fail –

Halina   I won't fail.

Neville   But if you *did* know in advance you couldn't possibly succeed, and would damage yourself in trying – that they were never going to let you in because of your story.

Halina   I might reconsider your plan. I don't know. Who knows!

Neville   I see. (*Moving away.*) Don't worry. I know what to do next now, everything will become clear.

Halina (*hardly listening*)   I can't sleep, no point trying now, too much of the night has gone. It's snowing so hard, maybe they won't be able to get me out of the country, even if they want to. (*Moving to exit.*) I'll make a tremendous breakfast. A *Polish* breakfast.

Neville   Is that wise?

Halina (*detached*)   You said you weren't going to make any Polish jokes.

She exits. Offstage she sings a fragment of a current English pop song.

Neville   I have to make her see sense. (*Punching out number from diary, on phone.*) Come on – where is the tone? Typical of the Immigration Service, forget to check the tone is working on their answering machine.

He gets a connection.

Right. (*His manner decisive, as if despatching some legal business.*) I have some information concerning Halina Rodziewizowna whose application for residency you received on December 12th.

Item one – she has been working illegally in the vicinity of Tottenham Court Road in a hi-fi and video store called the Sound Castle – without a work permit, or any authorisation, a simple check will reveal this.

Item two – her story of her dramatic ordeal in a Warsaw police station is a total fiction. The story is false, without foundation. If you now bother to look for any corroborative evidence, even a single witness, you will find none exist. That is the information I have. It is accurate. (*Signing off.*) An informed source. (*He rings off.*)

Halina *singing offstage, fragment of song.*

Neville   I should have done that before. It's the only sensible course. She would never have brought it off, her way. (*Looking down at phone.*) My voice tangled up with all those others on the tape, (*Sharp smile to himself.*) at least it's past the peak time for informing!

Halina *enters with two mugs of steaming coffee.*

Neville (*turns*)   I've just been clearing things up here, Halina.

Halina (*looking at cushions all over the floor*)   So I see. (*She hands him the coffee.*) First course.

Neville (*polite*)   Thank you. That's good of you. Why were you singing such an odd song out there?

Halina   It's very popular at the moment, didn't you know, it's sailing up the charts. (*Sings a fragment.*) I got a copy of it from the shop.

They stand watching the snow and the blue light breaking on the cyclorama. There is distant rumbling noise from outside.

Neville   My God – it *is* almost morning.

Halina   Neither of us will have slept tonight.

Neville   I never heard that noise before, another one! I wonder what it is, distant thunder of snow ploughs setting out, spreading across London.

Halina   Yes, the city's starting up again.

Blue light starting to break.

Neville (*by window*)   After what's happened these last few days, the sheer absence of logic, when the light comes up like now, I half expect to look out and see a different view there, a completely changed London. A fanciful whimsical mid-European version, full of eccentric deliberately perverse buildings, tilting at alarming angles and with perverse shaped people milling about across the square in the snow, old women with huge trunks on their backs and dwarves, all talking some incomprehensible language, which I can't reply to.

Light brightening all the time.

Halina (*sipping coffee*)   Well let's see what there is out there now.

As light increases.

You never know your luck do you.

Lights up to bright then blackout.

Act Two

Scene One

Sense of humming corridors in the blackout, of expectant noise, footsteps down the passage, foreign voices echoing and calling, phones ringing.

The mural, a mosaic of blue, green and silver stretching across the back wall where the cyclorama was.

Full expanse of the stage, bare except for a drinks machine and one chair.

The mural shows people arriving on a shore with blue and white water behind them, shadowy travellers facing an idealised glowing city on a hill, across an expanse of green.

Somebody has drawn one major piece of graffiti on the mural, a monster emerging out of the blue water with its teeth bared.

Neville *is upstage by a drinks machine, on the other side of the stage* **Waveney** *is standing, smoking with her back to him. She is wearing a red coat.*

Downstage sitting on a chair is an old **Turkish Woman***, scarf over her head, heavy boots and coat, and two large plastic bags bulging at her feet.*

Bright early afternoon sun. As **Neville** *approaches machine, a deafening but totally unintelligible announcement booms out.*

Neville (*stopped in his tracks*) They've got a nice way of making you feel welcome here.

Waveney (*without turning round*) Yes.

Neville *about to put money in,* **Turkish Woman** *lifts her head shouts over to him, loud Turkish.*

Neville Yes. Quite.

Neville *lifts his hand to put money in –* **Turkish Woman**

calls out again.

Waveney I think she knows something about that machine we don't. Maybe you should take her advice – it looks like she's spent rather a lot of time here.

Neville Yes, that's the feeling I get. (*To* **Turkish Woman**.) Thank you. (*He smiles pleasantly.*) She's probably lost a large part of her life savings in that machine.

Bells ringing in distance.

Neville (*to* **Waveney**) When's your interview?

Waveney Not today. I hope. (*She turns to face him.*)

Neville I'm dreadfully sorry, I didn't recognise you, you're the girl from the shop. I thought you were one . . .

Waveney So I see. Don't worry about it. (*Drily.*) Natural mistake.

Neville (*smiles*) I was dazzled by this monstrous mural, people arriving somewhere . . . where do you think it's meant to be?

Waveney (*staring at the glowing city*) I don't know, maybe Southampton on a sunny day.

Neville *smiles.*

Waveney A nice place, wherever it is.

Neville Why are you here today?

Waveney To give Halina a helping hand. (*Sharp.*) Why are you here?

Andrew *enters briskly.*

Andrew (*to* **Neville**) There you are. (*Glancing over his shoulder.*) I shouldn't be here of course.

Neville Why not?

Andrew I might be recognised, by either side. It's awash with people back there in the other section waiting for general interviews. There might be somebody there I failed to help – if they see me it could make the officers suspicious. (*Glancing around.*) It should be all right in this section. (*Worried.*) Where is Halina?

Waveney   She'll be here.

Andrew (*hardly taking in* **Waveney**)   She better be. We just got in under the wire before Christmas. Last interviews today. (*Anxious.*) She'll be able to find it will she?

Waveney   She wouldn't miss this for the world.

Neville (*breezily*)   Yes. You know I never thought she'd get this far. That they'd actually see her about her story, I'm very surprised . . .

Waveney   Why?

Neville   A reason of my own.

Andrew (*looks at* **Waveney**)   When's your interview?

Waveney   Not yet, not today.

Neville   She's with us (*Slight smile.*) I think.

Andrew (*surprised*)   Really? A friend of Halina? (*Glances at the* **Turkish Woman**.) People can wait months for special interviews, this looks like a good example. (*He smiles at the* **Turkish Woman**.) At last the day has come.

Neville (*smiles at* **Turkish Woman**)   Yes, she's had to wait outside these doors before.

Turkish Woman *lifts head, she is near machine.*

Neville   No, I'm not going to touch now, I assure you.

Andrew (*pacing busily, pointing at mural*)   This is interesting – like an illustration from a children's book. It's been through several important phases this building, first the strictly functional, just let's process the people without fuss and get the hell out of here.

Then, at the height of immigration the brutally unwelcoming, the benches so hard and so few of them, to flush out the people that weren't really serious about waiting for days without end. And now, for some bizarre reason, when there's practically no chance of ever getting into this country, they've decided to soften the place, murals, CHAIRS, we may even get some music . . .

Halina *enters. She's wearing a lilac coat, a pale yellow hat, as if for a wedding.*

Waveney   She's here!

Neville   My God, I didn't imagine you would dress like that!

Halina   Why not?

Neville   You look like the Queen Mother.

Halina   Did you want me to wear black? That would have been a little predictable wouldn't it. (*She smiles.*) I thought I should try and surprise them. (*To* **Waveney**:) What do you think? I borrowed everything.

Waveney   I think you look just right.

Halina   I'm glad you're here. I didn't think you'd be able to get away from the shop.

Waveney   That was easy. It's closed today for good. So I'm free.

Halina   Really? Closed? As soon as that!

Waveney   Yes. (*Holding bag.*) This is full of spare parts! Hundreds of little leftovers from the shop!

Halina (*rummaging in her bag with bits of plastic*)   Yes, I've got some still, the ones I studied, I was going to give them back . . .

Waveney (*exuberant*)   NO, NO! You might as well get something out of me losing my job! (*She smiles.*) I'm going to be your cheerleader today Halina.

Andrew   Now I just want to issue a few guidelines.

Halina   Guidelines?

Andrew Yes everything they say and do here has only one purpose, to prove you're *not what you make yourself out to be.*

Halina Yes.

Andrew That you're lying. Fraudulent. They may try any tack . . .

Halina Yes.

Andrew And be prepared for the extreme banality of the questions.

Halina (*slight glance at* **Neville**) I'm always prepared for that.

Andrew Some officers favour the geographical approach, to find whether you're really a *native* of the country you say you are, it can be very blatant. (*To* **Halina**:) For instance what is the highest range of mountains in Poland?

Halina I don't know. I have no idea.

Neville The Karkonosze, isn't it, in the Sudety mountains?

Andrew And the tallest individual mountain?

Halina I don't know. I'm sorry. I'm not very good on mountains. What about the cinemas and cafés of Warsaw?

Neville I should think it's Mount Sniezka.

Halina (*looking at him*) That's very good.

Andrew It's strange, nobody ever knows the geography of their own country.

Neville (*smiles*) Do you want the oldest churches in Warsaw? (*To* **Halina**:) If I'd known we could have done some last-minute coaching.

Andrew Don't worry – the watchword must be consistency, either be consistently knowledgeable or consistently ignorant. Don't mix the two.

Halina   I'll do my best not to.

Andrew (*brisk*)   I have to leave very soon. It's my perpetual fate to always have to exit before the *real* events occur, for obvious reasons – I could be recognised. So the final guidelines . . . Aim for a clean interview.

Waveney   You mean no filthy jokes, won't that disappoint them?

Andrew   By which I mean don't be over-ambitious, you have to convince them of your worth, and the worth of your story. The best way . . .

Booth *appears wheeling a bicycle.*

Andrew *immediately moves upstage.*

Booth (*stops*)   Miss Rod, Rodz, Rodzi . . .

Neville   Miss Rodziewizowna.

Halina   Yes?

Booth (*holding out card*)   Your number.

Halina   What is it?

Booth   Number one.

Halina   Good.

Booth   One, six, five, zero.

Halina *takes number.*

Booth   The size of the number is not necessarily of any significance. If you're called today you may bring only *one* friend in with you.

Waveney   Guess who that's going to be.

Neville (*to* **Booth**)   We understand. That will be me. I'm advising Miss Rodziewizowna.

Booth (*moving to leave*)   And please try not to bring slush, snow, or mud into the office.

Turkish Woman *calling after him 'Excuse, excuse me' . . . he* *goes.*

Andrew   Good we're making progress, we're into the first round.

Waveney (*to* **Turkish Woman**)   He'll return with your number, I'm sure, very soon.

Turkish Woman *replying, excited, worried stream.*

Neville (*indicating* **Woman**)   I've got it now, I think that's Turkish. (*Moving up to* **Halina**.) Relax Halina, just relax, as much as possible.

Halina (*very calmly*)   I am.

Neville (*animated*)   You really are through to the interview you *realise.*

Halina   I realise.

Neville   No need to be nervous! (*Up to her.*) You know I was certain for a particular reason of my own, that you didn't have a chance in hell of reaching this stage, but the reason seems to have disappeared into thin air. It's evaporated. It's unrecorded! In fact, now you are here, I really want you to do well, Halina. I do . . .

Halina (*drily, slight smile*)   That's good to know.

Blackout.

Scene Two

The wall of the office rolls across with a very large door in the middle of the wall.

Peirce's *office now fills the stage. The door is oddly large for the scale of the walls. Around and above the door is misted glass looking out on the passages beyond. We can glimpse the mural on the back wall, now looking smudged and diffused through the glass.*

There is a small picture on the wall of people on a golden beach mirroring the mural outside; it is the only ornament on the wall.

The stage is very bare, just the desk with papers on it, and three chairs, one of them a very ordinary wooden chair, empty in the middle of the stage.

Peirce *and* **Booth** *standing waiting.* **Neville** *also in the office. They are looking towards the large open door.*

Halina *enters, looking confident, almost flamboyant. She stops in the doorway.*

Halina *(surveying* **Peirce***)*   So you're the one that's going to be seeing me.

Peirce   Miss Halina Rodziewizowna.

Halina   Yes.

Peirce   I've pronounced it correctly?

Neville   Yes.

Peirce *(looking across the stage at her)*   If I may say so, you don't look at all like your photographs.

Halina   Really. *(She smiles, still in doorway.)* I hope that will not be held against me, *(Glancing around.)* nor my choice of clothes.

Peirce *(welcoming smile)*   I wouldn't have thought so. In this job I have to consume acres of newsprint, make sure I know what's happening out there. *(Indicates the outside.)* And I *kept* on coming across your picture.

Halina   So did I. *(She smiles, moving forward.)* I quite enjoyed that in fact. Things travel very fast through your media.

She moves to wooden chair.

Neville   This office has changed – it didn't look like this before.

The chair **Halina** *is sitting on squeaks every time she moves, rasping and rickety.*

Peirce *(invitingly)*   Can we offer you anything Miss Rodziewizowna? There's some tea here, yes, and there's a single biscuit left.

Halina   No. (*Lightly.*) I think I'll wait until I've got into the country, before I start becoming a serious tea drinker.

Neville (*taking the biscuit*)   Halina's a very cautious person.

Peirce   There is no mystery in what is going to happen – we're simply here to establish the truth. (*Pleasantly.*) Or to be more accurate what *I* think the truth is – that's all that matters.

Halina   Good, that could not be clearer. (*Looking at him.*) Your impression of the truth.

Peirce (*lightly*)   There are as many approaches in this building as there are interviewing officers. (*Moving to the desk.*) My colleague will not be saying anything, he is here merely to take notes.

Peirce *produces another full packet of biscuits from his desk. He bites into one.*

People have often been up all night before interviews, rehearsing.

Halina   I promise not to fall asleep.

Peirce (*pleasantly*)   And because they are nervous, lies can happen, sometimes almost by accident, and then people often seem to get into a spiral of untruths, which is unfortunately disastrous. If I unpick one false link usually –

Halina   The whole lot comes tumbling down – of course. (*She moves, rasping, squeak from the chair.*) And is this chair chosen on purpose? When people tense themselves up it squeaks. (*She does it, the chair squeaks.*) An English Lie Detector maybe? (*Slight smile.*) A very good idea.

Peirce (*watching her*)   Like everything else in this building it's feeling its age. Miss Rodziewizowna, there is a fact about your case which you are probably unaware of.

Neville   Which is what?

Peirce (*calmly*)   We have received certain information about you – alternative information, via a phone call to this building.

Neville   You mean somebody informed on her!

Peirce   Yes.

Halina (*blowing smoke from small cigar*)   How strange – somebody bothering to give false information about *me*.

Neville   I hope having mentioned it – you are going to tell us exactly what it consists of, and where it came from?

Peirce   The information was anonymous – which we take much less seriously. What this person didn't realise is, we get a torrent of malicious false information, as well as the truth.

Neville   Obviously this must all be withdrawn – I demand on Miss Rodziewizowna's behalf, these anonymous allegations be erased from the case.

Peirce (*ignoring him, to* **Halina**)   It merely makes this difference – before I was under pressure from those I'm answerable to, to make this interview a formality because of all the publicity, and the nature of that publicity. That can no longer be the case.

Neville   No, I must *insist* you disregard these flagrantly malicious allegations.

Halina *moving, chair rasping.*

Halina   The chair's getting excited. Please, I can't make you forget whatever you've been told – so I'll just have to demonstrate it's not true.

Peirce (*looking at papers*)   Your preliminary questionnaire – your answers seem very satisfactory, very clear, your education, the sudden halt, not married, no children, your father's loss of power and your time looking after him.

Halina (*lightly*)   Twenty-nine years.

Peirce   Twenty-nine years, yes, a long time. Your interests . . . by the way have you bought any records since you arrived here?

Halina (*meeting his eyes, smiles*)   You mean gramophone records to play on a gramophone?

Peirce   Obviously.

Halina (*stretching her legs out*)   I have been listening to the radio like a small child, all channels, it's started to grow on my ear . . . No I haven't.

Peirce   You've never been into a record shop?

Halina   I didn't say that, I've wandered into a few.

Peirce (*effortlessly, casually*)   What have you done since you arrived here, what jobs?

Neville   She hasn't.

Halina (*cutting him off*)   I haven't a job, it's illegal isn't it. I see now you ask an innocent question and then slide one underneath, the one with the kick. (*She smiles.*) That's good.

Peirce   You haven't worked in a store selling hi-fi video equipment?

Halina (*calm smile*)   If I'd been offered such a job I might have been tempted (**Neville** *twitches.*) but I wasn't.

I know nothing about hi-fi. (*Casually.*) You've checked of course!

Peirce (*briskly*)   Yes. The stores we contacted, none of them had ever heard of you.

He looks at her.

Miss Rodziewizowna – I think I want to move straight to your story, your dramatic story.

Halina (*smoking small cigar*)   Good, I have been waiting for this.

Peirce   Because the merit of your application so clearly depends on that. (*Looking down at notes.*) I see you were picked up by the police while speeding . . .

Halina   No. (*Calm smile.*) You are quite wrong right from the beginning. We were 'picked up' while driving normally late one evening. We were taken to the police station in Karmelicka Street . . . (*The chair squeaks.*) One of the legs of this chair is vibrating . . .

Halina *continues talking effortlessly as she gets up and moves to change her chair for the one* **Booth** *is sitting on.*

There were five of us, we were told there was something wrong with the license of the car. At first we were put in this normal room in the police station. Excuse me. (**Booth** *forced to vacate his chair, she takes his.*) Thank you . . . which even had magazines on the table, (*She sits on new chair.*) that's better, we sat there for . . .

Peirce   What are the colours of the walls in this room?

Halina   The walls? A pale green.

Peirce   You remember it just like that, you didn't have to think.

Halina (*leaning back on new chair*)   You know for a fact, or you ought to, I was in that police station – so obviously I know the colour of the walls, what you want to prove or disprove is what happened there. (*Innocently.*) Isn't it?

Neville (*coolly*)   Do you want Miss Rodziewizowna to continue or not?

Peirce   Very much.

Halina (*very casual, smoking cigar*)   In fact there was a picture of the American movie ET on the walls with its feet sticking out. I hope we can leave the walls now. The youngest of the guards then came in, he said we all had to come down the passage with him. I thought they must want to take photographs of us, I even looked at myself in the mirror.

Peirce   What were the exact words he used, this young guard?

Halina (*brushing this aside*)   I don't remember – some things

I remember, some I don't. We found ourselves at the end
of the passage, in a large old washroom full of baths, that
were unused, dead.

Peirce (*incredulous*) Baths?

Halina Yes, *baths*, you know that you wash in; the taps
were rusted up, I remember seeing some spiders at the
bottom. Suddenly one of the guards shouted, 'Take off
your shoes. Take them off now.' We all did.

Peirce You were barefoot now, by these baths.

Halina No, it was *winter*, as you know. I was wearing
blue tights. (*She smokes calmly.*) An old more senior police
guard came in, he started shrieking at us, we had been
found guilty, crimes against the state, they had checked our
files, we were the ones they had been searching for, they
had proof, at last they'd found us. (*She turns to* **Booth**.)
Please be quiet on that chair of yours, if possible.

She looks back at **Peirce**.

I thought they were drunk, this being New Year's Eve.

Peirce (*casually*) And you were all standing in this old
decaying kitchen?

Halina No, the *washroom*. Please *try* to listen. (*She pauses,
flicking the ash off her stubby cigar.*) We were taken outside,
which was brightly lit, with very high walls, a small pond
in the middle, with two large goldfish swimming in it, I
remember thinking there's hardly any room for them in the
pond. We were told to go over to the far end of the
courtyard.

Peirce (*sensing an opening*) These fat goldfish in *winter*, Miss
Rodziewizowna, this pond in fact was frozen solid of
course, wasn't it?

Halina *No*, there was a pipe running into it. Please
remember Warsaw is often no colder than London. (*Tone
changing to firm.*) I will go on, we were lined up against the
wall, arranged carefully, we were forbidden to turn round.

They stopped shouting, there was a curious silence, (*Perfectly
matter-of-fact.*) I heard this click behind us, and there was a
moment, a very clear moment of realisation, then of panic,
almost like a blow punching you in the stomach – they
were going to shoot us. We . . .

Peirce   One moment Miss Rodziewizowna. Did you turn
round, at this moment?

Halina (*momentary pause*)   I'm trying to remember the exact
order, yes, the lights were shining in my eyes.

People started screaming, then somebody dropped their
spectacles, there were three men behind us with machine
guns, they were yelling at us this abuse, both maniacally
and then very deliberately and all this time, there was this
song playing on a radio from somewhere, a Polish pop
song of that Christmas, a really banal song.

Then suddenly they started whispering to each other, the
police, and said they had decided to select only half of us,
we –

Booth   Could you say that again, I didn't get that.

Halina (*sweeping this aside*)   IF this is a device – it's not a
very clever one, get someone who can take shorthand
properly next time.

We were led back, into a different room, long low room,
and there . . .

*She gets up. Having seemed very casual, she shifts gear, now with full
authority.*

This is the very clever thing they did, their one stroke of
genuine imagination, one of the most alarming things I've
ever seen, there was this pile of clothes in the corner, other
people's clothes, shoes, stockings, spectacles even false teeth,
in these heaps, and all over the floor these buttons staring
up at you.

We all thought of course, this must be the group before us,
they had been shot, we really believed it was real then. (*She*

moves.) *No*, don't interrupt.

Four times, *four* times they took us out there, and put us through that, (*Loud.*) until there was *nothing* left inside us, *nothing*, and the final selection had been made. And I was in it, I was one of the chosen, come through this door they said, come through, and we did, we went though – only to find ourselves out in the street, and free.

Pause.

Peirce (*drily*)   I see.

Halina (*lightly*)   We never got our shoes back either.

The door flies open, the **Turkish Woman** *holding her bags, asks excitedly where her interview is.*

Peirce (*immediately*)   Not in here, your interview's not in here . . . along the corridor . . . you'll find your officer somewhere else.

She nods and leaves with her bags.

(*To* **Halina**:) It must have been an ordeal Miss Rodziewizowna.

Halina   It was yes.

Peirce (*sharp*)   Having to tell me all that.

Neville   Of course it was.

Halina (*having been wrong-footed, recovering immediately*)   No, not really, it was all right. There's even a certain pleasure in retelling something you've survived. I've told it so much in the last few weeks it just comes out now. (*Looks at him.*) And you *listened*, in the end.

Neville   I feel now we should –

Peirce (*sharp at* **Neville**)   Please, be quiet. (*To* **Halina**, *watching her closely*:) You complained of course about this appalling event.

Halina   Two days later, the official response was – it never happened. And when I got in touch with the others who went through it with me, they'd all been let go that morning, they didn't want to talk about any of it, or even hear it mentioned.

After my official complaint, I never felt entirely safe again, from the police.

Peirce   Not entirely safe.

Halina   No. That is why I'm here. Before you ask I think the reason it happened was a kind of manic spite from the guards, revenge for bad publicity, or simple, terrible boredom.

Pause, **Peirce** *watching her.*

Peirce   That seems conceivable, yes.

Halina (*to* **Booth**)   Can I see your notes please, you can have your seat back in a minute. (*As she flicks through* **Booth**'s *notes.*)

(*To* **Peirce**:) Something I don't understand, if you want to prove I'm lying, you don't have to prove anything, you just *tell* them that I am.

(*Pleasantly, turning to* **Booth**, *with his notes.*) These aren't too good, no, a little imprecise you've missed some detail – I'll correct them later for you.

(*Innocently looks up at* **Peirce**.) What's next please?

Peirce *suddenly exits sharply, frustrated movement,* **Booth** *scurrying behind him.*

Halina   Round one. Reasonable.   ·

Blackout.

Scene Three

Halina *and* **Waveney** *alone on stage in* **Peirce**'s *office, with the large door wide open and the vista of the mural seen through it. Warm mid-afternoon sun, distant music, dance music drifting from the* *bowels of the building, mingled with the announcements for interviews booming out.* **Waveney** *stands in the open doorway, back to the audience, staring towards the music.*

Waveney   Listen to that! Can you imagine anything worse than a Christmas party full of immigration officers? All trying to work out who in the room hasn't been invited. (*She turns smiling.*) I wouldn't like to try to gatecrash that party!

Halina   Maybe that's why they haven't come back – they are dancing with each other down there.

Waveney   They'll be back for more, don't worry! I've lost count of the times I've been stopped out there, (*Indicates through door.*) given a number, and told to wait for my interview. If I'm here any longer I'll start wanting to tell an officer my life story.

Halina   He doesn't believe me yet Waveney, I can feel it.

Waveney   He believes you, you are doing well.

Halina   How do you know?

Waveney   It's being relayed out there, live coverage, another giant screen, people are crowding round to see, betting on the outcome! No, you're doing fine – you're still here aren't you.

Halina   He's fifty-fifty. Sometimes I think I've got him, and then he gets away from me. There's too little room for error.

Waveney   I don't know why I want you so much to get in, but I do you know. Badly.

Halina   I had noticed.

Waveney   There's nothing at all logical about it. (*Sharp smile.*) Maybe I wouldn't mind somebody I know winning something for once. (*She moves.*) So don't let me down.

Halina   Thank you! (*Looking down at her hands as she smokes.*) I don't what to smoke too much. (*Lightly.*) I want to unnerve him with a dizzy calm. (*She fiddles with plastic bits in her bag.*)

Waveney You will! (*Moving loudly to wall where plaster has come away.*) Look at this – the 'gateway' to the country is falling to pieces! I don't know why I feel things so extremely today, of all days, vividly. It must be having to be out there in those passages, I keep getting twinges in them, bits of smells, bits of the floor, bring back memories.

Halina Yes, official passages affect me like that too: You feel absolutely nothing's secure, not even the linoleum under your feet, trap doors suddenly might spring open.

Waveney My first few days in this country a lot of it was spent in passages like those back there, about our papers. The *waiting* started right here, I was clinging to my mother, I was only four, everything was so blotchy and pale, I kept on not being able to work out the expression on people's faces, they were just blanks and blobs bending towards me.

Halina I've been having that problem over these last few weeks – and I am not four years old!

Waveney Even the first racist remarks I ever heard came spitting out of this bland round pebble of a face.

And I remember when I was staring out of the bus window, coming in from the airport, the day we arrived. I saw these people working in their gardens, they must have been wearing very pale clothes because they looked completely *nude*, and I thought how odd, all these people must go naked in this country all the time, even though it's so cold, will I have to? (*She really laughs.*) I don't think anybody's first impression of here has ever been more wrong!

Neville *enters holding tray with paper cups on it.*

Neville Here! Some drink.

Halina At last. (*Her head goes back, drinking deeply.*)

Neville (*smiles*) It's tap water. I avoided all the machines.

(*Looking at* **Waveney**.) I think the rules may be being broken – there are at this precise moment, three of us together in this room.

Waveney *not moving.*

Halina (*as she drinks*)   No sign of them?

Neville   No, they've gone away to regroup obviously.

Waveney (*indicating* **Halina** *drinking*)   They're being towelled down in their corner, and you in yours.

Halina   Yes.

Neville (*very animated*)   I can tell you Halina, it's an extraordinary sensation when you're listening to someone telling a story who you know is *lying*.

Waveney (*sharp*)   Don't use that word here – what do you think you're doing?

Neville (*ignoring this*)   First reaction – nobody, but nobody is going to believe this, stop! Just tell as little as possible. I wanted to go up and gag you, shout keep it simple for Godsake! And you were so outrageously casual, I thought she wants to get into this country so much and this is the best she can do – but then (*Pause.*) it really did begin to sound not at all bad.

Halina   Given time, is that going to grow into a compliment?

Neville   Maybe. There were too many details of course, the goldfish were severely unnecessary, but it was a skilful mixture, aimed accurately at several nerve-ends, traces of Kafka, a touch of cheap cold-war thrillers, from all that reading you've done, (*Moves, indicating building.*) it should appeal to people here, on the edge of being too much but not quite.

Waveney   I think it's really irresponsible of you to talk like this – why the hell don't you stop it?

Neville   What for? You're not suggesting they've bugged this room?

Halina   I don't think this particular one would want to bug – it would take all the skill and art out of his job.

Neville (*moving over to* **Halina**)   Anyway we have to concentrate on what they're planning next for you.

Halina   I wish they'd come back!

Waveney (*calling across*)   And why don't you leave her alone – I think she can look after herself you know.

Neville   I have no idea why you're being so hostile.

Waveney   Don't you?

Neville   You don't even know me.

Waveney   I know enough.

Noises ringing, **Waveney** *moves to the door.*

Neville (*turning*)   It has noises all its own this building. (*To* **Halina**:) Now, please don't overdo it this round, don't allow yourself to be tempted, you'll forget what you've said and they'll trip you up.

Halina (*quiet*)   Yes, Neville.

Neville (*lightly*)   And have *some* grace under pressure – you have to persuade them you're worth having, remember. (*He smiles.*) At least you have undoubtedly achieved one thing already – the informing has been neutralised, wiped off the record – totally annihilated!

Waveney   Informing? Who's been informing on you?

Halina   They won't tell us.

Peirce *and* **Booth** *moving into doorway.*

Waveney   The terrible duo – are they going to hand out parking tickets because there are three of us in the room at the same time?

Noise of voices, music and bells as **Peirce** *and* **Booth** *move into room.*

Peirce   I would like now, if possible, just to have a word alone with our friend here.

Neville   Me? Of course. Absolutely. (*To* **Halina** *and* **Waveney**.) Just leave us alone for a moment could you.

Halina (*sharp*)   Why is it necessary to talk to him?

Neville (*confidently*)   Yes, just step outside, I won't be long. (*To* **Halina**:) It's time to do business, I'll be with you in a minute.

Waveney   Aren't either of us allowed to stay in here – and keep an eye on him?

Neville (*smoothly*)   No, no it's best if we do this on our own, settle up – OK!

Halina *and* **Waveney** *exit,* **Halina** *taking a look back at the door.*

Peirce *and* **Booth** *stand together.*

Neville   As you can see, she is patently telling the truth.

Peirce (*looking at his papers*)   Mr . . .

Neville   If you are concerned about the publicity, we can do a deal about that – there'll be no press release from us saying she's been granted residency.

Peirce   Sit down please, Mr Gregory.

Neville (*amused smile*)   You want me to sit down? Of course.

He sits on the wooden chair centre stage.

Peirce   You don't mind helping us for a moment?

Booth   Just one thing we want to ask you.

Peirce   Why are you here?

Neville (*smiling confident*)   Why am *I* here?

Peirce   Wouldn't you say it's a little odd someone like you representing a . . .

Neville (*interrupting pleasantly*)   It's not odd, I am a solicitor who happened to meet Miss Rodziewizowna, and is giving her free advice.

Peirce (*sharp*)   But you work for a firm specialising in the entertainment industry.

Neville   Yes – but before then I worked in a general inner-city practice, I encountered every conceivable problem – like you do here.

Booth   And why did you leave?

Neville   Survival.

Peirce   You mean money.

Neville (*expansively, one professional to another*)   No – the money was about the same, but I began not to be able to cope with them all. Everything suddenly started to multiply wildly, you must know the feeling. These worried faces spattering the walls with their problems, shuffling in every day, full of rage and grievance before they even get up to my desk, sometimes with tiny problems that had grown inside their head – other times with problems so heavy they weighed on *you* the whole week. (*He smiles.*) I found I couldn't help them so I moved on.

Dipping about in copyright law is a little less interesting though.

Booth   How would you categorise your involvement in this case?

Neville   Categorise! I don't know why you're so interested. I am advising Miss Rodziewizowna, I was introduced to her by a friend.

Booth   Who was this friend?

Neville   The friend? (*About to say, then stops himself.*) An acquaintance, a woman who happened to –

Peirce (*suddenly*)   A woman! What's her name?

Neville (*brushes this aside*)   Why do you want to know her name – she only introduced us, it is irrelevant, there is absolutely no need for me to give you her name.

Booth   So you would categorise your involvement as one of polite interest?

Neville (*effortlessly*)   Determined to have your category aren't you – concerned, detached interest.

Peirce (*sharp*)   You're *living* with Miss Rodziewizowna.

Neville   I am not 'living' with her.

Booth   She's staying in your house.

Neville   Yes – she's staying in my house because she had nowhere else to go.

Booth   Nowhere else to go!

Neville   That's right. (*Thinking quickly.*) When she decided to go public with her story – she didn't feel secure where she was before. I expect you now want to know the colour of the walls in the house.

Peirce   No, we know that.

Face appearing of the **Turkish Woman** *staring through the fan-shaped window above the door, directly above* **Neville**'s *chair. Her face staring down at him, watching, occasionally mouthing something.*

Neville   What is she doing looking in here?

Peirce (*hardly looking up*)   Don't take any notice – they stick like limpets at this time of year, when we're closing down for the holiday.

Booth   Where does your family originally come from Mr Gregory?

Neville (*startled by the question*)   Originally come from? I have no idea. (*Then confident smile.*) Luton, I think.

Booth   Luton where?

Neville (*staring in disbelief*)   Luton, England, do you know of any others?

Peirce   Were both your parents English? No foreign connections? No foreign blood?

Neville   Of course. I'm wholly English. (*Sharp smile.*) What the hell is this?

Waveney *staring down with the* **Turkish Woman** *through the window, later joined by three or four other faces gathering to watch, a cluster of faces watching him on the chair, through the glass.*

Booth   How long have you been in this country?

Neville   How long? I have lived here all my life.

Booth   And where were you born?

Neville (*loud*)   Born?

Peirce   It's not necessary to repeat the question!

Neville   In India.

Booth   In India!

Neville   Yes – my father was a minor official in the diplomatic service, who was sacked for chronic unpunctuality. So he started selling cars, extremely successfully. Back here in the old country of course.

And now – I have no idea what you two think you're playing at, but I'm moving this on to other matters, Halina is waiting to . . .

Booth (*pronouncing his name with a foreign lilt*)   And it is your belief Mr Gregori, that your parents are wholly British?

Neville (*flicking this away*)   My mother, not that it's anything to do with you, was half Belgian.

Booth *makes an 'aha' noise.*

Neville   What's more you know (*To* **Peirce**:) you've broken your word – you said this character here (*Pointing to* **Booth**.) was not going to say anything, he'd be a silent notetaker – but he keeps piping up, asking idiotic questions.

Peirce (*standing facing him from desk*)   He asks the bread-and-butter questions – I ask the interesting ones.

Booth Your parents Mr Gregori.

Neville (*swinging round, very sharp*) My God – I have no other foreign blood whatever! I'm British. I'm fucking English for Godsake. (*Pause.*) You're going to ask me for my passport next!

Peirce And it is your belief that your parents were married at the time you were born?

Neville (*savage smile*) These questions are rapidly becoming objectionable as well as ludicrous. Have you two gone out of your tiny minds? I'm Miss Rodziewizowna's advisor.

Booth A little chipping away and we find you're not quite as wholly British as you make yourself out to be. It's so often the way with people who think themselves so English, scrape away the surface . . .

Neville *I'm* not applying for anything, you idiots, I live here!

Peirce (*calmly*) You don't have to answer any of our questions of course Mr Gregory, but that may not help your client.

Neville (*ebullient, ridiculing them as he moves*) It's a wonderful thought isn't it, a true paranoid's fantasy, some innocent wanders in here to help a friend and ends up being deported himself! (*Inspired by his own thought.*) Anybody who happens to come into this building, the places closes round you, and you have to explain your whole existence. (*Pointing out* **Peirce** *and* **Booth**.) Suddenly you two take a look at these perfectly respectable people, does he justify the place he takes up, is he worth keeping? (*Mimics.*) 'I've reason to believe you are no longer entitled to stay in this country owing to your irredeemable mediocrity'? (*Looking at them.*) I can think of a great many candidates!

(*He stops.*) Shall we now return to serious subjects?

Peirce Sit down and calm down Mr Gregory. I simply

want to establish your motive for being here, which I don't
understand.

Neville *pointing up at the collection of faces,* **Waveney** *and the*
Turkish Woman *looking down at him through the fan-shaped
window.*

Neville   And is that a public gallery now, are you selling
tickets! What the hell are they doing up there watching me.

Peirce   The corridors have been re-routed because of
redecoration – take no notice of them.

The faces staring down. The sun has gone a late afternoon red.

Booth   Have you ever been behind the Iron Curtain?

Neville (*to* **Peirce**)   You were right – he certainly does
ask predictable questions, the answer is yes.

Booth   Where Mr Gregori?

Neville   I have spent a week in Czechoslovakia as a
tourist.

Booth   Czechoslovakia! And that's all Mr Gregori, no
Polish connections?

Neville   What is this Gregori shit – No, I have never
been to Poland, nor Russia, nor surprisingly Afghanistan.

Peirce   Do you speak Russian?

Neville (*to* **Peirce***, sarcastic*)   *That's* an interesting question!
Yes 'O' level Russian and I also have to confess I once
went to a Bulgarian movie.

Faces staring down, he gets up.

Neville   I am now bringing this part of the interview to a
close. It is over.

*He moves the chair upstage and places it firmly against wall, smiling
and shaking his head.*

I love the idea! Being evicted from one's own country,
escorted to the airport with just a toothbrush and pushed

out!

Peirce (*watching him*)   You work Mr Gregory, are you happy with your work, your job?

Neville (*surprised*)   My work, of course, yes.

Booth   I thought you said it didn't interest you. (**Neville** *turns round.*) You *did* say that, didn't you?

Peirce (*before he has time to answer*)   The firm doing well is it?

Neville   Yes, very.

Peirce   And you?

Neville *standing in the middle of the stage.*

Neville   Me!

Peirce   Yes, your position inside the firm, how successful would you say *you* were?

Neville   That of course is none of your business at all, but as it happens things are going very well, extremely well in fact.

Peirce   A large firm isn't it. (*Idly.*) Several lawyers of around your age, what if I were to suggest to you that they were about to let you go?

Neville (*incredulous at this, then white with fury*)   That's a *complete* lie! That's a total fiction!

Peirce   Knowing how competitive these firms have to be in the present climate, would it surprise you to find that they are seriously thinking of dispensing with your . . .

Neville   That is *not* true!

Booth   How can they keep on somebody that's not interested in their job?

Neville (*loud*)   You're guessing, this is totally malicious and unfounded, to unnerve me, just grubby innuendo, which I refuse –

Booth (*cutting him off*)   Can you tell us Mr Gregori as of this moment are you considered *necessary*?

Neville   Necessary? Necessary where?

Booth   At your job. All things considered, in the end, *are you necessary*?

Neville   I will of course be making an official complaint about this.

Booth (*very loud, bearing down on him*)   ARE YOU NECESSARY OR NOT?

Pause.

You're not necessary are you.

Neville (*forced to reassure himself*)   Yes of course I'm necessary. Very necessary. There is no doubt about that.

Faces staring down.

Peirce   You are naturally aware that it is a criminal offence to aid and abet someone to enter this country under false pretences. If a member of the legal profession was involved, they might never . . .

Neville   How *dare* you try to do this, how dare you subject me to these insane questions. (*Shouting, pointing.*) Whoever heard of an interview taking place watched like a squash match by the gallery of ghouls and weirdos up there. It is totally irregular and surreal! I reject *everything* that's happened here.

Booth (*with notes*)   We have so far, you were born in India, with Belgian parents, you speak Russian, you have travelled behind the Iron Curtain, you may be about to lose your –

Neville (*incandescent with rage*)   I utterly deplore this attempt to create a crude destabilising situation, (*Loud.*) I want this recorded! This despicable attempt to undermine my status so I will reveal something about Halina. (*Pointing.*) I'm going to get you two for this! I promise you, you've had it –

absolutely. You're finished. I am now going to summon
Miss Rodziewizowna. (*Calling.*) Halina, Halina. (*Moving.*) You
may ask me no further questions, you have absolutely no
right –

Peirce   Allow me to be the judge of that. There is
something that troubles me about you Mr Gregory and has
been from the first moment I met you. Why?

Neville (*completely enraged, picking up chair*)   This discussion is
terminated! It is *concluded*! (*With chair.*) You cannot threaten
me or question me – I forbid you to make any remarks
about my future or my employment, which you know
nothing about . . . (*Shouting, waving chair.*) this has to stop right
now, or there'll be really ugly consequences, I warn you, I
WARN you.

Halina   *standing in doorway.*

Neville   *holding the chair out in front of him,* **Peirce** *and* **Booth**
facing him.

Peirce   Miss Rodziewizowna?

Halina (*to* **Neville**)   I see you are getting on just fine.

She moves into the room.

It's all right Neville – I will handle this.

Blackout.

Scene Four

Bells, and cacophony of voices, giving way to party music. **Peirce**'s
office a few minutes later.

Christmas lights have come on around the mural on the back wall.

*Dark outside, the sun going down rapidly. Behind the blind covering
the window in the side wall, orange neon blinks from a sign outside.
And heavy institutional lamps have come on above their heads.*

Halina, Neville *and* **Waveney** *facing* **Peirce** *and* **Booth**.

Christmas party music and noise of laughter really gets going as scene progresses, wafting towards them.

Peirce   Do we have the key?

Booth (*staring straight at* **Halina** *and* **Neville**)   The key?

Peirce   Yes to this . . . (*Indicating bottom drawer of desk.*) It's Christmas. (*He smiles.*) People tell me. Let us have some sherry Alan. (*Indicates* **Booth** *to unlock cupboard.*) Everybody steals in this building, so let's hope there's a bottle still there.

Halina   I think we'd rather have a decision than a drink.

Neville   Yes. (*Very sharp.*) If that's not asking too much.

Booth *serving sherry.*

Peirce   Mr Gregory and I were just having a relaxed chat in here, I was taking a short cut, a holiday indulgence, a little horseplay. Something about Mr Gregory bothers me – but no hard feelings I hope.

Neville   Why don't you just cut the crap and tell us what you're thinking.

Waveney   And going to do?

Peirce (*casually*)   Haven't I told you that? (*Moving by desk.*) There is just one thing that still worries me.

Halina   Just one, I thought there were many many more.

Peirce   Your story convinces me – except for one small thing.

Halina (*moving along wall*)   Yes?

Peirce   Snow, darkness, a courtyard . . . a mock-execution, people up against the wall knowing they are going to die, there is an echo going on in my head, a sense of recognition, the Russian novelist Fyodor Dostoevsky with whom you are no doubt familiar, the same thing happened to him, the mock execution, thinking he was going to die in the snow.

Neville   I don't recall this, I think you are –

Peirce (*sharp*)   You knew the story and borrowed it, made it your own.

Halina (*stopping, turning*)   *That* is what you're worrying about.

Peirce   Yes.

Halina   Just that?

Booth   Yes.

Halina (*watching them*)   You're *right*. (*Pause. Very controlled.*) I have memories of the story – it would be difficult for me to come here and tell you of any example of arbitrary cruelty which did not have some parallel, the banality of the minds of the people who do such acts means they must often imitate each other. (*She smiles.*) There are no exclusive rights, no copyright on any one method. Anyway it happened to me, and possibly to Dostoevsky – I think that is probably the only thing that we have in common. (*Lightly, looking straight at him.*) Though you never know.

Peirce (*not taking his eyes off her*)   That is your explanation? (*Loud.*) Alan! Could you leave us please.

Booth *looks startled.*

Peirce   And try to get rid of the last stragglers.

Booth (*slight smile at door*)   See you again, Mr Gregori.

Booth *opens the door, the* **Turkish Woman** *standing there, stammering 'I've missed my interview, it's gone, it is too late now, they won't give me another . . . please find me another one'.* **Booth** *ushers her away.*

Peirce (*as* **Booth** *closes door*)   I think it's beginning to grate on him, still being a nuts-and-bolts man. (*Turning sharply.*) You're right of course Miss Rodziewizowna.

Halina   I am?

Peirce (*suddenly, sitting informally on desk*)   I'm sometimes

offered two examples of the same grotesque experience
from totally different parts of the world, on a single day.

Halina   Exactly, yes.

Peirce (*orange neon behind him*)   People come in here some
times, with the most appalling stories, you listen to these
terrible details, and then you walk out of these doors into
the bland streets of Croydon, a lukewarm London evening,
red buses blundering by, and even after several years, the
contrast is for a moment extremely sharp and vivid.

Waveney   What's he playing at?

Peirce (*serious*)   Miss Rodziewizowna – this is a firm
request. Please sit down.

Halina *sits centre stage.*

Peirce   I have to tell you, I am inclined, I think I have
to believe you, and *will* recommend your application is
accepted.

Halina (*immediately jumping up from chair*)   You will? You
have!

Waveney   You've done it.

Neville   Is this absolutely definite? We have the right to
assume this is the final –

Peirce   You may have elaborated a little here and there,
people seem unable to resist, like a corridor is in reality
bright pink – but they think that sounds too cheerful so
they make it brown, the colour of excrement.

Halina   The walls really matter to you don't they!

Peirce   But I believe you.

Halina   I don't dare open my mouth in case I push
things the wrong way again.

Neville   That's very wise.

Halina (*suddenly it really hits her*)   YOU BELIEVE ME? HE
BELIEVES ME!

Peirce (*loud, injured tone*)   NO! You mustn't think of leaving yet.

Neville *has already moved to door.*

Peirce   One has so little chance to get to know people in this job. (*His legs go up on his desk.*)

Waveney (*whispering*)   Don't relax . . . don't relax.

Peirce   Sudden intense meetings and then nothing. I have a feeling there are some cheeseballs here somewhere. (*Pulling open a drawer.*) Completely off the record – when I recommend against people, I have no idea what is going to happen to them.

Halina   No you can't, how could you?

Peirce (*his tone suddenly personal, opening up,* **Halina** *never taking her eyes off him for a moment*)   I could be sending them back to a very uncertain future, I have an image of these people orbiting the world, going from frontier to frontier, desperately trying to find anyone who will let them in.

Halina   I feel terribly lucky, I can tell you.

Peirce (*leaning forward*)   And you know sometimes I'm interviewing somebody, and a hand, a gesture, a certain phrase jolts the mind, makes it compute backwards and I realise I've seen this person under another name, another passport, another identity, years before.

Halina   How awful! For both of you!

Waveney (*cynical smile*)   It's a very difficult job what you've got, we know.

Peirce   Yes, you have to budget for people's innate creativity, their unpredictability, the endless variations in how they are going to lie.

There is the sound of an alarm bell, hooters suddenly clammering, **Peirce** *uncoils his legs.*

That is my summons, the typical greeting from one officer to another! (*He smiles.*) I hate this time, the dregs of the

year. I have to try and face the terrible prospect of the
Christmas party, can you imagine anything worse than a
party full of immigration officers?

Halina *laughs spontaneously, as does* **Waveney**.

Peirce (*smiles*) Yes, lots of bad jokes about the passengers,
about rats scrabbling to get on a sinking ship, all my
colleagues, dancing wearing party hats!

Peirce *smiles, leans forward casually and touches* **Halina**'s *knee.*

By the way what's that you've been playing with during the
interview, I've been trying to work it out?

Halina This? (*Automatically, holding plastic box.*) It's a
Nagoaka moving permalloy stereo cartridge – MP 30 XX.

Peirce Really? Nagoaka.

Halina Yes, moving perm – (*She stops.*)

Music in the silence.

(*In Polish.*) Oh my God.

Her head goes down, sudden shout in Polish.

Peirce Yes – a small but vital item of hi-fi equipment.

Halina's *head goes back, another shout.*

Neville (*loud*) Just something she picked up in my flat, I
have lots of spare equipment lying around, (*Loud.*) it means
absolutely nothing!

Waveney I gave it to her just now, it's mine – she knows
nothing about it.

Halina *Please* – don't, there is no point in doing that
now, he knows that was a bad mistake.

Waveney Something told me you weren't safe – not until
you were out of this building.

Peirce Miss Rodziewizowna is about to admit she
worked in this country illegally.

Halina (*answers in Polish*)

Pause.

You will have to settle for it in Polish. Undone by a gramophone needle! I can't believe I was so stupid.

Neville   What are you doing with this absurd object anyway! Moving permalloy! (*He crunches it up and throws it aside.*)

Halina   Neville, just leave us for a moment, both of you, please, wait for me outside now.

Waveney (*very animated to* **Peirce**)   You really are a fool as well as a shit, if you can't see she's worth having, worth keeping, (*Loud.*) why don't you take me instead, if you have to have someone! Fair exchange! Let me take the chair, (*Loud.*) are you interested? . . .

Halina   Waveney.

Neville (*at exit*)   Don't say anything further to him Halina.

Waveney   Give him nothing.

Both exit leaving door open.

Halina *sitting on wooden chair in lilac dress facing* **Peirce**.

Halina   Now.

Peirce (*facing her*)   Yes?

Halina   How simple that must have seemed, you caught me off guard for one instant.

Peirce   That's all it needs.

Halina (*getting up, picking up paper spike from his desk*)   You got me to relax, let my defence slip, by talking about yourself. Not bad. (*Turning on him.*) I made one mistake which is not, I repeat *not*, going to prove fatal. I have no intention of letting it.

She swings round with a sharp but controlled movement and drives paper spike into wall, as her frustration boils.

You shouldn't keep these things on your desk, somebody next time might go between your eyes.

Peirce I have had some near misses with those, yes.

He moves other spike carefully into a drawer. **Halina** *facing him.*

.**Halina** What do I have to do to get in?

Peirce Do?

Halina How small do I have to make myself? What shape do I have to become to squeeze myself in, to crawl through the net?

What do you want me to say? What international incident needs to erupt to make me suddenly useful and desirable?

Peirce I'm afraid it may not be possible now.

Halina (*suddenly powerful*) Let me in! You have to. You're not certain about the decision, that's clear, I can feel it.

(*Straight at him:*) LET ME IN!

Peirce Don't do that please. First time you've tried to bludgeon me with direct appeals, they never work, I can promise you.

Halina (*looking at him*) They might. (*Slight pause.*) I *have* to get in you know. (*With force:*) How many other people have you seen standing right here, trying for the same thing?

Turkish Woman *outside in the passage, seen through the open door, calling in support in Turkish to her.*

Halina At least somebody's on my side.

Peirce (*watching her*) Occasionally you know, I wonder if I changed places with a passenger what sort of place, and people would be staring at me as I came in to land.

Halina (*straight back*) It won't work a second time! That technique.

Music in distance.

Peirce (*matter-of-fact*)   I *really* do hate the idea of the party.
Moves.

It was good your story, very professional – rather, and this
is a very uncharacteristic word for me . . . a wonderful lie.

Halina (*very sharp*)   *Who* says it's a lie?

Peirce   I do.

Halina   You haven't proved that yet. And until you do, I
think I have a chance.

Peirce   What would you have done in this country
anyway if you'd managed it?

Halina (*with feeling, looking about her*)   I would have done
just fine. (*Correcting herself.*) I will do.

Peirce (*facing her from behind the desk*)   Sometimes, even
quite often, I come across passengers I find personally
appealing, people seething with energy, with things to offer
– of more interest than most of the people who work in
this building.

One finds oneself thinking why on earth shouldn't I
recommend to let them in, that their application is valid.

Halina   That's what you're going to do now.

Peirce   *NO.*

Halina *sitting on chair, looking straight at him, they face each
other.*

Halina   You seem quite a reasonable man, though you
need careful watching.

She leans forward.

Of all the thousands of people you've processed through
this building, you can make *one* exception, (*Loud:*) who will
ever know! The building won't fall down – not because of

that anyway.

Peirce (*calmly*) I'd never be able to do this job again.
This is the best controlled border in the Western world, the
UK, and I'm the best in this building – though I wasn't at
my best today.

That is the only thing that makes it worthwhile. (*Pause.*)
Just.

Staring straight at her. Music playing.

I will do everything in my power to stop you getting into
this country.

Turkish Woman *calling at door.*

Halina You are *not* going to succeed though. I've lost the
skirmish maybe, but I am still going to win. (*Indicating*
Turkish Woman.) I am not going to look like that in a
few days' time.

Peirce You have an appeal against our decision – but I
must warn you, you'll find we can use the media too.

Halina We'll see.

She stands very calm and strong in the middle of the stage, smoking.

Now my friend, I think we understand each other, you are
going to tell me something of great interest.

She looks at him.

Who betrayed me?

Peirce I can't tell you that.

Halina I think you can. I think you know and you quite
want to tell me. *Who was it?*

Pause.

Peirce (*staring at her*) IF you ask me the right questions
about that, Miss Rodziewizowna, I may be able to reply.

Blackout.

Scene Five

A smear of Christmas carols, mixed with seasonal adverts, followed by the news, a news story about **Halina**, *'the case of the mock-execution housewife ... Red Halina ... Home Office spokesman, her story under investigation has proved a pack of lies ... Future uncertain'. Sense of channels being switched, pieces of other stories about* **Halina** *come piling on top of each other, a blitzkrieg of anti-stories 'lying Halina ... KGB plant? ... Polish housewife spreads fraudulent stories ... attempt to undermine media credibility ...'*

Andrew *and* **Neville** *stand with back to audience frontstage, the walls of the office have slid back, the mural on the back wall is in shadows, bare stage with just two wooden floorboards leaning against wall and a roll of wallpaper.*

Andrew   What on earth's happening here?

Neville (*staring towards floorboards*)   I had a compulsion to redecorate the flat – of course now they have ripped everything up, they are stopping for two weeks over Christmas! Leaving it looking like a war zone. I can't find where anything is.

Pause.

Andrew   Have you seen her?

Neville   Of course not. Have you?

Loud crash, another floorboard is thrown on stage. Both **Andrew** *and* **Neville** *start.*

Andrew   No. Have you seen this? The evening paper? (*He waves it.*) 'Red Halina, mad housewife, KGB prankster, a weaver of falsehoods, malicious intent etc ...'

They are making out she was sent by the Russians to be deliberately rumbled, so as to discredit any future unfavourable reports coming out of the Eastern Bloc! (*Flicks paper.*) There's even a cartoon.

Neville   I have to admit I've rather enjoyed some of the things that have been said about her!

Andrew (*sharp*)   Really?

Neville   And she may well have had quite an
irresponsible effect.

Andrew (*sharp*)   She didn't intend to! (*Pause.*) Somebody
informed on her.

Neville   I had a dream about her the other night. (*Slight
smile.*) Very easy to interpret like most of my dreams.
Halina as this small curly-haired girl staring at me through
a wire fence, asking me for a cigarette, then this mad
bloated old tramp, covered all over in travel labels, outside
the window, refusing to look at me. Like some batty
avenging angel clawing her way out of obscurity, up the
side of the house, but refusing to meet my eyes.

He moves.

They've moved so quickly! I never expected it, detaining
her, locking her up, the deportation order. I wasn't even
here when they took her away!

Andrew   They're like large reptiles, departments in the
Home Office, most of the time they don't move at all,
lying motionless in the sun, but when they want to, they
can move like hell.

Another crash, a second floorboard thrown across the stage.

Neville (*looking at* **Andrew**'s *pale face*)   You look terrible.

Andrew   Thank you. I feel it too.

Neville   Why?

Andrew   The contrasts in my life are particularly clear at
this time of year. I went to a party last night, when I got
there I realised it was a theme party, fancy dress, do you
know what it was, a *fin de siècle* party!

Neville   My God already!

Andrew   Yes, everything and everybody dressed in black
and white, people into end-of-the-century ennui, into
celebrating their boredom, the years are silting up for them

already.

Neville Silting, that's right, people with no appetite for anything . . .

Andrew Imagine London in the nineties, if it's like this now!

And then I raced off to one of my absurd rendezvous, in a deserted bus station at one o'clock in the morning, with a Cypriot family. The people I *manage* to get in usually have a pretty miserable time. It's such a waste. Some of them disappear without trace. They think they are coming to a land of opportunity, a multi-racial society! A home! (*Very sharp.*) God knows if I've ever actually helped anybody!

Neville Of course you have.

Andrew (*suddenly turning on him*) You think so do you – that's your considered opinion is it Neville?

Neville *startled by his tone.*

Andrew I know you've always found what I've done pretty ridiculous, really rather comic.

Neville (*very surprised*) I have!

Andrew Yes, of course you have. So I don't really need your reassurance now.

Neville What's the matter Andrew?

Andrew Time for me to scuttle off to another meeting.

Neville But what will happen to Halina?

Andrew What indeed? She's dangling on the edge. Her future doesn't look too bright does it?

Andrew *moving.*

Neville Why on earth wouldn't she accept the original plan Andrew?

Pause.

Andrew You don't understand that? That's easy.

He looks straight at **Neville**.

Who would want to land right *here* – if they could possibly
help it?

Blackout.

*A still of a rather fetching small girl in forties clothes appears on the
screen. She is staring gravely at us through a fence.*

Scene Six

*The sound of aircraft taking off and landing very loud. A metal grid
slides across the whole length of the mural on the back wall, the
mural visible through the metal mesh.*

A door with a barred grid upstage, left of the back wall.

*The world at the detention centre, on the edge of the runway, among
the warehouses at the airport. Carols grinding out, only half audibly
from a tannoy, foreign voices calling, visitors' area, a wooden table
and two chairs, upstage a second table and chairs.*

Halina *is standing, she is wearing a plain black dress, and looks
elegant. She has a bruise around her eye.* **Waveney** *is standing
holding a large bag.*

Waveney (*as planes go directly overhead*)   Christ! The planes
fly so low here they are scraping the top of the building! Is
it always like this?

Halina   Yes, you feel all you have to do is stretch out
and you could easily grab hold of a passing undercarriage
and get a flight out of here.

Waveney (*calling up as one goes over*)   Clapped-out old
planes. Really have to heave themselves into the air,
probably start falling out of the sky. (*She moves.*) It's a weird
place to put a prison, right at the end of the runway. (*She
points to brightly-coloured saris drying on the radiators.*) Clothes
from all over the world drying here. Look . . . (*She delves into
her bag.*) I brought you a Christmas present.

Halina You shouldn't have.

Waveney Somewhere in here. (*Bits of plastic fly out of bag.*) I ground up a fistful of styluses, (*To* **Halina**:) styli, pulverised the moving permalloy, (*Scatters fragments.*) all that remains of them and the shop, ashes of a sunrise store!

Halina Good.

Waveney (*produces present*) I brought you an atlas.

Halina An atlas? So I can improve my Polish geography!

Waveney No. So you can select where you're going to go. Stick a finger in the world.

Halina (*smiles*) There's no point – nobody will have me. I've been refused permission everywhere.

Waveney Really? There must be somewhere on the whole planet – what about the Falkland Islands!

Halina (*slight smile*) You have to draw the line somewhere. (*She moves.*)

Anyway it's been *here* that I wanted to come to, not America or Paris but here. Always – now I can't get into any country, I'm being sent back to Poland.

Waveney What's going to happen to you there?

Halina God knows.

Waveney I'm sorry. (*She moves.*) You know I told that bastard immigration officer to take me instead – I don't think that's such a bad idea. (*Sharp smile.*) I mean I haven't exactly got much to keep me here. If I could take my little girl, and if there was anywhere to go, which there isn't! (*Shouts at back wall.*) So don't get any ideas! (*Ironic smile.*) Do you think anybody would notice the difference if I changed places with you, (*She laughs.*) I don't think so, if I just wear your hat and did your walk.

Halina You are certainly welcome to the Christmas dinner I'm going to get here.

Plane going over.

Waveney   What a strangled wail that one's got!

I know I hitched a ride on what you were doing, your campaign, for no real reason. I projected your story so big on such a large screen maybe it seemed more important, more likely to win, than it really was.

Halina   Don't be stupid, it's not your fault. (*She turns.*) I've been so obsessed with getting in, I haven't thought about you Waveney, and you losing your job.

Waveney   Yes. I don't much like this feeling I can tell you – hard as I try it's like I always return to the same place. I used to think I was just waiting till my luck changed, I don't now. It's very simple, why shouldn't I do something with my life for chrissake.

Voices calling from building with anger.

And I don't like what's happening inside me either.

(*She turns.*) Anyway – a real Christmas present would be me finding a way of springing you from here in the next twenty-four hours wouldn't it?

Neville *enters in grey suit carrying briefcase.*

Neville   Halina – there you are. (*He looks around him.*) For some reason I thought the bars would be a little more discreet.

Halina (*staring at him across the stage*)   You always look so crisp Neville.

Waveney   He certainly looks like a lawyer doesn't he.

Neville   What has happened to your face Halina?

Halina   It's a bruise.

Neville   I can see that.

Halina *is half turned away.*

Halina (*lightly*)   It's shaped like a strawberry don't you think?

Neville (*sharp*)   You are not going to tell me you were beaten up by maniacal guards – they strapped you to the floor I suppose.

Halina (*firmly*)   No. I did it myself. I suddenly lost control, I wanted to get out of here rather a lot.

Neville   And you did that?

Waveney   Yes.

Neville (*to* **Waveney**)   Now – I have some business to conduct. (*Moving.*) I have come to help Halina. Only one visitor is allowed in here with you at a time, and to make sure we're left alone – (*He looks at her.*) I will tell you who informed on you to the immigration authorities.

Waveney   You know who betrayed her?

Halina *with her back to him, not moving.*

Halina   Tell me, I'm interested.

Pause.

Neville   It was I. (*She doesn't move.*) Me. I did it.

Waveney   My God. *YOU* – why didn't I think of that? It fits doesn't it.

Halina (*turning from wall, loud*)   Leave me alone with him! (*Quieter.*) Please. You can come back a little later to check if he's still alive.

Waveney   Yes. (*Sharp smile.*) I'll try not to get locked up back there as one of the inmates. (*In exit.*) Be careful Halina, never take your eyes off him.

Waveney *exits.*

Neville   I informed on you. I supplied the necessary information on you.

Halina   You lousy ... fucking bastard.

Neville (*facing her*)   That's what I did, Halina, yes.

Pause.

Halina   But *in fact* you see, you didn't.

Neville   What on earth do you mean?

Halina   It wasn't you at all. You had nothing to do with it.

The person who informed on me was one of my fellow Poles – one of our group.

(*Staring across at him.*) If you did try to do it . . .

Neville (*loud*)   I did do it! I did!

Halina   You couldn't it seems even do that properly. It was obviously unrecorded.

Neville (*swings round, very sharp*)   God – does absolutely *NOTHING* work in this country, (*Loud.*) can't even rely on their informing service!

He stops and looks at her.

My one big action . . . my spontaneous and dark manoeuvre, and nobody gets to hear about it.

Halina   Precisely.

Sound of people, voices, foreign calls and shouts from the bowels of the building, increasing in volume.

Neville   Don't you want to know why I did it?

Halina   No. I know why you did it.

Neville   No you don't, you don't at all. I did it because I knew you were heading straight for disaster. I had to make you see sense, before it was too late.

Halina (*straight at him*)   Really?

Neville (*watching her*)   Why should I believe you anyway, you are probably lying like you usually are.

I can't trust you about anything.

Halina (*loud*)   You not trust *me*!

Neville   No. (*Moving around.*) Why do I keep getting the feeling that all of this was planned?

Halina   What was planned?

Neville   My world being deliberately turned upside down, a carefully structured and malevolent scheme – leading to my outrageous humiliation at the hands of the immigration officer. Fortunately I've discovered my job is safe – I think. (*Loud.*) I had to justify my existence to him – me – in my own city!

Halina   That was due to your incompetence and clumsiness.

Neville   It was pure malice.

Halina   And you think I had something to do with that!

Neville   (*shrewd look*)   I don't know. It's very strange isn't it, we had a straightforward plan, which you decided to reject.

Halina   Yes.

Neville   And what have you managed instead, what have you actually achieved? One tiny and brief piece of fame, ending in you being torn apart, and a jousting match with an immigration officer for an afternoon.

Halina   One of the best afternoons of my life.

Neville   Before he cracked you and you lost everything. That's *all* your extraordinary decision has –

Halina   (*advancing on him with aggression and precision*)   The really interesting question is not about me at all. It's about *you*. Why a fairly successful solicitor should want to enter into this scheme in the first place – and I'll tell you the answer.

Neville   I rather felt you might.

Halina   Because you thought you were in need of a little distraction, isn't that right, to get rid of the stale claustrophobia you were in, all around you, bored with life, here was a nice idea for a little suspense. And the candidate was this weird spiky Polish woman – might provide a few comfortable surprises.

Neville   I'm absolutely sick of being told what I'm feeling by you, that I'm predictable, have no imagination.

Halina (*advancing on him*)   And I knew this desire of yours, this *mild* need could vanish overnight, before the marriage, cancellation, leaving me nowhere at all. Or worse, far, far worse, it could continue *after* the arrangement was over, this new interest of yours, and you'd return again and again to have a look, you'd have a claim on me, I'd be one of your possessions.

Neville   My God you're so pleased with yourself Halina! The thought never crossed my mind.

Halina (*moving*)   Especially when you started being intrigued by this tiny pimple of history, having her right there.

Neville   *I* never called you that, I did not . . .

Halina   And when my real history, the slow drip drip of my existence with my father was far too humdrum to get me in, and I had to expand myself, give myself a little notoriety, that proved even better, didn't it –

Neville   That's not true.

Halina (*loud*)   And when you saw this appetite for nearly everything coming out of me, this hunger, straightforward selfish hunger, spurting everywhere, all over your apartment, and over other parts of your life, that was even *more* interesting, (*Straight at him.*) almost fascinating.

Staring at him.

So you decided to own me after all didn't you. (*Straight at him.*) Simple!

She moves.

And now I'm locked up here with all these other caged people, feeling like me, beating on the walls, you should hear all the different languages echoing around here! And I can't do anything about it. I can't get myself out in time. (*Loud with anger.*) I'm not enjoying it. I hate myself for losing.

Silence.

Neville (*drily*)   Marry me.

Halina *by wall, not facing him.*

Halina   For what reason?

Neville   Don't start that Halina – you know the reason.

Faces appearing at the grid staring in at them, noises and echoes from the rest of building.

Because you're in a brutally simple situation. You took on enormous odds and lost. If you're thrown out of this country, which you're going to be in forty-eight hours' time, you're finished. You won't have done anything with your life and you never will.

Slight pause.

Halina   That's not good enough Neville.

Neville (*very sharp*)   What do you mean it's not good enough? (*Moving.*) And *I* don't want to see your life a total waste Halina, I certainly don't want you on my conscience.

Halina   What's the other reason?

Faces at the grid watching them.

Neville (*furious*)   I'm not going to be interrogated by you, treated like this, as if I'm –

Halina (*cutting him off, not facing him*)   Why else Neville?

Pause. A plane taking off nearby.

Neville (*not looking at her*)   All right – Because over the last few weeks I've been propelled out of my normal existence. (*Moving, not looking at her.*) You know, people that almost die, like in a car crash, for a moment they actually stop breathing and find themselves floating out of themselves and staring down from above at their own bodies, and surroundings – for once I forget the medical term for it – I've had that without the crash, find myself peering at a world full of dying video shops, with graveyards for their machines, black girls full of startling hostility towards me from the first moment they see me! Those disturbed carol singers, outside the window, and old clients pursuing me full of dark city paranoia – even immigration officers that read Dostoevsky! It's like a map of the city where all the streets have been re-named.

Slight pause.

(*Sharp.*) I've been evicted from my normal certainty Halina, and the person responsible for that is you.

Halina (*not facing him*)   Quite possibly, yes.

Neville   While lying through your teeth about everything else – you've revealed things to me! Whether deliberately or not, I still don't know, you've never said anything about what you feel about being here, about how you find this country.

Halina   I told you I wouldn't till I'd lived here – so you'll be spared that now.

Neville (*very sharp*)   What right you had to cause all this, I have no idea, but you have.

Pause.

Will that do? (*Sharp.*) So marry me.

Plane taking off.

Halina, don't try to be so calm, we're here in this ghastly place, with all these trapped people.

Indicating faces clamouring at the grid.

You can't get out of it any other way.

Halina   You reckon that is so do you?

Neville (*sharp*)   I think you have a duty to stay here now.

Halina *turns.*

Halina   A duty! (*Forced laugh.*) 'England needs me' you mean ... I don't think so! (*She moves.*) And tell me – how would you categorise our relationship, Neville?

Neville (*loud*)   Don't do this.

Halina (*loud*)   How?

Neville (*loud*)   You really infuriate me, Halina!

Pause staring at her.

It's hardly *love* that's for certain.

Halina   Love? No.

Neville   God knows if we'll ever touch each other either.

Halina (*with full agreement*)   Yes.

Neville   I ... I don't know why you're doing this ...

Slight pause, watching her.

I suppose if I have to describe it, if you're making me, I suppose I'm impaled on you. (*Watching her.*) On this Polish spike.

Halina   That's better.

Neville (*loud*)   Don't patronise me, Halina.

Halina *moves.*

Halina   Yes – snarled together.

Neville (*louder*)   Snarled, *yes*. (*Looking across at her.*) What are your feelings for me?

Halina   I like you, (*Pause.*) quite.

Neville (*loud*)   No quites – you're not allowed any *quites*. None.

Noises of bells, end of visting hours.

Halina Time for you to go.

Neville (*furious, passionate with anger*) For chrissake, Halina
– don't be so incredibly proud and obstinate. You're too
proud to do this, aren't you!

He hurls chair against wall.

Halina There're people watching Neville please.

Couple of the faces applauding from behind grid.

Neville (*really angry*) I don't care who's watching – you
want to be like them, stay amongst them do you, wherever
they're going, be locked up for the rest of your life! (*Shouts.*)
You stupid, perverse woman. You need to do it!

Halina Neville . . .

Neville *grabs her and gives her a violent shake.*

Neville Don't you realise, you need me, you've got to
accept that, you need to do this, you do!

Halina I need you . . . ?

Neville (*loud*) Yes! Halina – see some sense now.

People at the grid.

Are you going to do it or not?

*Plane suddenly flies directly over them, much lower than all the rest.
As it does so* **Halina** *replies.*

Halina I need you . . . maybe . . .

Neville What did you say?

Halina You mean you weren't listening.

Noise and bells, plane dying away in distance.

I don't want to. But I said maybe.

Neville Maybe!

Noise of plane dying away.

Halina Will they let us get married?

Neville   If we make them believe it. IF we're seen a lot together. And if we live in the same place afterwards for say a six-month period.

Halina *turns.*

Halina   Three months.

Neville   Four months.

Halina *nods.*

Neville   Do you want a contract to that effect, that it won't be longer?

Halina   No ... (*Slight pause.*) Not yet.

Sound of doors being locked, slamming shut.

You're probably locked in now for Christmas.

Neville   Good, my apartment is a wreck because of you, the oil went everywhere. At least I can keep an eye on you.

Halina   You mean we're glued that tight together – already? When you move, I move. I'm not sure I like the idea of that at all.

Neville (*sharply*)   It's happened.

Halina (*sound of aircraft in distance, she moves to grid*)   What a place to get engaged, among the warehouses, and this low flat prison, and the cages full of quarantining animals, both monkeys and people locked up around here, and the dead planes parked amongst the long grass, and all the other flotsam of the airport. I've been pushed right into the jaws of the exit.

Neville   You've dragged me with you there, too. One of the edges of the country, you can look back into it from here. Have you noticed, the snow's gone at last Halina, the mild weather's returned. (*Looks at her.*) At least now I may have put a stop to the careering nightmare you've put me through.

Pause.

Of course this might mean merely a continuation . . .

Halina (*moving*)   Yes.

She stares back at him.

Or even just the start.

Blackout.

Close My Eyes

Close My Eyes opened in the UK on 6 September 1991 with the following cast:

Sinclair	Alan Rickman
Richard	Clive Owen
Natalie	Saskia Reeves
Colin	Karl Johnson
Jessica	Lesley Sharp
Paula	Kate Gartside
Philippa	Karen Knight
Geal	Niall Buggy
Scotsman	Campbell Morrison
Stony-Faced Woman	Annie Hayes
Balding Man	Maxwell Hutcheon
Dark Haired Girl	Geraldine Somerville
Scottish Girl	Helen FitzGerald
Noley	Christopher Barr
Hotel Porter	Gordon Salkilld
Maid	Choy Ling Man
Pimply Young Man	John Albasiny
Selina	Marie Passarelli
Doreen	Jan Winters

Directed by Stephen Poliakoff
Produced by Therese Pickard
Music by Michael Gibbs
Director of Photography Witold Stok
Production Designer Luciana Arrighi

A Beambright Production for Film Four International released by Artificial Eye

Interior: **Natalie**'s *room: Night:*

The camera moves through a modern room, in a small but quite elegant flat, towards the figure of **Natalie** *who is standing in a thin summer dress with her back to us.*

We pass some candles, beginning to burn low, records strewn around, one playing loudly on a battered gramophone. The camera passes an old ornamental oil lamp on a modern table and without a cut we move with **Natalie** *onto the balcony into the night air, where a spread of glittering city lights falls away below us.*

The area is surrounded by tall modern flats. **Natalie** *stares down to the concourse below as if waiting for someone.*

Natalie *is in her late twenties at the start of the action. There is a musky, hot atmosphere as she waits, the candles burning round her, and the music playing.*

Exterior: City streets: Credit sequence: Night:

Below us we see a figure approaching, very small at first, seen from a great height, as the credits play.

We cut to the figure of **Richard** *and track with him along the concourse past an eerily empty landscape of wide walkways and bridges, across night roads. But the atmosphere is not desolate, the night lights, the music and the lettering of the credits make it seem velvety and expectant.*

Interior: Staircase: Night:

We watch, under the final credits, the figure of **Richard** *weave his way up the staircase towards us, seen from a great height.* **Natalie,** *leaning over the bannister.* **Richard** *running up floor after floor without apparent effort.*

A caption comes up – '1985' – as we stare down into the stairwell.

Natalie (*calling*) You're late.

Richard Sorry, it was unavoidable. Trains on Sunday . . . you know what they're like.

Natalie Unavoidable – I don't believe it. I've eaten all the food.

Richard (*grins*) You've eaten all the food? Now that's serious. (*He looks at her.*) Aren't you pleased to see me?

Natalie (*lightly*) NO!

Interior: **Natalie**'s *room: Night:*

Cut to a wide shot of the two. **Natalie** *lighting a couple more candles.* **Richard** *sitting on the floor, scraping the last traces of food out of a bowl.*

Richard Is this all there is?

Natalie I told you.

Richard (*glancing round*) What are all the candles for anyway? – it's spooky. (*He grins.*) Is this what you used to get up to with him every night?

Natalie I just like it – that's all.

Richard (*lightly*) You've got to stop it. It looks like you're grieving – grieving for a relationship! Must make it ten times worse.

Natalie Thank you Richard, I've been waiting here for the last six hours just to hear you say that. It is all I need.

Richard (*licking bowl*) It *is* what you need. (*Moving.*) Come on, I'm going to get you out of here, this place is bad for you.

Natalie No, there's nowhere to go round here on a Sunday.

Richard (*affectionate smile*) Now she can't go out of the house! – come on Natalie, there's no need to over-do it!

Natalie's *pale worried face looking at him.*

Exterior: The concourse: Night:

Cut to **Natalie** *and* **Richard** *moving through the night landscapes.* **Natalie** *has put on an old fur coat over her light red summer dress.* **Richard** *tugging her on.* **Natalie** *stops to light a cigarette.*

Richard (*disbelieving*) She can't even get down the street without one! (*He tugs her on.*)

Interior: Restaurant: Night:

A long thin Wimpy-style restaurant with ceiling fans going round in the hot night air, a half-hearted mural along the wall, and most of the restaurant in semi-darkness. **Richard** *and* **Natalie** *are sitting in the shadows below the mural, far away from a couple of waitresses standing together by the counter in a pool of white light.*

Richard Can you believe this! They boast of a waitress service and then they take no notice of you. (*He calls out.*) Excuse me . . .

Natalie It's OK. You've got me out of the flat. (*Lightly.*) We can just sit here and enjoy the decor.

Richard (*looking at the mouldy fur coat*) Why are you wearing that?

Natalie *moves back in her seat.*

Richard I don't like seeing you unhappy.

Natalie Well, I am unhappy. (*Self-mocking smile.*) I'm incredibly unhappy – I mean you buy a flat with your lover and then he leaves you within two months. Six and a half weeks, actually! Not many worse things.

Richard No.

Natalie And now Mum and Dad have both gone – you are the only person I can tell (*She begins to laugh.*) which is terrible!

They both laugh.

Natalie (*looking at him*) I haven't seen you for ages.

Richard (*who is unscrewing the top of the mustard, peering in*) I'm sorry, I've been very busy.

Natalie Students aren't busy. (*Poking him gently.*)

Richard (*charming smile*) It's a good course planning pretend cities . . . I'm very happy.

Natalie I bet you are, plenty of girls.

Richard Absolutely.

Natalie Endless time to lie around and talk, (*With a trace of envy.*) raving it up in London.

Richard *has picked up the plastic red tomato and put it on his plate.*

Stop playing with those. What are you doing?

Richard (*unscrewing top of tomato*) You should always look in these wherever you go – can judge a town by what's in its tomato.

Natalie (*lightly*) Stop it – that's disgusting.

Richard (*pulling out of tomato*) What have we got? Not a bad catch . . . some chewing gum, a few coins . . . and what's this . . . A tooth! Natalie, somebody's popped a tooth in here.

Natalie (*horrified but really laughing*) Jesus – I am never using those things again. EVER!

Exterior: City: Night:

Cut to a shot of **Richard** *and* **Natalie** *alone in the city, crossing a square at night, seen from a great height.* **Richard** *is moving ahead of her.*

Richard Come on, Natalie . . . you're out of condition. Take the coat off, for goodness' sake, it's so warm. (*The coat coming off in a swirling movement,* **Natalie** *in the red dress running, trying to catch him up.*) . . . too much smoking . . . look at you . . . Come on!

Interior: Bedroom: Night:

They move into a room with two bunk beds for children and a mobile brushing them in the middle of the room. Wallpaper showing elephants in brightly coloured hot air balloons.

Natalie Come on, you can sleep in here.

Richard (*laughs*) Kids' beds – you were already planning for two kids. (*Lightly.*) No wonder he left – fled in terror!

Natalie (*slight laugh, playfully nudging him*) Stop it! No, we bought it like this – we were just going to have them removed.

Richard (*touching the thin walls*) Not too bad, this flat, but the finish is cheap . . . It's not built with love.

Close-up of **Natalie,** *looking vulnerable, musak playing.* **Richard** *notices a little pile of belongings in the corner, large men's shoes left behind.*

Natalie (*looking up at him, indicating the pounding music from next door*) It's not usually as loud as this. He must have known you were coming.

Interior: Bedroom: Middle of the night:

Cut to **Richard** *lying in bed, his eyes flick open. Music still playing, a dull, audible pounding. Clock ticking by his bed showing it's 3.30.*

Richard Jesus!

He gets up, in underpants. He pulls a shirt round his shoulders.

Interior: Main room: Night:

Richard *moves angrily into the main part of the flat. Music is still very audible. He suddenly sees* **Natalie** *lying in the shadows, a large glass pudding dish full of water beside her. She's floating small, lighted candles on the water.*

Richard *kneels beside her hunched shape on the floor, the lighted bowl between them.*

Natalie Oh Richard . . . make it better! I wish I could wake up and be *happy!* Just one morning, it would be gone, this feeling, and never come back.

Richard, *nonchalantly playing with her lovely thirties necklace.*

Richard You can make that happen, get out of town, start all over again.

Natalie A new career? I'm too old to start again.

Richard You're not too old! Don't be stupid. That job was never what you wanted – a buyer for that bloody awful store, you wanted to be *artistic.*

Natalie But I'm not artistic.

Richard (*smiles*) But you want to be.

Natalie (*turns her head, looking very vulnerable*) Kiss me . . .

Richard *kisses her, a brotherly kiss. She suddenly hugs and kisses*

him with surprising intensity, pulling him so close, so tight.
Richard *pulls away, slightly taken aback by the intensity in her eyes.*

Natalie Sorry – I just needed something to hug. Even you
. . . (*She smiles.*) Even my little brother. (*She moves away in the shadows.*) Go back to sleep. And you haven't made me feel better, so don't look so smug.

Interior: Main room: Early morning:

We see the empty room in the early morning sun, sweet papers, chocolates, and ashtrays strewn round where **Natalie** *had been lying in the little nest on the floor, the candles all out.*

Interior: Passage/staircase: Day:

Cut to **Richard** *emerging in shirt, jeans, barefoot, carrying one of the large shoes, moving along the passage towards the door from which the music is* still *pounding. He wallops the door with the shoe.*

Richard Switch it off, you moron, for Chrissake!
(*Thumping door.*) Go on.

Natalie *rushes out after him, restraining him.*

Natalie Stop it, Richard! Stop it. (*Laughing.*) I've never seen the guy, he might kill us! Come on.

They move off down the passage towards where the sun is splashing down the staircase from the next floor.

Exterior: Roof: Day:

We cut to them emerging onto the roof, surveying the view. Tall buildings jutting up behind them, dwarfing them. **Richard** *moving around the ducts on the roof.*

Natalie Where are you going?

Richard Getting away from that music. (*Touching the thirties necklace.*) You have *definitely* got to leave here.

Natalie OK. OK.

Richard I mean it. (*Quiet smile.*) You could do anything if you set your mind to it.

Natalie That's not true. (*Looking at him.*) *You* are always so confident, Richard.

Richard (*suddenly exclaiming and pointing*) Look, look! Look at this!

Natalie *looks down horrified. Out of a crack in the roof several giant cockroaches are happily marching around.*

Natalie (*appalled smile*) Oh my God!

Richard I told you about this building, didn't I? Now you've *got* to leave. You ought to come and join me in London. Oh yes.

They are moving away from the cockroaches.

Natalie Jesus, they're following us! *They are!*

Richard (*laughing*) You see, no choice now!

They are hopping around among the cockroaches on the roof.

Exterior: Kings Cross Station: Day:

We cut to a pan down from large advertisements of escapist images, beaches or mountains, high up on the walls of Kings Cross Station, to find **Richard** *strolling nonchalantly along the concourse, he is smartly and expensively dressed, and pulling an elegant little luggage trolley of an unusual design.*

A caption comes up: 'Two Years Later'. **Richard** *stops in the middle of the station, he feels in his inside pocket, mumbles to himself, shakes his head.*

Richard Shit.

Interior: Office: Day:

Cut to heavily designed office, full of plants, mid-eighties chic, very young men and women sheltering among the plants and computers. **Natalie,** *the oldest person there, is sitting typing on a word processor when she picks up the phone. She is trying to look chic in this atmosphere but is obviously ill at ease. She has to share a table with another girl.*

Intercut with:

Interior: Phone booth: Kings Cross Station: Day:

Richard *in phone booth at Kings Cross.*

Richard It is me.

Natalie What's the matter?

Richard I've left my wallet at your flat.

Natalie So go and fetch it.

Richard I haven't got a key! Please . . . they've announced the train!

Natalie I don't believe this, you appear out of nowhere, use my flat as a hotel, I hardly see you and –

Richard Natalie . . . just this time, please.

Interior: **Natalie**'s *Office: Day:*

A **Dark Haired Girl**, *who is no more than 22, is talking to an older secretary.*

Dark Haired Girl Look, how many times do I have to tell you, I don't want it done like this – you really disappoint me, Alice, when you don't *listen.*

Natalie (*to phone, staring at girl*) I'll have to get permission . . . have to ask my 14-year-old boss.

Natalie *stares with apprehension towards the* **Girl**.

Exterior: Kings Cross: Day:

Natalie *appears on walkway above platform.* **Richard** *sees her across the concourse. They meet on the platform among a maze of empty, blue trolleys.*

Natalie (*handing wallet*) There! The things I do for you, I can't believe it.

Richard (*grinning*) I can . . . I'll pay you back sometime.

Natalie (*indicating* **Richard**'s *luggage trolley*) And what is that? I've never seen a trolley like this.

Richard It's Swedish – a new design. It's great, isn't it?

Natalie (*laughing*) Trust you to have one, and (*Picking up lunch box.*) a cordon bleu packed lunch!

Richard Naturally! (*Whistle blows, he glances round, then back.*) How's the job?

Natalie Now he asks! It's horrible there. I've become a *secretary*. My boss is terrifying, I'm going backwards.

Whistle blows, both heads move.

I look for somewhere trendy to work, 'creative', and see what happens. I feel like I'm 150 – *and* six years old!

Richard (*reproachfully*) Stop it.

Natalie OK, OK, yes. I can do anything – you told me. (*She smiles.*) So it must be true. You're not listening.

Richard (*looks towards platform, whistle blowing*) It's just . . . no, it should be OK.

Natalie I've been meaning to talk to you – and now I try to do it here!

They look at each other, a tense, strained moment, **Richard** *wanting to go but not wishing to seem callous.*

Natalie This is stupid! Go on then, GO.

Richard *hesitates.*

GO.

Richard It's just the train . . . (*Gives her a little peck of a kiss.*) 'Bye.

He moves off purposefully.

Natalie You'd better write, or I'll kill you. And ring too. Scotland's not that far away.

Richard (*calling back*) I may be busy!

Natalie (*calling*) No, you won't. Building a new town, that's nothing. You'll have plenty of time!

Richard *falls into step with a tall blonde, helps her with her luggage.* **Natalie** *watching him disappear with the girl, then realises she's holding the special packed lunch. She smiles to herself, walks off with it, swinging it as she walks.*

Interior: Empty office and passage: Day:

A phone ringing somewhere, as the camera moves through a new empty open-plan office towards a glass partition. Everything is still wrapped in paper and plastic sheets, whole building still in cotton

*wool. As the camera moves we hear giggles and laughter. A caption
on the screen: 'One Year Later'.*

Interior: Old office: Day:

Close-up of **Natalie** *on telephone wiping her nose, she has a
streaming cold. She looks puffy and harrassed.*

Natalie (*on phone*) Come on . . . where are you?

*We see in a wide shot she is in a large almost Dickensian office with
heavy mahogany desk, tall windows, huge dusty files. It is grey
outside, a dismal rainy atmosphere. Opposite her a* **Pimply
Young Man** *is giving her knowing smiles. He has a large blotter
in front of him and is making a series of patterns out of coffee
stains, rings from the bottom of his coffee cup.*

Natalie (*more urgent*) Richard, be there.

Interior: Modern office: Day:

*We cut back to the modern office. The camera moves through the
glass partition. Then a bare arm suddenly shoots up and answers
the phone.* **Richard**'s *face appears slightly sweaty, broad grin.*

Richard Hello . . . Natalie! It's you!

Wide shot, we see he is naked with a **Scottish Girl** *in the middle
of an empty office where everything is still covered in plastic
sheeting.* **Richard** *moves very relaxed, naked with the phone, as he
talks, warm in the air-conditioned office.*

Intercut with:

Interior: Old office: Day:

The very draughty office **Natalie** *is in.*

Natalie Richard – what's the matter?

Richard Nothing . . . I was busy.

The **Scottish Girl** *gets up naked, beginning unhurriedly to put on her clothes.*

Richard (*to her*) It's only my sister.

Natalie Only! Who's that you are talking to?

Richard (*lightly*) My secretary. We're all alone here.

Natalie What are you giggling for? (*Suddenly.*) I suppose you were in the middle of screwing her.

Eyes flash all around **Natalie** *in the silent office.*

Richard As it happens, yes. But this is not a regular occurrence. (*He watches the* **Scottish Girl** *put on her jeans.*)

Natalie Jesus – I'm ringing off. You're incorrigible, it's 4 o'clock in the afternoon.

Natalie *stares down at a revolting cup of milky tea on her desk. The* **Pimply Young Man** *is watching her.*

We cut to **Richard**.

Richard (*relaxed and naked*) We're celebrating our last days of freedom. They've finally got the office finished. People will be moving in . . . (*Watching the* **Scottish Girl**.) It's going to get a lot more formal here.

Natalie (*staring about her*) I'm so cold, Richard, it's dismal here.

Richard The one thing we've got is marvellous central heating.

Natalie (*angry*) You're meant to be cold in Scotland!

Cut back to the **Scottish Girl**, *standing bare-backed by the* *window in her jeans, letting her hair blow in the air from the heater.*

Richard (*gently*) I know.

Natalie I thought I needed a drastic change. I've got my own desk! But the place is like out of a horror movie, it was out of date before the war. (*Staring at files.*)

Richard Maybe it's time to move on again.

Natalie You always make it sound so easy.

Richard Well, *I've* got a new job.

Natalie Another one!

Richard This one is on the continent . . . if I get it.

Natalie (*real alarm in her eyes*) What, you mean? You'll be going abroad?

Richard Maybe. Yes.

Close-up of **Natalie**.

Look, I've got to put some clothes on, (*Gently.*) I'll call you tomorrow, I promise.

Natalie (*furious*) Yes, it might be an idea to get dressed, wandering about naked in the middle of your office, that's ridiculous. I don't like this conversation. (*She slams down the phone.*)

Interior: Modern office: Day:

Cut back to **Richard**'s *office, he is pouring wine into paper cups. The* **Scottish Girl** *sitting opposite him. They are both now dressed in shirts and jeans.*

Scottish Girl I didn't know you were going abroad.

Richard (*warm smile*) Yes – it's a big job, Pan-European,

integrated transport planning, and other buzz words. I
never thought I'd get it.

Scottish Girl (*letting the heater blow her hair, moving her head
from side to side*) You get jobs very easily, don't you.

Richard (*self-mocking smile*) Yes, I don't know why that is
. . . maybe other people forget to apply.

Scottish Girl (*teasing smile*) Means I can try for your job,
can't I. (*Sensual smile.*) Let's have another little celebration,
shall we?

*We stay on her head, her hair blowing in the draught from the
heater, a warm relaxed moment.*

Interior: The old office: Day:

Natalie *now alone in the grey office, with just the* **Pimply
Young Man**, *who is making another coffee ring on the blotter,
and smiling at her, in a slightly predatory fashion.*

Natalie *starts feverishly circling new jobs in the 'Jobs Vacant'
section of a newspaper. The* **Pimply Young Man** *staring at her,
giving her little knowing smiles.*

Natalie *heaves and pushes the heavy desk away, so she can get out
from behind it and escape. A desolate image with the rain on the
windows.*

Exterior: London: Day:

*Cut to wide shots of London. Canary Wharf, ghostly, growing in
the early morning light, massive structure climbing into the sky. The
river, and the changing landscape, new development sprouting
around the river. In the shadow of these a large old warehouse
building, unconverted, walls still grey. The camera peers down at it*

from a great height. A caption on the image says 'Two Years Later'.

Interior: 'Urban Alert' offices: Day:

Large high-walled interior with flaking plaster dominated by the peeling decorative crest of the merchant company that once owned the warehouse, on the wall. The interior is divided into loosely planned office space, with rough and ready partitions. And there is a wide passage with tall quite elegant windows leading towards some large ancient service lifts.

Through the Venetian blinds covering the glass of one of the partitioned offices, **Jessica**, *a woman in her late twenties, is staring into the passage. She can see* **Richard** *sitting waiting there, in a fine suit, looking sleeker, slightly older, successful. Sun splashing the passage, dust visible in the sun.* **Colin**, *a very pale thin-faced man in his thirties joins* **Jessica** *by the blinds.*

Colin Is that him?

Jessica It must be.

Colin I don't like the look of him at all. (*Sharp smile.*) Let's keep him waiting.

Cut back to **Richard**, *his arms stretched out along wall as he sits, looking elegant and coolly detached.*

Interior: **Colin**'s *office: Day:*

Cut to **Colin** *in mid-sentence, interviewing* **Richard** *in his cramped office, spilling over with files, but they are neatly stacked, and there is a computer on the desk.* **Colin** *is sitting on the window sill, and* **Richard** *on a very low seat, so he has to stare up at him.*

Colin Frankly, I'm amazed to see somebody like you here.

The salary cut you'd be taking is immense, I mean all these jobs you've done, Pan-European, Brussels . . .

Richard Yes, take no notice of that. I've always for some reason been very good at landing terrific jobs . . .

Colin *stares at him coldly.*

. . . without having the right qualifications for them. It was just luck. And I wasn't happy doing them.

Colin So you think you're going to get this job do you?

Richard Not at the moment, no.

Colin You mean you only get *terrific* jobs and this isn't one of them.

Richard No, I meant this interview is going rather badly so . . . (*He pulls out a cigarette.*) I don't smoke, I just fiddle with them.

Jessica *looking through window.*

I've changed you see, I saw there was more to life than planning new roads, (*Self-mocking smile.*) I discovered the 'environment', a bit late maybe . . . I'm not putting this well. I've seen so much incompetence among developers . . . bad planning – I want to do something about that.

Colin (*staring straight at him*) You realise we have no money to speak of, we get *some* funds from the local council. There are no planning controls in this part of town, all we can do is *hound*.

Richard (*smiles*) A sort of urban Greenpeace . . .

A shot of **Jessica** *watching outside the office. Cut back to* **Colin**.

Colin (*cold stare*) It might be useful to have a professional town planner, who'd respond really quickly with alternative plans to any situation.

Richard That's right. (*Very slight pause.*)

Colin (*briskly*) I'll let you know. I'll call you.

Richard No. You tell me now.

Colin *'s eyes narrow.*

Richard I prefer to cut the bullshit. And I imagine you do too.

Colin *'s arm suddenly goes up, plucks a file from above his head and chucks it down at* **Richard** *so it lands with a thud in his stomach.*

Colin We have a meeting with Lappenshaw Mercantile at the end of the week, we're only 'granted' face to face meetings very occasionally, it's a chance for us.

Richard (*taking the file*) Great.

Richard *getting up,* **Colin** *watching him.*

Colin We may look like a bunch of ex-hippies but I fire people at a moment's notice. You ought to know that. It's much worse here than at a merchant bank.

Interior: 'Urban Alert' offices: **Richard** *'s office: Day:*

High shot, mid-afternoon light, the camera moving across the office, phones are ringing, people working hard, we see **Richard** *in his office, behind a makeshift partition. He has covered the walls with an eclectic collection of posters, some nostalgic, some very urban and modern. He is pacing up and down, reading a file, with paper chaotically spread all around him.*

Jessica *pushes back books on top of partition, speaks through the gap.*

Jessica Phone call for you.

Richard I can't take it.

Jessica It's your sister.

Richard (*offhand*) Oh shit, yes, I was meant to . . . I
suppose I better take it.

Interior: **Natalie**'s *bedroom: Day:*
Natalie *in profile, lying on her bed, just her face in semi-darkness,
and the afternoon light through the bedroom window.*

Intercut with:

Interior: **Richard**'s *office: Day:*

Richard I've been really busy, I'm sorry, I've been
meaning . . .

Natalie You've been back six weeks – you haven't called.

Richard (*not concentrating, looking at file*) I did call! I left a
message on your machine.

Natalie Took till yesterday! (*Her face in shadow.*) You want
to come over and·meet Sinclair?

Richard Who?

Natalie Don't do that . . . *Sinclair.* Since you didn't
manage to make it to the wedding.

As **Richard** *is on the phone,* **Jessica** *calls out.*

Jessica (*calling at him*) Food! Food's up!

Richard *looks up, a very pretty girl,* **Paula**, *in some sort of
restaurant uniform, is handing out take-away food boxes dropping
them on desks.*

Richard ‚(*on phone, very abstracted*) Sure . . . Yeah . . . why
not. Lunch on Saturday, fine. I'll try to make it. (*He
replaces the receiver, looks at* **Jessica**.) Families!

Interior: **Natalie**'s *bedroom: Day:*

We settle for a second back on **Natalie**'s *face in semi-darkness, lying on pillow, her eyes staring out.*

Interior: **Richard**'s *office: Day:*

Jessica (*watching* **Paula** *with food*) He may work us hard, but Colin does send out for great take-aways.

Richard (*staring at* **Paula** *as she comes towards him*) So I see.

We cut to **Colin** *and* **Jessica** *staring at* **Richard** *as he chats up* **Paula** *among the piles and piles of paper in his office.*

Colin (*watching* **Richard** *flirt with* **Paula**) I'm beginning to think we've made a real mistake.

Interior: **Natalie**'s *kitchen: Day:*

Cut to ingredients being laid out as if for an operation, spotless utensils, magnificent ingredients, for the making of a summer pudding.

Interior: Developer's office and passage: Day:

Colin, Jessica, Richard *and a couple of others from the office walking towards us down a plush passage. Then we see their approach being watched through an open door by* **Geal** *and three other city types sitting behind a desk.*

Geal (*watching their approach*) What a miserable looking bunch.

Richard *staring at* **Geal** *as they approach through door, into the* *room with its blinds drawn against the sun, gold and black light, half-light.*

Richard It looks like they've modelled themselves on those banking commercials on TV.

They sit opposite each other. The businessmen the same age or slightly younger than the pressure group.

Geal Delighted to see you all here. I'm sure you're going to give us a clean bill of health.

*Interior: **Natalie**'s kitchen: Day:*

*We see food being prepared, fruit, meringues, and especially a summer pudding being finished, the blackcurrants gleaming, the pudding a rich dark red. **Natalie**, cooking on her own, licking the juice from the pudding off her fingers.*

Interior: Developers' building: Day:

*Cut back to **Colin** awkwardly in the middle of a speech to the businessmen, stuttering, realising he's not having impact.*

Colin . . . However many times you say that, the fact is you said there'd be access to Threepenny Street . . . and . . . and an open space there, and there.

Geal I think you will find we have done everything we stated we would – there is not a single public statement, or a single promise that we've made, which we've failed to honour. If there is, I'd be interested to see what it is!

Colin But that is not the case, your wording was ambiguous, maybe, but everybody took it to mean . . . (*His papers suddenly fluttering everywhere scattering across desk and room.*)

Noley (*sidekick to* **Geal**, *slightly older, watching* **Colin** *with great contempt*) Want any help with those?

Interior: **Natalie**'s *kitchen: Day:*

Cut back to **Natalie**'s *kitchen, the bread soaking in the blackcurrant juice, the pudding being moulded into shape by delicate fingers, more dark juice being poured over it, and more fruit squeezed inside it, fresh raspberries and blackcurrants.*

Interior: Developers' office: Day:

Geal Gentlemen, (*Correcting himself.*) and to the lady present, I don't want to seem impatient – but we are under no obligation to see you, and it is Saturday, we have now spent fifty minutes, and I think nobody would quarrel with that. You have not been able to show us one instant –

Richard Just one moment.

Richard *gets up and opens the door, they all stare at him surprised.*

Geal (*smiles*) You leaving us?

In the passage two **Security Guards** *look up in surprise.*

Richard Exactly what has happened here?

Geal (*grinning*) What do you mean?

Richard This passage, the guards.

Geal Our security system. (*To the others.*) Your friend is not making himself clear.

Richard (*suddenly producing a piece of paper from back pocket*) You know you said on August 4th, 'Our new block will be an asset for the whole area, we want to share it'.

Geal Exactly.

Richard 'We are proud of it, and as is the regular practice in America, the public will be allowed to see the full glories of our foyer at any time, and there will be public tours of the building every day of the week.' (*He smiles.*) But getting in here, Mr Geal, is more difficult than entering Fort Knox – this promise was crap, wasn't it?

Geal I'm not aware of having made this statement, but it is a small matter . . .

Richard (*producing another piece of paper*) Absolutely, and talking of small matters, let us now move on to the matter of Threepenny Street. On September 3rd in a speech you made . . .

Shot of **Geal** *looking discomfited.*

Interior: **Natalie***'s kitchen: Day:*

Cut to the pudding reaching its climax, its completion.

Exterior: Canary Wharf: Day:

Cut to the group moving along the road by the river, the vast building works behind them, towering above.

Richard *is walking slightly behind the group.* **Colin** *still formidably aloof, the others obviously impressed with* **Richard**.

Jessica (*coming up to him*) Well done.

Richard Yes, well Colin doesn't look too pleased.

Jessica (*she smiles*) What do you expect, applause from him!

Richard (*suddenly stops*) Shit, I was meant to go to lunch with my sister, Jesus!

Smoke blowing from road works.

It's too late now. Forget it! She's married some boring guy. I was meant to meet him.

Richard *moving into smoke, stops dead again.*

Jessica (*staring at him amazed*) Why don't you go?

Richard I better go, hadn't I?

Exterior: Surrey approach: Day:

Cut to the voluptuous views of Surrey, the Thames Valley, the large houses sheltering behind thick foliage, exotic, rich shots, Surrey seen as surprisingly, almost disturbingly lush, and large vistas almost un-English in their size and contrast. The shots starting high and distant and closing in on **Richard** *driving an old open-topped Triumph Herald, but well kept, moving along the sleepy streets. The car slowing, as we see houses, surrounded by clusters of roses, and the car stops completely as* **Natalie** *and* **Sinclair***'s house slips into view, imposing red brick Edwardian house with a huge conservatory and a tower.*

Exterior: The house: Day:

Cut to **Richard** *on foot now, moving up the path, glancing at the garden packed with flowers, it is heavy with colour and scent.*

He rings the bell and the door opens a second later and **Natalie** *is standing there. A vitally important shot: her face moves out of the half shadow, slowly glimpsed as the door opens.*

She looks stunning. Her hair is different. Her eyes alive. She is beautifully dressed. For a moment **Richard** *stares at her in surprise.*

Natalie You are unbelievably late.

Richard (*very quiet*) I know.

Natalie There is practically no food left.

Richard (*amused, remembering*) I've eaten all the food.

Natalie What?

Richard Don't you remember? (*He looks into her eyes.*) Nothing? This house, Natalie . . . it's extraordinary. I thought I'd come to the wrong place.

Natalie Are you going to come in – or are you going to admire it from out there?

Interior: The conservatory: Day:

We cut to a group sitting around a round table in the massive conservatory. A vine climbs up the conservatory walls with grapes hanging ripely all around. There are other plants and flowers, late afternoon hazy summer light. This is our first sight of **Sinclair**, *a dynamic sharp-faced man, full of energy, quick-witted eyes, warm chuckling laugh. He is sitting commandingly at the centre of the group, next to* **Philippa**, *a woman in her early twenties, with two golden-haired girls sitting near her, all of them in expensive summer clothes, a young man by her, and two other handsome women, lying in a post-prandial lazy way, the remnants of a gorgeous meal spread on the table.*

Sinclair The brother! This, at last, must be the brother.

Richard (*he smiles*) Yes, at last, it is.

Sinclair (*pointing at summer pudding*) I've been eyeing this last portion wondering if I could possibly eat it. (*Warm smile.*) But now you've turned up! . . . sit, sit . . . have some cold soup.

Sinclair *ladles the soup out.* **Richard** *is glancing round at the other women, the golden-haired children and* **Natalie** *moving in the conservatory. He keeps glancing back at her, taking another look.*

Sinclair It's all your fault we have eaten so much. (*He stares at* **Richard**, *a warm but shrewd look.*) I've heard so much about you – most of it extremely interesting.

Philippa (*a warm smile*) It's lovely to meet you.

Something plops from the ceiling of the conservatory into **Richard**'s *soup.*

Sinclair (*smiles*) Take no notice of that, it adds to the flavour.

Richard (*looking about him at the profusion of flowers and foliage*) This is amazing, this place – it's like a grotto or something.

Sinclair You've seen nothing yet.

Exterior: Garden by river: Day:

Sinclair *moving along the lawn overlooking the river, imposing houses on the other side, one of them with palm trees.* **Philippa**, *the children, and* **Natalie**, *moving behind them across the grass.*

Sinclair This is the 'estate'.

Richard Very impressive.

Sinclair I love it here. (*Staring across the water.*) I thought when we moved here we'd stand out, eccentrics amongst all these rich pricks, but not a bit of it, the place is full of madmen, dreamers, psychopaths, (*Waving at the houses across the water.*) bank managers who want to be painters, deep-freeze merchants who want to be poets. We're really rather boringly normal and restrained in comparison.

Natalie *is moving among the flowers,* **Richard** *watching her out of the corner of his eye, fascinated by the change in her appearance.*

Sinclair (*suddenly up to him*) I see you are reading the guilt-book!

Richard (*startled*) What?

Sinclair (*plucking book from* **Richard**'s *jacket pocket*) Proust ... Volume 7, or is that just for our benefit? If you carry that around people automatically think – 'Jesus, I feel so *guilty*. I've never read it'. Proust! I'm afraid, though it's nauseating to admit it, I've read the entire book in French.

Richard I've read some in French.

Sinclair You're very good at languages, I hear. (*Smiles at* **Richard** *and breaks into Spanish.*) Mi burro favorito vive en Salamanca. ¿Ha estado ustéd allí?

Richard No conozco bien España.

Sinclair (*changes immediately into Italian*) La prossima volta che vieni a Verona invita mi a prendere il te. (*A sudden burst of Dutch.*) Mign vriend Herman van der Horst hasst zojuist een nieuw supermarket complex ge-opened.

The strength of his personality is overwhelming, but it's also warm and funny.

Sinclair That's Dutch – an amazingly ugly language – how about Norwegian – (*He bursts into Norwegian.*) Har du vaert i den del av skogen før. Actually, I'm not fluent in Norwegian. I have to admit.

Natalie (*quiet*) Stop showing off Sinclair ... please.

Sinclair Rubbish, he's enjoying it. (*He begins to move off.*)

Natalie (*slight laugh*) Apart from anything else, it makes me feel so ignorant.

Sinclair (*heading off*) He must see the car. (*Charming smile.*) You want to see the car, don't you?

Exterior: Garage: Day:

Cut to the garage door opening, slowly going up as they watch.

Richard It's not a Rolls I hope.

A beautiful vintage Bentley is revealed, shining in the darkness.

Sinclair Very predictable I know, and it's very vulgar showing it to people, but it's a magnificent car. (*Charming smile.*) I just can't help it!

Richard *watching* **Natalie** *who has moved nearer the car.*

Natalie He doesn't let me drive it.

Sinclair Nobody drives it – we've got other cars for that. I do believe, I have to confess, in spending money, not just hoarding it.

Richard (*amused*) Of course.

Sinclair And fortunately there's a lot of money in being able to tell people what's going to happen! Business trends, analysis. The wonderful thing is you can make an awful lot even if you're wrong. Most people don't realise that. (*Shrewd look.*) But I'm not wrong. Not often. (*He moves off.*) Come on Nats, tea time.

Natalie Oh no, Sinclair, not more eating. What about your diet?

Sinclair The diet starts tomorrow. Tea is definitely overdue.

Interior: Boathouse: Day:

Natalie *staring at* **Richard** *in the boathouse, a moment between them, alone together.*

Natalie (*quiet*) So what do you think!

Richard (*looking round*) Oh, it's . . . amazing, and everything is wonderful.

Natalie And Sinclair?

Richard Oh he's . . . great. Does he ever stop talking?

Natalie (*smiles*) Not when he's eating – as you will see.

Richard Does he ever let you say anything?

Natalie Oh yes, of course. (*Slight smile.*) Once a week, at least.

Richard (*imitating her new Home Counties voice*) And how did you get to speak like this?

Natalie (*self-mocking smile, exaggerating her new voice*) I've always spoken like this, haven't I?

Natalie *is wearing the same thirties necklace as when he saw her at the beginning of the film. Involuntarily he reaches out and touches it.*

Richard Why are you wearing this?

Natalie What do you mean, why?

Richard You wore it that night when I visited you in your flat. You remember . . .

Natalie (*looking at necklace*) I don't think so.

Richard You look all . . . all . . . (*Embarrassed smile.*)

Natalie (*staring at him*) All what?

Richard (*laughs*) All different. I wasn't expecting –

Natalie I know you weren't.

Sinclair *comes in.*

Sinclair A brother and sister reunion. I intrude. (*He smiles.*) I'll withdraw. (*Suddenly to* **Richard**.) But you'd forgotten it was her birthday hadn't you? Nat's birthday.

Richard *surprised. He has forgotten.*

Interior: Conservatory: Early evening:

Natalie *blowing out the candles on cake.*

Sinclair (*ebullient, the force of his personality, he catches hold of* **Natalie**'s *arm*) Not like that! Blow them out separately, one by one.

Natalie *hesitates.*

Sinclair No, go on darling, do it, a wish for *each one*. What are you waiting for? *Go on.*

Natalie *begins blowing them out separately, embarrassed in front of everyone.* **Richard** *watching her, their eyes meet over the cake.* **Natalie** *blowing out the candles.*

Sinclair (*as this is happening, with cream dispenser*) You see this is a new sort of cream dispenser – market research showed people hated cream coming out of tubes, like toothpaste, so they've made this cow – it's meant to be an elegant cow.

Philippa *laughing at him.*

Go on, squeeze its udders, go on . . .

Natalie *is still blowing out the candles.* **Sinclair** *notices her again.*

Sinclair Come on darling, haven't you finished yet!

Natalie *blows out the last one.* **Sinclair** *hands her the knife.*

Sinclair That took long enough. Anybody would think you'd never done it before!

We stay on **Natalie** *looking embarrassed and vulnerable.*

Exterior: Field near the house: Evening:

Natalie *and* **Richard** *walking in a field dotted with flowers.*
Sinclair *walking a little behind, wearing a floppy hat. The gnats
chasing each other in the evening air.* **Natalie** *plucking the tops off
the long grass as she walks. A particularly fine view from the field
across the river.*

Richard I never realised the Home Counties were so
beautiful. All this so near the City.

Sinclair Yes, all sorts of things happened here. It was the
site of a great Victorian party at the end of the last
century. They had columns of elephants here.

Richard *walking side by side with* **Natalie**, *getting further away
from* **Sinclair**.

Natalie (*quiet*) What about your new job?

Richard That's fine . . . they're very serious.

Natalie (*slow smile*) You mean they don't laugh at your
jokes?

Richard And my boss looks rather ill . . . the office is
amazing, it's all decaying, but they're quite efficient . . .
it's OK. (*He looks her full in the face.*) Are you happy?

Natalie Oh yes.

Richard But this isn't you, is it? . . . This house . . . and
everything?

Natalie Oh, it's me all right. (*She turns on the path, looking
lovely.*) It's very much me.

Richard (*watching her*) Really? Even though you never get
to speak . . . (*Quiet.*) You do remember don't you . . .
(*Touching necklace.*)

Natalie (*quiet smile*) You keep saying that – I don't know
what you mean.

Sinclair *behind them on the path.*

Sinclair Do I pass?

Richard (*looking back down the path*) What?

Sinclair (*calling out, waving his hat*) Do I pass? Do I meet with the brother's approval?

Richard (*smiles*) Oh yes.

Natalie Very definitely.

Interior: 'Urban Alert' offices: Day:

Wide shot of the office, and then we move closer to **Richard** *and* **Jessica.** **Richard** *in full flood, talking to* **Jessica** *through the partition.*

Richard It was really rather astonishing, the house and . . . and, it's like being *inside* a colour supplement, pretty women draped about the place, golden-haired children, food on every available surface.

Jessica *watching him closely.*

Jessica Were you envious?

Richard Envious, no, no. (*He smiles.*) Maybe a little. It would drive me mad in less than a week living like that.

Jessica Are you close you two, you and your sister?

Richard Not particularly no. (*Definite.*) Not at all. My parents separated when she was a teenager – she went to live with Dad.

Jessica (*smiles*) And now she's married a rich man?

Richard Yes, a complete cop out. (*He grins.*) She applied for a job, he was the boss. She didn't get the job, but she got him! Anyway you must come and see.

Jessica (*amused*) Is that some kind of invitation?

Richard Yeah, maybe.

Jessica Thanks!

Colin's *face suddenly appears round the partition.*

Colin Don't know what you two are up to. Chat, chat, chat. (*Makes derisive movement of his hand.*) Always at it. I want those figures by the end of the day. *Understand.*

He moves off, his face tense and pale.

Richard Jesus – what's the matter with him?

Jessica (*amused smile*) He doesn't like you – that's all. I know you find that impossible to believe.

Richard (*self-mocking smile*) I'm not used to it.

Jessica I know!

Richard *glances around.* **Paula,** *with food boxes, is waving at him from across the office, a playful wave.* **Jessica** *watching things, amused.*

Interior: 'Urban Alert' offices: Day:

Cut to plans on large graph paper, beautifully drawn plans, the pencil moving along the paper. We see **Richard** *bent over the paper, drawing in the afternoon light. He is concentrating very hard. We see the plans in close-up again.*

Suddenly an orange rose drops into shot, drops onto the middle of the plans.

Richard *looks up,* **Natalie** *is standing there, dressed in surprisingly formal clothes as if for a wedding reception, a rich red dress and hat.*

Natalie Hello.

Richard *looks up, the afternoon light is behind her.*

Richard What on earth are you doing here?

Natalie We were just passing on the way to a wedding in Greenwich, couldn't resist dropping by, having a peek. (*She surveys the room.*) Sinclair's here . . . can he come in? He feels a bit over-dressed for this place, because of the wedding.

Sinclair *in grey suit and top hat approaches round the corner, in mid-afternoon light, looking splendid and formidable.*

Sinclair Forgive this invasion Richard. I feel ludicrously incongruous for a place like this.

He puts the top hat on **Richard**'*s desk.*

Richard It's fine . . . don't worry.

Sinclair But Nats was so eager to have a nose around.

Natalie *staring at a pudgy girl in jeans, sandals and baggy sweater, who's working away.*

Natalie So this is what you wanted?

Richard Yes – so it appears.

Sinclair (*looking at the drawings on* **Richard**'*s desk*) What plans are these? Oh, this is interesting, this is very interesting, Richard. I know about this, as it happens. (*Quiet.*) I feel there may be an obvious solution which nobody seems to have mentioned because they are all so obsessed about the river frontage.

As **Sinclair** *has been saying this,* **Richard** *and* **Natalie**'*s eyes meet fleetingly. She has been taking in the place, and picking up some of the things on his desk. Suddenly* **Richard** *is aware of an odd sensation, the office sounds begin to fade, a phone ringing on the table next to him remains unanswered.* **Richard** *is watching* **Natalie**, *he looks down and then up at her again.*

Natalie Shouldn't that phone be answered?

Richard (*turns slowly*) Yes, probably.

The phone stops.

Natalie Sinclair, we've got to go.

Sinclair (*running his finger along the plans, deeply interested*) Yes, just one moment, this is extremely interesting.

Natalie (*leans low by* **Richard**, *whispers*) You don't belong here, this isn't you.

Richard (*smiles*) Oh yes, it is, very definitely.

Natalie (*casually*) I need to see you properly. Talk about something. I'll make an appointment. Can you fit me in?

Richard Sure, why not. Yes.

Natalie Good.

Natalie *moves off,* **Richard** *watches her go, rich light.*

Richard (*picking up the rose*) Do I keep this?

Sinclair (*taking rose*) No. I believe we need that.

Interior: **Richard**'s *flat: Wet afternoon:*

Shot of the television with test match cricket on, a damp field, with the covers on. No cricket.

Richard *pacing in front of the television. The flat consists of a large room tapering into a much smaller kitchen and bedroom, but it is a fine atmospheric room. Outside there is some large building works, the sound of scaffolding falling, being thrown about, through the whole scene.*

The doorbell rings, **Natalie** *is standing there.*

Richard You're four hours late.

Natalie I'm sorry – I had to go shopping for Sinclair. (*Putting the bags down.*)

Richard Is this deliberate? I've been stuck in here waiting. I couldn't go.out!

Natalie *You* were late for lunch! Even later than this!

Richard So it *is* deliberate!

Natalie What's the matter with you Richard!

Richard At least I might have been able to watch the cricket – but it's raining for fuck's sake! It hasn't even started!

Natalie Sssh relax – for Chrissake. (*Involuntarily touching him.*)

Richard You're wearing that again – (*Touches necklace.*)is that on purpose too?

Natalie Maybe this time, yes.

Their eyes meet for a second. Pause. **Richard** *surprised by this admission.*

Natalie Anyway this is not much of a greeting, you haven't even shaved.

Natalie *touches his cheek, and then finds she's kissing him, a full kiss on the lips, but quite a short kiss. She breaks away, her hand goes up to her lips as if trying to rub it off.*

Natalie I'm sorry – (*Smiles.*)don't know what that was for.

Natalie *moves into the small kitchen.*

So this was what was for lunch was it?

Some carrots are boiling in a saucepan on the stove. Nothing else.

Richard *moves after her into the kitchen. Suddenly they are kissing again, she is pressed up against the wall of the tiny kitchen, next to the stove. This time they are much more passionate and sexual as they kiss.* **Natalie** *breaks away.*

Natalie Come on, this is . . . this is . . . (*She moves.*) OK, it just happened. We won't mention it again.

Richard Yes, I knew you'd say that.

Natalie (*switching off the gas on stove*) I don't know why it happened – but it's stopped. It's over . . . let me look at your flat.

She opens the bedroom door. Immediately shuts it. Nervous laugh.

Natalie Don't want to go in there. How many girls have been in there recently?

Richard (*watching her*) Hardly any, I've been very celibate.

Natalie Really? (*Moving into the large room.*) This is nice.

Richard I spent my savings on this place.

Richard *touches her from the back, kisses the nape of her neck.*

Natalie No . . . this is not a good idea.

But she lets him kiss the back of her neck.

Natalie Please Richard . . . I shouldn't have started this . . . we don't mention it. Go. And sit over there.

Richard Is that an order?

They sit opposite each other, on either side of the room.

Natalie (*flicking her hair back*) So is it convenient?

Richard (*nervous grin*) Convenient?

Natalie This flat, for buses?

Richard For buses? (*He flicks off his shoes,* **Natalie** *looks away.*)

Natalie Yes, buses. (*She does the button up on her blouse.*)

Richard (*taking a ginger biscuit out of an old packet*) I think there are probably some buses.

Natalie (*moving her hair again*) What number? The buses?

Richard (*munching soggy biscuit*) I don't know . . . you know

small buses, those small buses that beetle about . . .
Hoppers.

Natalie (*staring at him*) Hoppers . . . you've got some
crumbs . . .

Richard's *hand goes up to his mouth.*

Natalie (*undoes the button on her blouse*) The cricket has
started.

*Highlights of a dramatic one-day game played in a thunderstorm
being shown on the television silently.*

Richard No, that's old highlights.

Natalie (*staring at the white figures in the thunderstorm on TV*) I
never knew they ever played cricket when it rains.

*Pause. Their eyes meet. They move at the same moment, the same
impulse towards each other, kissing passionately, pulling each
other's shirt and blouse off.*

*We cut to close-up of the cricket in the rain. English and Australian
cricketers, dramatic light, dense rain, but also the sun is out, the
water dripping off the players.*

We cut back to **Natalie** *lying on top of* **Richard** *on the floor.
Both of them are naked.*

Natalie (*quiet*) You're going to stop me aren't you? (*She's
kissing him.*) You're going to stop me.

Richard I don't know.

Natalie Come on stop me. (*She half kisses him, stops.*) I'm
just lying here, I'm not doing anything.

Richard (*warm smile*) OK . . .

Natalie OK what? (*Pause.*) Are you clean, are you clean
everywhere?

Richard (*nervous laugh*) Yes of course.

Natalie I don't believe it, maybe you are . . . (*She can't stop* *herself kissing him.*) Stop me . . . (*She smiles.*) Please . . . (*She can't stop the kisses.*) Please . . . (*She continues to kiss.*) Please . . . stop me.

Richard *breaks away, gets up.*

Natalie (*quiet*) I knew you would.

Richard (*nervous grin*) I'm just putting some music on . . . I . . .

He looks for tape, they're scattered everywhere, he just bangs on the radio.

Natalie *comes up beside him, they kiss against the wall.*

Natalie Oh Richard.

We cut to the cricket, the rain and the players, water dripping everywhere, and then back to **Richard** *and* **Natalie** *not trying to resist any more, kissing longingly. Entwined together, kissing passionately.*

Interior: **Richard**'s *flat: Rain heavier:*

They're lying in a corner of the room, curled together, naked and quiet.

Natalie That noise.

Richard It's the scaffolding.

Sound of it dropping.

Natalie Must drive you mad.

Richard No, I like it . . . I don't know why. (*She kisses him, a sexual kiss.*) And to think we never really liked each other as kids. (*Another kiss.* **Natalie** *stops decisively.*)

Natalie OK, that's the last bit.

Richard What do you mean, 'last bit'?

Natalie It just happened.

Richard (*smiles*) 'And we don't mention it. Don't know what got into us' etc, etc.

Natalie (*lightly*) Precisely . . . it's never going to happen again. It's your fault for being away so long.

Richard (*lightly*) It's always my fault.

Natalie Of course.

Natalie *puts his shirt on, and walks over to the kitchen.*

Natalie I'm going to make the carrots – with lots of butter.

Richard They'll be the best I've ever tasted I'm sure.

Natalie (*by stove, half to herself*) We tried to stop it happening and it's finished. (*She glances up from stove.*) By the way Sinclair wants to have lunch with you.

Richard Sinclair. Jesus! You mention that now.

Natalie (*stirring carrots calmly*) Sure . . . (*She looks up.*) There's no problem is there?

Interior: Atrium of office block: Day:

Cut to atrium of a huge new office building with the customary glass lifts gliding up and down its sides. **Richard** *staring about him,* **Sinclair** *appears suddenly from the right of frame.*

Sinclair Here you are! Good! Just have to drop something off – come with me.

Cut to them going up together in a glass lift.

Sinclair These lifts are interesting.

Richard *staring down at the people miles below, as the lift gets higher and higher.*

Richard Are they?

Sinclair Yes – they've become such a common feature, but people hate them, they much prefer the old claustrophobia, now they all have to pretend they don't suffer from vertigo – and feel so *exposed*. (*He gesticulates.*) Everybody can see them! Imagine coming out of a truly terrible meeting and seeing right down there.

Richard *reluctant to look down.*

Sinclair It's frightening! But nobody admits it.

Cut to them moving down large passage with huge doors.

Sinclair These doors are interesting aren't they – ridiculously large. People try to proclaim their importance in such a crass fashion. What will a historian make of these doors?

Richard (*amused smile*) You're interested in everything Sinclair.

Sinclair Oh yes, lifts, doors . . . (*He looks at* **Richard**.) this secretary here, *you* . . . Just stay there for a moment. (*To the Secretary.*) He's expecting me.

Sinclair *goes through one of the massive doors, the Secretary eyes* **Richard** *coldly.*

Sudden euphoric laughter from behind the door, **Sinclair** *sharing a joke, the laughter climbs louder and louder.*

Sinclair *emerging through large door, he smiles.*

Sinclair All done. Simple.

Interior: Bar: High up, view over London: Day:

Cut to **Sinclair** *and* **Richard** *having a drink,* **Sinclair** *incisive, leaning towards* **Richard**.

Sinclair You see I believe in a personal service. People are amazed and flattered that I deliver files of data myself, *walk* around with them! I'm successful enough now for it not to seem a sign of weakness. So many people pretend they're busy don't they, meetings about meetings, most of it is bullshit – just a way of protecting themselves. I like to get to know people.

Richard (*sips drink*) Of course.

Sinclair I like to find out about my clients, poke into their personal lives, and I can tell you there's some interesting things going on, so much *cocaine* being taken – drink too, that's massively on the increase, sudden hysterical temper tantrums flaring up from nowhere –

Richard (*mischievous smile, looking straight at him*) Do *you* have a temper Sinclair?

Sinclair Oh yes, horrendous, unfortunately . . . (*He leans forward.*) We're having one of our great picnics soon. They are not to be missed. You must be there. (*He drinks, puzzled tone.*) Natalie didn't want you to come for some reason.

Close-up at **Richard.**

Interior: 'Urban Alert' offices: Day:

We move with **Richard** *as he enters the office in the early morning light.* **Jessica**'s *face tense and pale, the small pudgy girl blowing her nose like a trumpet, the atmosphere awkward and hushed.*

Richard (*at his desk*) So what's the matter? What's happened . . . What's going on?

Jessica It's about Colin. He's sent us a memo. Yours should be somewhere. (*Staring at his mass of papers.*) He's ill.

Richard Yes. I thought so . . . I knew he might be. (*Pause.*

He reads the memo. He looks up surprised. His eyes flick across towards **Colin**.)

Jessica Don't stare – don't do that.

Richard I'm sorry. I didn't know he was gay.

Jessica He isn't.

Richard (*quiet*) He's not?

Jessica He's had it for some time. *I* knew, actually. He's letting the office know because he may be spending more time in hospital. (*Watching* **Richard**.) Don't worry.

Richard (*sharp*) I wasn't.

Jessica You don't need to talk to him about it. Life goes on as normal.

Richard (*quiet*) Yes, of course.

Jessica So get to work.

Exterior: Lift of Docklands Light Railway: Evening:

Richard *running for the lift just as its heavy doors are closing.*

Richard Hold it!

He gets to the lift, the doors close.

Richard Thanks.

He sees he's alone with **Colin** *as the heavy lift grinds upwards.* **Colin** *glances at him perfectly normally, his usual sharp expression.* **Richard** *embarrassed for a moment, not certain whether to say anything.*

Richard Hi.

Colin I want to see the Threepenny Street plans by the end of the week, OK?

Richard Yes of course. I'll make sure that happens.

The lift clanks downwards.

Exterior: Canary Wharf: Day:

Cut to **Colin** *and* **Richard** *walking along by the river. The great development behind them. It is very windy.*

Colin (*moving off*) So don't forget – I've got a very full diary, so the sooner the better.

Richard Understood.

Colin *moving down pavement.*

Richard Have a nice . . .

Colin *turns.*

Have a good weekend.

Exterior: The picnic: A field near the river: Day:

A crane shot, the picnic spread below us. The Bentley parked in the middle of a field of long grass and poppies, hampers bursting with food spread around. Girls in orange dresses, the atmosphere is drenched in sensuality.

Natalie *has a red umbrella/parasol shielding her from the sun.* **Richard** *is taking photographs.* **Jessica** *is lying there, drinking in the sun.* **Sinclair** *pouring himself wine,* **Philippa** *is rubbing cream on herself. The children are picking flowers and looking for snakes.*

Philippa (*rubbing herself with cream*) The sun is getting hotter every year. I heard in New Zealand –

Sinclair (*knowingly*) New Zealand. Ah!

Richard *photographing* **Natalie,** *she keeps moving her head.*

Philippa People were getting burnt, when they've never been burnt before.

Sinclair Wouldn't it be interesting, if because of the greenhouse effect, people started using parasols again. So we ended this century using them just as they did at the end of the last. Maybe you could market them Richard, make your fortune.

Natalie (*with red parasol*) They do look good.

The shadow on her face, **Richard** *close to her with the camera.*

Sinclair Of course there will be winds of 170 miles an hour too, storms like we've never seen, umbrellas will not be much help during those!

Richard *continues to take pictures of* **Natalie,** *their eyes meet,* **Natalie** *telling him silently to stop.* **Sinclair** *is still talking in the background.*

Sinclair And these miniature hurricanes we've been having are going to get worse and worse, trees in southern England are going to become something of a rarity.

Jessica So you're a disaster freak are you?

Sinclair No, these are just facts.

As **Richard** *moves closer to* **Natalie,** *lazy movements over the picnic food,* **Philippa** *is watching* **Natalie** *under her parasol.*

Philippa (*to* **Jessica**) Did you know her *before?*

Jessica Before?

Philippa Before Sinclair of course. (*Whispering as she gazes at* **Natalie.**) He's changed her completely apparently – I wonder if she's really clever enough for him.

Close-up of **Natalie,** *we can't tell if she's heard or not.*

Natalie (*getting up, stretching her body*) I need to go for a walk.

We cut to them crossing a field of blue herbs with **Philippa** *carrying the parasol, and the children running behind.*

We then cut to them moving along a narrow path running along the river bank, the water glimpsed to the left, through the leaves. Couples are entwined in the grass, enjoying the sun, half hidden by the leaves.

Natalie *is moving ahead along the path, occasionally looking back towards* **Richard,** *on the path.* **Richard** *follows her.*

Sinclair Look for mushrooms, Nats – but don't kill us, you know the ones to pick.

Natalie *stoops to pick a mushroom,* **Richard** *gets up to her.*

Natalie You shouldn't be here.

Richard Don't be silly.

Natalie *moves off.*

Richard (*half whispered*) Natalie!

Richard *moves fast after her, he stops her on a little boating jetty, where the path opens out.*

We cut between them on the jetty and the rest of the group catching them up, looking towards them.

Richard I need to see you.

Natalie Listen we agreed.

Richard We agreed nothing – and you want to see me . . . we just can't pretend it never happened.

Natalie (*staring at him*) Can't we?

Richard Don't you want to talk about it, ask why?

Natalie No.

Richard Is it because . . . our parents are dead, is it because we didn't see each other for a long time, or . . .

Natalie There *isn't* a reason.

Richard That's right. .

Richard *can't take his eyes off her, her brown arms, her summer clothes, she looks so self-possessed.*

Natalie Please don't touch me.

Richard *touches her.*

Natalie Sinclair's coming – he can see.

Richard He'll just think –

Natalie I don't want him to think anything.

Richard You are just my sister, what can he think?

Cut to **Sinclair** *and* **Jessica** *moving along towpath.*

Jessica (*staring at them on the jetty*) What do you think they are talking about?

Sinclair (*smiles, unabashed*) Me, I shouldn't wonder.

Richard (*close to* **Natalie***, more forceful*) Please . . .

Close-up of **Natalie.**

Interior: Conservatory: Evening:

Sinclair*'s head tilted back, his hat down over his eyes,* **Jessica** *picking at some grapes,* **Richard** *is sitting opposite her, but he is watching* **Natalie** *who is in the hall, taking her shoes off.*

Richard *moves into the hall.*

Intercut with:

Interior: Hall: Evening:

Richard (*whispers*) So where?

Natalie Where what?

Richard Where can we meet?

Natalie You're not going to take no for an answer. (*Decisive.*) Maybe we need a proper meeting to clear this up.

Richard (*whispers*) Exactly.

Shot of **Sinclair**, *sitting dreamily in chair.*

Natalie I'm not coming to you again. It's just possible – occasionally I go out of town for work.

Richard (*teasing, dismissive*) Oh yes, the employment agency.

Natalie Thank you! Nearly made me change my mind . . . sometimes I go away to interview people. Perhaps I can say I'm doing that.

Richard (*very close to her*) Yes.

Natalie Don't whisper like that – I don't want us to look as if we are plotting.

Richard But we are!

Natalie (*whispering*) But I'm just making normal arrangements with my brother.

Sinclair (*suddenly calling, from conservatory*) Tell her she doesn't need to do that job. Pokey little agency, it's ridiculous.

Natalie (*lightly*) I'm a partner in it now.

Sinclair Oh, makes all the difference! Tell her it's silly just to work for work's sake, meeting morons every day. (*Pulling hat down.*) She won't listen to me.

Natalie (*stops whispering but pulls* **Richard** *close*) We can meet in Sinclair's parents' flat.

Richard (*truly astonished*) What! Are you crazy! What are you trying to do?

Sinclair *looks up idly from conservatory, then tilts back his head again.*

Natalie (*calm*) Don't worry, they're away on a cruise. I've got the keys, I often use it when I'm in town. It's being redecorated, it's a bit grotty . . . but it's somewhere to talk. (*She stares at him.*) But this won't be for a fortnight Richard, if at all.

Richard I can't wait that long.

Natalie (*softly*) Oh yes, you can. Yes you can . . .

Interior: **Natalie** *and* **Sinclair***'s bedroom: Night:*

Natalie *in white nightdress,* **Sinclair** *lying naked, half covered by sheet. It is extremely hot, they are both sweating. She rolls over, as we cut into the scene, as if they've just finished sex. She looks quite happy. She kisses* **Sinclair***'s shoulder.*

Natalie I do love you.

Sinclair (*self-mocking smile*) Of course you do.

Natalie Do you love me?

Sinclair Of course I do.

Natalie Even though . . . I'm just me?

Sinclair What does that mean?

Natalie I don't know – (*Pause. Slight smile.*) IT'S ONLY ME – (*Pause.*) go on, you can read it, I don't mind. (*She smiles.*) I can see you edging towards it.

Sinclair *picks up a volume of Proust in French.*

Sinclair Just one chapter. (*Warm smile.*) It's the only thing that shuts me up, isn't it? (*He starts reading. Pause.*)

Natalie (*watching him*) I may have to go away, one weekend . . . I don't know, it's not decided.

Sinclair No problem.

Natalie (*staring at him*) It may be cancelled . . .

Interior: **Natalie**'s *office: Day:*

Cut to a medium-sized high street office in a nondescript Surrey town. Hot warm light. **Natalie** *is sitting at her desk conducting an interview with a small balding man.*

Balding Man Yes, before that I worked for Tesco's, deputy store manager, quite a big branch, just off the M25, and then before that in Guildford. I was acting deputy manager at –

Natalie *is not making notes, a drop of sweat falls on the form. She is curling one of the ends of her hair. The* **Balding Man** *stops, watches her. She looks up, their eyes meet. He senses she's in some sort of sexual reverie.*

Natalie Just a moment . . . (*She grabs any piece of paper off her desk.*) I need to get copies of this.

She moves off, she's kicked off her shoes under desk.

We cut to **Natalie** *by the photostat machine in back room. Without putting any paper in, she switches on the machine. She leans against the wall, puts one of her bare legs up on the wall opposite. The photostat machine flashing green. The room is in shadow. A woman appears in the doorway of the room.*

Natalie Ah, Doreen – I . . . I . . . will be away next weekend. If my husband should ring and mention it – you *will* remember that.

Their eyes meet.

Natalie It's just . . . I *have* to do something, Doreen.

Interior: Mansion flats: Lobby: Afternoon:

Key shots of **Natalie** *standing in a fine dress, coat over her arm, calm, poised, one suitcase by her side, in the lobby of grand old mansion flats, evocative light.* **Richard** *comes towards her – the shot pulling him, drawing him closer.*

Richard I am on time, aren't I?

Natalie (*slight smile*) Yes, for once, you are.

They begin to move up the staircase. An old upper-middle class woman, an inhabitant of the flats, is coming down with a shopping trolley, **Richard** *helps her down the last few steps, watching* **Natalie** *as he does so. Old woman mutters, glancing at their faces beadily.*

Interior: Mansion flat: Afternoon:

Richard *and* **Natalie** *come in to mansion flat – which has extremely large rooms, fine plaster çeilings, huge windows with lace curtains, blowing gently in the breeze, a balcony and balustrade overlooking a sleepy leafy garden square, a richly evocative square. The furniture is heavy and old, the colours subdued greys, greens, browns,* **Natalie** *in her bright dress moving amongst them.*

Richard Jesus, it's like Rosemary's Baby! This place. It's enormous.

They move about the flat, avoiding each other, skirting past each other, not touching as they explore. **Richard** *takes off his jacket as he moves,* **Natalie** *puts down her coat, lets down her hair. Moments later she has kicked off her shoes.*

Natalie (*as she does this*) Sinclair's grandfather made a fortune out of margarine, before the First World War . . . they had three flats like this once.

Richard (*staring out at the leafy old gardens*) Margarine . . . so long ago, I didn't know the money went back that far . . . I love these sleepy old gardens.

Natalie (*moving, businesslike*) We're just going to talk, OK, that's all . . . get things . . . get things . . .

Richard *touches her as he moves past her, turns her around.*

Natalie (*a slight excited laugh*) Out in the open.

They start to kiss, unable to stop touching each other, passionately entwined, **Richard** *unbuttoning her dress, pulling it off above her head, in the mouth of the cupboard, among all the old elderly clothes and shoes. They fall down together at the base of the cupboard and begin to make love.*

Interior: Mansion flat: Early evening:

Cut to **Richard** *and* **Natalie** *lying on their fronts, naked on the bed, as if after sex. But apart, not touching. The linen on the bed, starched, crisp.*

Richard It's so warm. (*Stretching his arm out.*) It's great. Why do you think . . .

Natalie (*calmly*) No whys.

Richard (*smiles*) You don't know what I was going to say.

Sound of a key in lock, front door opens, **Richard** *sits up looking startled. Very alarmed. Small mid-European cleaning woman bustles into hall, they can see her through the open bedroom door. She is hunting for something, nosing around.*

Natalie It's all right – Just get under the sheets. Come on. And *sleep*!

Natalie *calmly gets up, pulling on stylish dressing gown out of her half unpacked suitcase. She intercepts cleaner.*

Natalie Hello Selina, you've forgotten your keys have you? Yes?

Cleaning woman snuffling around, looks straight into bedroom.

Natalie My brother's sleeping in here. See – sleeping, like a baby. I'm getting ready for the theatre, giving myself a treat. *(She smiles.)* I'm up in town on business.

Cleaning woman muttering in some incomprehensible language, disappears, bangs front door.

Natalie *turns, laughing.*

Natalie Don't look so worried!

Interior: Mansion flat: Night:

Night. **Richard** *and* **Natalie** *in loose summer clothes sitting in semi-darkness on the floor of the biggest room, passing a wine bottle between them. Fruit from a jug, mangoes, apricots, oranges. During the scene* **Natalie** *rolls them over to* **Richard**. *Very little light.*

Natalie *(laughing)* Sometimes . . . I feel this big with Sinclair. *(Fingers close together.)* No, this big . . . *(Getting smaller.)* Even this big.

Richard *is smiling at her.*

Natalie It's nice being able to tell someone . . . at last. *(Wipes a dribble of wine from the corner of his mouth, fondly.)* That's all that's going on here, *understand?*

Richard Of course. *(Pause.)* *What* happens if he tries to ring you?

Natalie He won't. Not tonight. Fortunately he's out. Tomorrow I have to remember.

Richard Oh, really? Out? What's he doing? What's he up to? Maybe he's cheating too.

Natalie (*emphatic*) This isn't cheating. Absolutely not. Anyway, that's an American expression.

Richard (*solemn*) Is he faithful?

Natalie (*slowly saying the word*) Faithful. Yes, I think so. (*Slight laugh.*) It's never really occured to me he wasn't. (*Staring at* **Richard**.) We can see – he always works on a Saturday morning. Even when we have people over for lunch, he insists on going in. Nothing stops him. (*Looking into* **Richard**'*s eyes.*) We can take a look at him tomorrow.

Interior: City office building: Foyer: Day:

Subjective shot of the modern foyer, **Natalie** *beginning to move across foyer,* **Richard** *behind her.*

Richard But don't they know you, here?

Natalie I don't think so, no. I hardly ever come . . . we'll see.

Natalie *up to reception desk,* **Stony-Faced Woman**.

Natalie I wonder . . . if you could see if Sinclair Bryant is in his office.

Stony-Faced Woman Mr Bryant? One moment.

She phones up, shot of **Richard** *watching.*

Richard (*whispers*) What you going to say if he *is* there . . . this is silly.

Natalie *seemingly totally calm, gives the woman a little smile, stares straight at her.*

Stony-Faced Woman No reply.

Natalie What?

Stony-Faced Woman (*as if for a two-year-old child*) There
is – no – reply.

Natalie *looks startled.*

Exterior: Road outside City office: Day:

Natalie *walking along slightly in front of* **Richard**.

Natalie I don't know . . . I don't know what I feel. He's
probably just . . .

Wide shot of **Natalie** *from across the street. We see her suddenly
stop dead in her tracks.* **Richard** *who hadn't noticed, has to go
back to fetch her.* **Natalie** *is staring through glass window of a
cafe.*

Richard What's the matter?

He looks down at one of the tables. In front of them is **Sinclair**
*eating a quite enormous breakfast – a fry-up spilling over three
plates, with fried bread, mushrooms, sausage, eggs, tomatoes, chips,
even a piece of steak.* **Sinclair** *is eating voraciously and reading.*

Natalie *presses herself against the glass, fascinated, amused.*
Richard *pulls her away, but she moves back for a second look.*

Richard (*suddenly loud*) Natalie – come here!

Natalie *turns her head, across the street her car is being clamped,
it is parked almost opposite the restaurant on the other side of the
road.*

Natalie Jesus! That's all we need!

She runs across the road, and up to the men doing the clamping.
Richard *follows.*

Natalie (*although excited, she is not hysterical, in command*) Now
that is not fair – absolutely not. We've only been here ten
seconds, twenty seconds at the most.

Clamping Officer I'm afraid, once the clamps are out of the van madam – there is no going back.

Richard (*eyeing the restaurant across the road*) Natalie, please, you're meant to be in Nuneaton. Come away, come on, you can never ever talk your way out of a clamp.

Close-up of **Natalie** *staring into the eyes of the* **Clamping Officer.**

Natalie (*very direct*) I'm having an affair with that man there.

Indicating **Richard** *who is peering at the other clamps in the van, trying to distance himself.*

Natalie And my husband is right across the street having breakfast, and about to come out. (*Slight smile, gazing at* **Officer.**) You wouldn't want to break up my life would you?

Officer's *face intrigued. Shot of clamping van roaring off, and* **Richard** *and* **Natalie** *jumping into car, double quick.*

Richard What on earth did you say to him?

Natalie (*laughing*) Let's celebrate.

Interior: Jewellery shop: Day:

Natalie *with several carrier bags from expensive shops, peering at jewellery with* **Richard.** *A very sober male shop assistant watches them.*

Natalie I want to get something for Sinclair . . . (*To* **Shop Assistant.**) I want something for my husband.

Shop Assistant (*to* **Richard**) What do you like the look of sir?

Natalie (*smiles*) No point asking him! I think that gold tie pin looks nice.

Richard Does he use tie pins? (*Correcting himself.*) Do *I* use tie pins?

A giggly exuberant mood between them.

Natalie Oh yes. They're very fashionable again. We'll take it.

Interior: Mansion flat: Night:

Evening light, dying in the big room. **Natalie** *comes out of the bedroom in a beautiful new evening dress.* **Richard** *stares across the room at her, rather overwhelmed at the sight of her. Deep sense of attraction and love from him.*

Natalie (*makes a self-mocking fanfare noise*) Do you like it?

Close-up of **Richard**.

Cut to **Natalie** *with phone, dialling the last number.* **Richard** *near her.*

Natalie This is important, don't distract me. (*Phone is answered.*) Sinclair?

Interior: The kitchen: Evening:

Sinclair *on phone in kitchen. We intercut with* **Natalie**.
Sinclair *during conversation is trying to extract a knife from the washing-up machine which is open and bulging with dirty plates and cutlery. At the beginning of sequence he opens a drawer to find no clean knives left.*

Sinclair Natalie . . . great. I was just wondering when you'd ring.

Intercut with:

Interior: Mansion flat: Evening:

Natalie I'm fine. Bit tired . . . fine.

Richard *touching her hand during the conversation, kisses her neck, running his hand down her neck, over her arms, over her breasts.* **Natalie***'s head goes back.*

Sinclair How's the hotel?

Natalie A little gloomy . . . but the rooms are very big . . . (*Trying to push* **Richard** *away but responding to him.*)

Sinclair Yes . . . those big old provincial hotels can be very depressing, how's the food?

Natalie The food. (*She smiles.*) You would ask that! The food . . .

Richard *kissing her.*

Natalie Excellent, I'm just going out to get a quick bite now . . . and then I'm going straight to bed. Very early tonight, OK?

Sinclair OK my darling.

Natalie *about to ring off.*

Sinclair How are the beds?

Natalie The beds? The beds are . . . I've only got a single – average, I'd say. Quite nice.

Sinclair Fine. Good. Is there a view?

Natalie (*her head goes back*) No. No view – not to speak of, not here in Nuneaton. Goodnight, darling. (*She rings off, kissing* **Richard**, *just brushing his lips, not real kisses.*) I'd hate to have a real affair. Lies . . . deceit . . . all that.

Exterior: Canary Wharf by the river: Night:

Richard *and* **Natalie** *walking in the hot summer night, her dress shining.*

Richard You don't feel –

Natalie No questions, I told you they were forbidden.

Richard (*lightly*) You're so calm, we're doing something illegal, a major taboo, could go to gaol! – and you just seem to find it mildly relaxing!

Natalie We're not doing anybody any harm; we're not sticking needles into our arms, killing ourselves with drink. Just enjoy it, the last moments.

Richard What if it wasn't the last moments?

Natalie What do you mean?

They move around a corner, searchlights are stabbing the sky as if for an opening of a nightclub by the river, among the otherwise dead offices.

Richard I mean we could go off together somewhere.

Natalie Like where?

Richard (*lightly*) I don't know. Mexico. People always go to Mexico in stories and things, don't they, when they are fugitives.

Natalie But we're not fugitives. And how would we live?

Richard (*charming smile*) Oh there are plenty of ways of making money. We could write a blockbuster novel, you know the sort you buy in airports, that's easy enough, or – (*He suddenly turns.*) I mean it. We can both escape!

Natalie *looks alarmed at this.*

Natalie (*touching him*) Sssh . . . stop it . . . we can't go anywhere, don't think it, not even as a joke.

They get to where the searchlights are positioned, revolving round. Kids standing outside the club, some in very short skirts.

Richard (*looks at the kids*) Being single –

Natalie What about it?

Richard It's not as simple as it used to be.

Natalie (*touching him*) Suddenly feeling older are you? – my little brother . . .

Interior: The kitchen: Night:

Cut to pouring water, gushing from the washing-up machine. It has already half flooded the kitchen. **Sinclair** *rushes into the kitchen.*

Sinclair Shit! . . . Christ!

Rips out plug from washing-up machine, water still spilling from pipe somewhere behind the machine, leaking.

Sinclair Calm . . . calm . . . come on, be calm. (*Pulls out 'Yellow Pages'.*) No, no, wait a minute, no rip-offs. (*His hand flicking through 'useful numbers' by phone.*) Nats will know . . . (*He dials briskly.*)

Shot of the water dribbling from behind the machine.

Sinclair Is that the Royal George? – I want to speak to Mrs Natalie Bryant . . . what . . . ? sorry . . . what? What do you mean there's nobody of that name? Don't be ridiculous. (*Slowly.*) Mrs Natalie Bryant – you *are* in Nuneaton are you? Then check again. I may have got the name of the hotel wrong, but it's highly unlikely . . . Right! Give me the number of *every* hotel in Nuneaton. It's urgent, there's a flood in the kitchen.

Close-up of **Sinclair**'s *face, puzzled, truly startled.*

Interior: All-night supermarket: Night:

A shot of **Sinclair** *pushing large wire basket through supermarket, deep in thought, muttering slightly.*

Sinclair Let's get this straight . . . the hotels . . . all the hotels . . . stop talking to yourself.

He sits on the floor for a moment to do his shoe-lace up, not an abject figure, but a deeply thoughtful one, coping with a possibility he'd never considered.

Sinclair There is an explanation . . . must be.

Cut to **Sinclair** *at the check-out, still with his large wire basket, the only thing in it is one packet of kitchen roll. He stares down at it.*

Sinclair (*to check-out girl*) This looks silly doesn't it? I was actually looking for something more substantial, a . . . a . . . looking for some absorbant . . .

Check-out girl looks bewildered.

Sinclair Something to *absorb* . . . a towel would do really, of course but, maybe I'll get another packet of this, do you think?

Interior: Bedroom: Night:

Sinclair *going through* **Natalie***'s drawers.*

Sinclair (*muttering*) No, this is too much, don't do this . . .

He stops himself, takes one more final riffle through her things, then stops himself again.

Sinclair Stop it . . . Stop *it.* (*He sits on the end of the bed.*) Do things logically.

Interior: Mansion flats: Bedroom: Morning:

Early morning sun, through the net curtains. **Natalie** *and*
Richard's *faces close to each other,* **Richard** *staring at*
Natalie's *sleeping face. He gets out of bed, naked, moves towards*
the curtains. Church bells are ringing from the square, Sunday
morning bells. He looks out at the golden peaceful square. **Natalie**
opens her eyes.

Richard (*gesturing at the view*) You know this place can
have hardly changed in the last fifty years . . . it's a time
warp, isn't it.

Natalie (*quiet*) Yes.

Richard Be nice to stay here, wouldn't it?

Natalie (*quiet, staring from bed*) No.

Exterior: Church and square: Sunday morning:

Richard *and* **Natalie** *come out into the sleepy Sunday morning*
square. He is wearing a shirt and jeans and is barefoot, **Natalie** *a*
short skirt and T-shirt. The bells are ringing out.

Richard We don't *need* to go back yet. Don't you see . . .
(*Lightly.*) we really don't . . .

Natalie (*suddenly up to him, pushing him against a brick wall in*
the sun) Now listen to me . . . we don't see each other –
listen! . . . we don't even set eyes on each other, until
you're going out with someone. Got yourself a girlfriend.

Richard You're setting me tasks now!

Natalie I'm not seeing you until that happens, because
you're getting addicted to this.

Richard It's only happened twice – that's not addiction.

Natalie (*touching him in the sun, his open shirt*) You see I
fancy you, and I love you as a brother – that's all, and you

fancy me, and you're beginning to love me as a *lover* and
that is going to end badly, messily, (*Touching him.*) unless
we're careful. Maybe I've always fancied you a little . . .
and probably should never have done –

Richard (*cutting her off*) Sssh. (*Pause.*) I find a girlfriend,
and then what happens? Can I see you?

Natalie You won't want to then.

Richard But if I do?

Natalie We'll see.

Richard That's a strange bargain. (*He smiles.*) But simple.

*Sound of choir practice coming out of the church, before the morning
service.* **Richard** *smiles.*

Richard Go into the church and feel no guilt. I dare you!

Interior: Church: Day:

*They go into the church, a group of young choristers singing,
stopping and starting.* **Richard** *and* **Natalie** *sit for a moment in
a pew listening to the young voices singing.*

Richard (*turns, touches her cheek*) You do look beautiful.

Natalie (*very firm*) I MEAN IT – I PROMISE YOU. (*Her
eyes half close.*) Oh Richard, please . . . please, don't try to
make this more . . . (*Very fond, touching his hair.*) *I* don't
want it to be more.

Interior: Hall/conservatory: Day:

Natalie *arriving back with her shopping bags, moving through the
hall to the conservatory,* **Sinclair** *is sitting waiting, very still, with
the light behind him.*

Natalie You're in here.

Sinclair (*watching her closely*) So it appears.

Natalie *looking tired, but her eyes still alive, excited.*

Natalie (*with bags*) I went on an orgy of shopping.

Sinclair You had the time?

Natalie I had some of the afternoon off yesterday, between meetings. (*Smile.*) Went on a spree to kill the boredom.

She puts tie pin down in front of him.

Sinclair That's lovely, very useful.

Natalie (*gently*) It's not meant to be useful.

Sinclair I had a disaster with the washing-up machine.

Natalie (*not taking this in, moving in the conservatory*) Doesn't matter. (*Warm.*) You're so hopeless with anything mechanical Sinclair!

Sinclair (*simply*) How was the hotel?

Natalie Gloomy. I told you. (*Lightly.*) Huge and draughty.

Sinclair What was it called? This hotel?

Pause. **Natalie** *with her back to him, she senses something.*

Natalie I told you what it was called.

Sinclair I just wanted to avoid it in the future.

Natalie You've never been to Nuneaton – never likely to go. (*Slight laugh.*) What is this?

Sinclair (*calm*) Fine. I don't need to know . . . I was just curious.

Natalie, *sitting astride him, pinning the tie pin on.*

Natalie The Royal George. (*Fondly.*) And it *is* a good idea to avoid it.

Sinclair (*quiet*) Right. Good.

Natalie *moving her hand down his face.*

Sinclair I'm glad you're back.

Natalie So am I.

Interior: 'Urban Alert' offices: Day:

Mixture of grey evening light, and electric light, all the table lamps on. **Jessica** *sitting behind* **Colin**'s *desk, in his office.* **Richard** *dropping some papers in front of her.*

Jessica Thank you, not before time.

Richard (*lightly, staring at the papers*) I wish we were getting somewhere.

Jessica So do I.

Richard *doesn't move.*

Jessica You haven't been to see Colin in hospital yet, have you?

Richard No, I will, I will . . . I promise. (*Not moving.*)

Jessica You *keep* putting it off. Is there something else?

Richard Jessica – what are you doing tonight? (*He smiles.*) I've been meaning to ask for some time.

Jessica What's that twinkle for?

Richard What twinkle?

Jessica I don't believe this, Richard. The vanity! Just get out of here before I lose my temper.

Richard I was just asking you out.

Jessica I thought you were meant to be something of an – expert. (*Sharp smile.*) You seem decidedly rusty to me.

Richard Rusty? (*He smiles.*) Certainly not. So what's the answer?

Jessica No. *No.* I've never seen somebody so obviously thinking about another . . . (*She stops.*)

Richard Another what?

Jessica (*sharp smile*) I was going to say another woman, but it's more likely to be a fifteen-year-old girl, isn't it? Who is she? At a loose end tonight because of her? Or are you trying to forget her?

Richard (*moving away*) OK. OK, that's OK, Jessica.

Richard *sees through the glass partition, a dark-haired young person in restaurant uniform moving among tables, with take-away boxes.*

Jessica Yes, why don't you try that – much better idea. (*As* **Richard** *moves.*) Why's it so urgent anyway? (*She laughs.*) Can't go one night without!

Richard *goes up to dark-haired person who turns to reveal herself as a stocky fifty-year-old woman.*

Richard (*non-plussed*) Ah. Sorry – I was looking for somebody else. Maybe you know where she is?

Interior/Exterior: Chinese fake world in Trocadero: Night:

Richard *moving from main concourse in Trocadero shopping centre into the fake Chinese 'streets', the narrow passages, the stalls of food, steam, street signs, red and yellow light.* **Paula**, *the first girl he saw with the take-away in the office, is serving out food to a couple of tourists.* **Paula** *sees him, leans out and calls.*

Paula Hi!

Richard So you remember me.

Paula Of course. Come behind here, help me serve some of these tourists. (*Sharp smile.*) Come on, it'll be good for you!

Cut to the false street lights flicking off, **Paula** *and* **Richard** *moving down the 'Chinese street', as the place shuts down, towards the back door and the outside world. Just before they get out,* **Richard** *sees a green neon sign saying 'Gents'.*

Richard Just a moment. (*He smiles.*) I've forgotten something.

Interior: Gents: Night:

Richard *slips into the Gents, where there is a massive Durex machine on the wall, with about ten different varieties, with different refinements. A large Scotsman is studying the choice.*

Scotsman Never know which flavour to pick, do you? (*He looks at* **Richard**.) Which do you get? (*Both stare at machine.*) I always get Strawberry Elite − (*indicating slogan on machine.*) you're 'safer' with Strawberry Elite!

Interior: Chinese fake world: Night:

Richard *emerging out of the lavatory,* **Paula** *watching curious,* **Richard** *with four different packets in his hand, slips them into his pocket.*

Richard (*charming smile*) Sorry to keep you waiting.

They bang through the back door into the alleyway behind.

Exterior: Alleyway behind Trocadero: Evening:

The back street, litter blowing over the pavement. Two girls standing in a seedy entrance, kids in the distance drunkenly marauding the street. Sordid, messy atmosphere.

Paula (*stretches her body, reaching towards the night sky*) Fresh air! At last!

Richard (*picking his way over the garbage*) Fresh air? *This* is fresh air?

Paula Oh yes – when you've had people grabbing at you all day – this is wonderful. (*She moves in front of him.*) Free at last.

Richard *looks around at the sleaze, tramps curled up in a doorway. We feel his disgust. Strong images of young beggars, people wandering in the night or asleep amongst the garbage.*

Paula (*warm smile*) What do you want to do now? Apart from *that* of course.

Richard (*gently*) Not sure I want to do *that*. Not just yet. Can I just be with you a bit. Can I?

Paula Maybe. (*Up to him.*) You know what you're like – you're like somebody who's trying to make an alibi for himself.

Richard Perhaps I am.

Paula An alibi for what?

Richard (*lightly*) Not murder anyway, something infinitely worse than that.

Interior: **Sinclair** *and* **Natalie**'s *bedroom: Night:*

Cut to **Natalie** *and* **Sinclair** *in bed, watching TV. Relaxed intimate atmosphere, sense of them growing together again.*

Sinclair (*pointing at TV*) It's the one with the yellow socks, I keep telling you. It's going to be him.

Natalie (*laughing, playfully hitting him*) Stop it, sssh, you always know what's going to happen! Don't tell me.

Phone rings, beside bed. **Natalie** *answers it.*

Intercut with:

Interior: Phone booth: Street: Night:

Richard It's me.

We intercut with **Richard** *in phone booth, in the back street,* **Paula** *close to the glass.*

Richard We can arrange to meet – your condition's being met . . . fulfilled.

Natalie Richard it is too soon. Much too soon. Who is she?

Shot of **Paula**.

Richard Just somebody I know slightly, why, are you jealous?

Cut to **Natalie**, **Sinclair** *watching TV.*

Natalie Doesn't sound a proper one to me. Can't talk now. (*Whispers.*) I'll think about it. (*She rings off.*) That was Richard – he's got a new girlfriend.

Sinclair Calling you with progress reports at this time of night. He must be drunk!

Natalie (*quiet*) Yes – yes, I think he is.

Interior: **Natalie**'s *dressing room: Night:*

Natalie *slips away into her dressing room, a small private space. She sits at the dressing table, light from an old lamp. She is so hot, sweat running down her neck. She moves a photo of* **Sinclair** *on the dressing table; behind it is a picture of* **Richard** *as we first saw him in the film. Her lips hover close to the picture, her head bends down, as if she is fighting something, torn. She slips the thirties necklace and the photo into a bottom drawer, closes it with a sharp movement. She begins to cry, fighting back tears, silent tears, not sobs.*

Interior: **Paula**'s *room: Very early morning:*

Small, upstairs room, dawn light through little window.

Cut to a cat, its eyes shining straight at us. Then to **Paula**, *who is lying sweating in the heat on the bed in T-shirt and panties next to the cat. Outside the window a boy in boxer shorts is roller skating in sleepy jagged circles on a slab of concrete below.* **Paula** *turns her head lazily.* **Richard** *is sitting on a chair, watching her in a detached way. He smiles.*

Paula Haven't you slept?

Richard Don't think so.

Paula It's not right, is it, that it should be as hot as this, in *England*!

Richard *moves over to the bed, begins stroking the cat.*

Richard (*lightly*) Do you worry, Paula?

Paula Worry? What about?

Richard (*gently stroking her leg*) Oh you know, anything and everything . . . the end of the world?

Paula Why bother? (*She smiles.*) Nothing much you can do about that.

Richard (*gently rubbing her bare feet*) And sex?

Paula (*dreamy smile*) What about it? (*Watching him.*) This is nice . . . let's just do this, no more.

Richard (*amused smile*) You mean it's better than nothing?

Paula No, it's too warm to do any more.

Richard (*lightly*) You think about sex a lot, Paula?

Paula You sound like a doctor! Some days I think about nothing else. (*Lightly.*) Around 4 o'clock, usually.

Richard (*tracing a bead of sweat down her leg*) It used to seem so simple, didn't it . . . (*He laughs.*) Except you're probably too young to remember – never had to worry about disease, not something that could kill. But now . . . there is a man at work who has Aids.

Paula Poor guy. I'm sorry.

Richard (*quiet*) Yes.

Paula (*calmly*) I suppose soon almost everybody will know somebody who's got it.

Richard Yes, but him being right there, now, in a strange way it's almost like a sign . . . (*Self-mocking smile.*) from I don't know where – that what I'm doing is right.

Paula (*staring dreamily*) And what are you doing?

Richard (*smiles*) Oh, just trying to escape.

Paula Where is there to go?

Richard Aha!

Paula (*sitting up, her face close to his*) Where are you going? Tell me! What do you have to do?

Richard Oh, I have found a simple way, better than any drug, any desert island.

Paula Really? (*Their eyes meet.*) So what do you need the alibi for?

Richard Oh, nothing very much. I'm just in love with someone.

Paula (*disappointed*) Is that all?

Richard (*smiling*) 'Fraid so.

Paula That's not very dangerous . . . I *knew* you were thinking of someone else.

Interior: Mansion flat: Lobby: Day:

We are inside the lobby waiting with **Richard**. *The porter in shirt sleeves, smoking, wanders out into the hot summer streets. Through the ornamental glass in the doors we see* **Natalie** *approaching dressed in yellow.*

Richard Natalie – I thought you weren't coming.

Natalie I nearly didn't.

Richard (*touching the yellow dress*) Is this new?

Natalie No, not very. (*Immediately breaking away.*) We're not going up; if you've got anything to say to me, you can say it here.

Richard Here?

Natalie Yes – go and sit over there.

Richard (*lightly*) You're always telling me where to sit!

He sits across the foyer, for a moment they are alone, beneath the big mirrors. **Natalie** *has the flat key in her hand, a big, old-fashioned key, she keeps turning it over and over in her fingers.*

Natalie So what do you want?

Richard (*staring across the foyer at her*) I want to touch you.

Natalie I don't want you to.

Richard Let's go up. Just for a little while, come on. (*Watching the key in her lap.*)

Natalie No . . . no . . . I'm not going to let you talk me into it.

Richard I did what you said, your task –

Natalie I don't believe you. I don't believe anything's changed.

Richard *moves his chair a little closer.*

Richard I'm not going to go away, Natalie. It's not something you can suddenly drop. (*He smiles.*)

The old woman we saw before in the flats, starts moving through the door pulling her trolley, making a great business of crossing the foyer, and climbing the stairs, muttering crossly.

Richard (*as the woman appears*) Ignore her . . . (*Lowering his voice.*) Let's go up, Natalie. Just today. It's what we both want. It's what you want.

Close-up of **Natalie**. *We feel she is about to weaken.*

Richard (*charming smile*) Haven't I always been right about you?

Natalie It's not what I want.

Richard (*getting close*) Why did you come then – if you don't want to?

Natalie Sinclair's been asking about the hotel I stayed in.

Richard Really? Did he believe you?

Natalie I think so. I don't know.

Richard Good, then this can last all summer then, can't it? At least . . .

Natalie No, Richard. You see, you really need it, and I won't have that.

The old woman dragging her trolley up in distance, muttering.

Richard (*lightly*) If it's an addiction, like you say, maybe I'm prepared to –

Natalie Don't say that.

Richard Don't say what?

Natalie Say the rubbish you were about to say that you're prepared to 'die' for it because that's crap. You want to pretend this is all going to end tragically, something enormously final, because you find that idea exciting.

Richard (*quiet*) No, that's not true.

Natalie I need you, Richard. I really need you – as a *friend.*

Richard A friend! . . . (*He's up to her, holding her.*) Come on, Natalie, give me the key and –

Natalie Stop that, get off me, go on, GET OFF!

She fights him, raining cuffs on him, the porter outside smoking with his back to them. They see the old woman's face staring at them through the bannisters.

Richard Sssh . . . ssh, Natalie . . . we don't want somebody reporting us.

Natalie (*against the wall*) No . . . (*More lightly.*) we don't want you to go to gaol, do we . . . (*Touches his hair.*) Hadn't you better get back to work?

Richard No, my boss is very ill. I told you he's got Aids.

Natalie Yes, I'm sorry. Have you seen him yet?

Richard No.

Natalie That's very cowardly – why not? You've got to go at once.

Richard You keep setting me tasks!

Natalie Why not? I am your sister, after all.

Richard And if I do go?

Natalie I make no promises. (*Their faces very close.*) You can have one kiss . . . just one. I shouldn't . . . but one kiss can do no harm.

She lets him kiss her, then breaks away.

Natalie If you keep away from me . . . till the end of next month, then you will have proved something to me. You can break it, Richard. I promise you.

She moves back out into the hot London streets. **Richard** *watching her go.*

Exterior: Mansion flat courtyard: Day:

We follow **Natalie** *across the courtyard, see her forcing herself to walk away, wanting to go back.*

Interior: **Sinclair***'s office: Day:*

Sinclair *in his fine office, tastefully furnished in pale grey and yellow, with modern pictures on the wall. He is sitting behind a striking black desk, totally occupied with a domestic answering machine – listening to calls* **Natalie** *has received, messages that have been left, a mixture of male and female voices. One of his own phones rings on his desk. A secretary is sitting opposite him, waiting patiently.*

Sinclair (*takes the call, while the tape still plays*) Alan? Yes, no. No, I'm fine. I'm busy at the moment. Call you back. OK? (*Watching tape, then looks up at secretary.*) Won't be a moment. This is my home answering machine. (*Matter of* *fact.*) We had a burglary last week. Just seeing if there's anything here, any wrong numbers, anything that doesn't sound right. (*He continues to stare down at tape, listening for a message left by* **Natalie**.)

Interior: Hospital: Day:

Richard *walking through the hospital ward, to the end bed, where* **Colin** *is lying, looking very, very ill, his face swollen with drugs, but his eyes sharply alive.* **Richard** *trying to cover the awkwardness he feels.*

Richard Hello.

Colin Hi. Sit down.

Pause.

Richard I didn't know what to bring – so I brought a couple of books, thrillers –

Colin (*quiet*) Great. Thanks.

Richard There's a third one here – it's got a little messed up, a biro burst in my pocket. (*Produces third book. It's covered in a large stain.*) I've been wondering if I should give it to you . . . (*He smiles.*) but it's the most fun of the three. So there it is . . .

Colin No, give it to me. Fine.

Richard (*looking at book*) I'm sorry, it looks awful. (*He begins instinctively to wipe at it.*)

Colin No problem.

A couple are sitting across the ward, next to a patient finding it very difficult to talk to him.

Colin (*quiet*) You can go when you like – don't feel . . .

Richard Oh, I'm sorry. I didn't mean to look . . .

Colin It's like someone made you come.

Richard *looks guilty.*

Colin (*watching group across ward*) My parents haven't been to see me.

Richard (*startled*) Really? I'm sorry, that's . . .

Colin (*sharp*) That's just like them. True to form.

Pause. **Richard** *fingering inky book, wiping at it.*

Richard I probably should have bought some fruit I know, I'm sorry. It seemed so –

Colin (*very direct*) Stop apologising all the time, it's nauseating – and stop wiping the book like that, it's driving me crazy – I'll read it with the stains. OK! Right!

Richard *grins, the outburst warms up the atmosphere.*

Richard Right. Are you allowed out of bed, out of here, for an afternoon?

Colin Yes, if I want. Can be negotiated.

Richard I've got a meeting with Lappenshaw Mercantile. (*Staring at* **Colin**.) Want to come?

Colin *doesn't react for a moment.*

Richard I could brief you on the way. (*He smiles.*) Why not?

Pause.

Colin Yes. OK. Why not?

Interior: **Natalie**'s *bedroom: Day:*

Cut to **Natalie** *wrapping up jewellery – she puts it into a case, as if beginning to pack up.*

Exterior: Docklands Light Railway: Day:

Cut to **Colin** *and* **Richard** *on the train.* **Colin** *in wheelchair,* **Richard** *sitting next to him in almost empty carriage, studying his papers. The train passing across the extraordinary Docklands urban landscape, rampant, unplanned.*

Richard (*with papers*) I think those are all the important ones. (*Staring at the view.*) Look at it, it's like fighting with a pea-shooter, what we're trying to do.

Colin (*light grin*) Yes, might get one extra zebra crossing – better than nothing.

Richard (*staring out of window*) You know I can remember when they first announced what was going to happen here, it was going to be a great new city, the new Venice, modern but magical – one of the wonders of Europe!

Colin (*laughs*) Yes, I can remember that too.

Richard And look what happened! (*Looks at the chaotic buildings.*)

Colin You're becoming an architectural reactionary, Richard.

Richard No, no, I'm a modernist – definitely. (*He smiles.*) Always *thought* I was.

Colin Oh yeah?

Richard (*suddenly laughing*) This is incredible, isn't it? You're the one that's ill – yet you're the optimist!

Colin Yes. Because you're determined not to be. (*Teasing smile.*) Aren't you? (*Jabbing him, laughing.*) Aren't you?

Richard (*grin*) Maybe.

Colin (*laughs*) We'll have to do something about that, Richard.

Interior: **Natalie***'s bedroom: Day:*

Cut to **Natalie** *putting a fur coat into a trunk. She is packing winter clothes.*

Interior: Developer's office: Day:

The low black and gold light. **Colin** *wheeled into the office by* **Richard,** *to face* **Geal, Noley,** *and third young man.* **Geal** *in the middle of eating sandwiches, looks astonished and deeply uneasy at the sight of* **Colin.** *The wheelchair bearing down on* **Geal.**

Richard Colin was able to make it after all.

Geal (*words almost sticking*) How good to see you. We're a little pressed for time today, so maybe we should –

Colin (*sharp smile*) In that case let's not waste any more of it. (*Flicks his fingers.*) Richard!

Richard *standing behind him handing him papers on command.*

Colin Right, it appears there've been interesting developments in the last few weeks. You made a statement saying you had absolutely no intention of going back on your plan for providing housing on the site, but then just a week after that there is a secret meeting between you and two civil servants from the Department of the Environment . . .

Geal Untrue. Untrue, untrue.

He is edging his one uneaten sandwich away from **Colin***'s hand, which is getting terribly near it.*

Colin We have a memo to prove it. (*He smiles.*) Would you believe! Written by A.R.A. with B.G. – I take it that's you – and B.F. present. It says 'meeting with Lappenshaw Mercantile about whether they will be held to promises – '

Geal How did you get hold of this? This is just 'let's get the wicked developers', standard knocking stuff.

Colin (*effortlessly*) We don't think you're wicked, just seeing what you can get away with, like everyone.

Geal This is all untrue. I question the authenticity of this document. Let me –

Colin *wheels himself out of range.*

Colin No, no, gentlemen, don't be so eager, you will see it all in due course when we publish it in five days. Now I think you should just listen. (**Geal** *edging his sandwich almost into safety along the table –* **Colin** *wheels himself right up to desk, staring at him with a sharp grin.*) You are getting a sneak preview of it, before it becomes public. (*Picks up* **Geal**'s *sandwich and sinks his teeth deep into it.*) I think that's very generous of us, don't you Richard? (*Mouth full of sandwich.*)

Richard Oh yes indeed.

Colin Very considerate of us. (*With sandwich.*) Is it curried tuna? I think it is. (*Pushing sandwich up to* **Geal**'s *mouth.*) Have a taste, see what you think. (**Geal** *looks astonished, terrified of the sandwich now* **Colin** *has touched it.*)

Interior: Developer's building passage and lifts: Day:

Colin *in wheelchair and* **Richard** *waiting by lifts, cleaning woman picking up paper cups strewn along passage.*

Colin (*ironic smile, looking at mess*) They're so proud of this building!

Richard Yes. (*Looking at* **Colin**.) That was great.

Colin Yes, the sandwich was nice anyway.

Richard I'll get you back then.

Colin Yes. (*His eyes tense and worried for a moment.*) I suppose you better.

The lift climbs up towards them, **Richard** *wheels* **Colin** *into it.*
We see **Colin**'s *pale face disappear behind the lift doors.*

Interior: **Richard**'s *bedroom: Early morning:*

Very early morning, **Richard** *lying in bed, hot, sweating, restless,*
his bare arms stretched out. He is staring at photographs of
Natalie *taken at the picnic which he's put on the wall. He's had*
some of them blown up. **Natalie** *looks imperious in some, seductive*
in others, staring back at **Richard**. *He looks at the clock.*
3.45 a.m. He looks back into **Natalie**'s *eyes.*

Richard (*muttered*) Just go there . . . GO THERE . . .

Exterior: **Natalie** *and* **Sinclair**'s *house: Morning:*

Richard *approaches the house, through the flowers. Curtains still*
drawn downstairs. The door opens surprisingly quickly. The
Maid's *sleepy face.*

Richard It is very early I know – (*Unabashed smile.*) I was
just passing . . . happened to be in the area.

Maid (*sharply*) We were already up.

Exterior: **Natalie** *and* **Sinclair**'s *garden: Day:*

Sinclair *appears through the garden, seeing* **Richard** *standing at*
the front door.

Sinclair Natalie's gone out already.

Richard (*startled*) She's not here!

Sinclair (*watching him carefully*) No – she's not. But I am.
Come with me.

Sinclair *moves off through the garden towards the river,*
Richard *following.*

Sinclair We're getting ready.

Richard Ready for what?

Sinclair *turns and smiles and moves towards the river.*

Sinclair It's very convenient you being here – because I'm
not going to work this morning. Definitely not.

Richard (*following* **Sinclair** *to the water's edge*) Where are
we going?

*They reach the river. At the bottom of the garden is a sizeable boat.
Its engine running.*

Sinclair Just a little trip. I've hired this for myself. But it's
perfect you should be here.

Richard (*very apprehensive*) I don't like boats, I think I'll –

Sinclair Don't worry. I know absolutely nothing about
boats either. But he does, Fernando does – he comes with
the boat. (*Indicating tall man driving boat.*) You've *got* to
come Richard.

Close-up of **Richard**, *looking very suspicious.*

Exterior: The river: Day:

Cut to broad stretch of the river, a ripe landscape. **Sinclair** *and*
Richard *sitting high on the stern of the boat,* **Sinclair** *in his
straw hat.*

Sinclair Relax – you're here now.

Richard (*very unrelaxed*) Yes.

*Seductive shots of the river bank, the houses, people in their gardens,
a child on a swing, people eating breakfast outside under a parasol,*

a figure in white standing watching them go past, a timeless, evocative feel. And then we cut back to **Sinclair***'s beady eyes.*

Sinclair So Richard, what is the matter with you? – you can tell me . . .

Richard I don't think so, Sinclair.

Sinclair What do you mean?

Richard There's nothing to tell.

Sinclair You turn up suddenly like this! You ring up in the middle of the night! There's something on your mind.

Richard No more than usual.

Sinclair Are you in love?

Richard No.

Sinclair You sound very definite.

Richard Yes, because I'm definitely not in love. Not with anyone.

Sinclair Who is she? Somebody I know?

Richard Sinclair – I assure you there is no one.

Sinclair *smiles. Shot of the bank, the boat moving into unspoilt countryside, rich landscape. A whole cluster of children are suddenly revealed in a field running down to the river, they all have kites. Big Chinese dragon kites. Large kites, small kites, getting ready for some sort of display, running with them, or moving them on the ground.*

Sinclair Other people's children are wonderful, aren't they?

Richard (*watching them*) Yes. Do Natalie and you plan . . . ?

Sinclair Oh yes, some day . . . Natalie doesn't feel ready at the moment, as I'm sure you know. Relax Richard . . .

Richard (*slight smile*) I told you – I hate boats.

Richard *watching* **Sinclair** *suspiciously. The river narrows, the overhanging trees get nearer the boat.*

Sinclair You know dinosaurs roamed this place more than anywhere else in England.

Shot of the receding river as they move.

Sinclair There was a sort of dinosaur rush hour at certain times of day along this river, great herds wading along here. I think that's why there's something dangerous and exotic about Surrey still, isn't there?

Richard (*avoiding* **Sinclair**'s *gaze staring at the view*) So what will remain of our world Sinclair, in a couple of hundred years?

Sinclair We spend too much time thinking about the end of the world!

Long lens shot of the boat moving through narrow part of the river, **Sinclair** *lying back, his hat half tilted over his eyes, watching* **Richard** *beadily.*

Sinclair It's not going to happen . . . today . . . I promise you. Not before we've had lunch. I'm a professional forecaster remember!

Exterior: Bank of river: Boat moored: Day:

Sinclair (*moving up a little path with hamper*) Come on, I know a secluded spot.

Richard Secluded spot! (*He glances at Fernando.*)

Sinclair Fernando will stay here, he prefers eating on his own.

Richard I'm sure Fernando would love to join –

Sinclair *moving up ahead. Fernando looking down at* **Richard**. **Richard** *smiles at him.*

Richard Is he going to kill me? Do you think?

We cut to a small lake full of lilies, old trees bending over the water, dense foliage, some junk floating among the lilies, but rich almost tropical atmosphere. **Richard** *and* **Sinclair** *on the bank, a white umbrella shielding them.*

Sinclair (*opening the hamper*) You can have anything but the lychees.

Richard (*staring at the bulging hamper*) You didn't know I was coming? You *couldn't* have.

Sinclair No. Of course not.

Richard (*staring at food*) So this was *all* for you?

Sinclair Sure. Why not? (*Staring at lake.*) Probably full of corpses. (*He turns suddenly to* **Richard**.) She's having an affair isn't she?

Richard If you mean Natalie . . .

Sinclair (*peeling lychees*) Who else would I mean! Don't give me dumb replies, please Richard. It insults both of us.

Richard If you mean Natalie. (*He breathes deeply.*) I'm sure Natalie isn't.

The still water, the lilies, the heavy, hot atmosphere.

Sinclair She's lying to me, all the time. When people lie to you, you suddenly can't think about anything else.

Richard (*quiet*) You've spotted little signs have you?

Sinclair Little signs! No, I didn't have to – she's been carrying a giant placard around with her saying 'I'm fucking somebody else'.

Richard (*staring at him, and then flicking a stone into lake*) So who is it?

Sinclair You tell me.

Richard I don't know.

Sinclair I don't believe that.

Richard Sinclair . . . I promise she hasn't talked to me about it. (*Pause. They stare at each other.*)

Sinclair You know I'll find out.

Richard Yes . . . I know.

Sinclair (*chucking stone into lake*) I have a plan now, anyway.

Richard You have?

Sinclair Oh yes. (*Pause.*)

Sound of roaring among the trees, getting louder and louder.
Richard *looks towards the noise with a flicker of alarm. The roaring gets louder still, through the thick foliage he glimpses a large eye, the eye of a creature, a great head. It is moving among the foliage, mysteriously roaming, then it gets bigger. And it erupts out of the bushes. It is revealed as the head of a kite, a dragon kite, more fierce and reptilian than a Chinese dragon. Three children are running with it, they whoop down the opposite bank of the lake, laughing, running and giggling.*

Sinclair (*laughs*) They must have known you were here Richard! Tracked you down.

The children shaking the kite's great head at them and laughing.

Exterior: River: Approaching house: Day:

Shot approaching the back of the house as the boat returns. **Natalie** *is standing in the garden watching them come back,* **Richard**'s *eyes and* **Natalie**'s *meet.*

Interior: The kitchen: Day:

Richard *coming into the kitchen, there are flowers everywhere, the place is heavy with lilies and other flowers. Vases being prepared,* **Natalie** *amongst the flowers.*

Natalie *(strong)* What on earth are you doing here?

Richard A surprise visit. I had to see you.

Natalie We'd agreed –

Richard I don't care what we'd agreed – *(Touching the flowers.)* What's going on here?

Natalie We're leaving –

Richard Leaving? What do you mean?

Natalie And I want the house to look nice for the last weeks we spend in it.

Richard Where are you going?

Sinclair *(suddenly appearing)* America – we're going to live there, in Connecticut.

Richard *(quiet, very startled)* What you mean live?

Sinclair *(breezily)* *Live,* you know – take up residence, change of scene.

Natalie For a few years or so.

Sinclair *(opening cupboard, sorting things)* Yes, this time I had to say yes. I've had many offers before of course – in my line of work it can't be avoided. But this was suddenly irresistible, and we succumbed, didn't we? It wasn't just the money; the house, the timing, everything seemed right.

Sound changing, dialogue fading. We stay on **Richard**, *his preoccupied face, he is stunned by the news. He moves among the lilies.*

Richard *(moving up to* **Natalie**, *who's been saying something to*

Sinclair) We've got to talk about this – (*He tries to move her.*)we have to –

Natalie Of course. (*Half whispers.*) But, but nothing can change, you do understand.

Sinclair (*going through cupboard*) There may be some things for you Richard, if you want. We can't possibly take everything – *Richard* are you listening, are you with us?

Richard *looks up, totally preoccupied.*

Richard (*quiet*) No.

Interior: Hotel lobby: Day:

Tracking shot moving at steady pace across the great expanse of a richly decorated old hotel lobby. **Natalie** *standing looking very smart against the white walls. People moving around her, and having tea in pools of sunlight in chintz armchairs. The genteel clink of china.*

Richard *moving up to her, as she stands looking controlled and elegant.*

Richard We can't talk here – this is ridiculous.

Natalie Can't we?

Natalie *glances around, a group of glacial looking women move past.*

Natalie People having tea. They can't hear.

Richard Why are we out here? You're expecting me to cause trouble are you?

Natalie (*slight smile*) Oh yes.

Richard's *face very close to* **Natalie**, *brushing her cheek.*

Richard (*strong*) We're going somewhere else.

Natalie No. Keep still. *Still.*

She produces a tie, starts to tie it round his neck, her mood febrile but quite happy, becoming a sister again, not sensing the extent of **Richard***'s intensity.*

Richard What's this for?

Natalie I'm meeting Sinclair here in a little while by the way. You can't go in without a tie. They won't let you in without this, *keep still. (She smiles.)* Promise me you'll behave yourself.

Interior: The tea rooms: Day:

The old ladies at tables – the main dining room of the hotel with a great glass roof, like the Waldorf. A pianist tinkling on the piano, cucumber sandwiches on the table, **Richard** *and* **Natalie** *opposite each other. All around them elderly couples, especially women, having tea, bobbing hats, afternoon conversations buzzing, gossiping.*

Richard Is it because of me?

Natalie *No.* It's time for a change. Sinclair wants to get out of England, the economy's going down the chute, the atmosphere's getting ugly, and working in an employment agency is not exactly the answer to my dreams. It's a good time to make a move – it's *our* decision.

Richard *(mocking)* '*Our*' decision?

Natalie Yes, it has nothing to do with getting away from you.

Richard *You're* running away now.

Natalie No – it makes sense. Sinclair's a wise man, he is a little over-whelming and maybe I thought I couldn't cope, but I love him and he's right.

Old ladies twitching in their hats, sitting surrounding their table, **Natalie** *watching them.*

Natalie If *they* knew . . . about us.

Richard You find that idea exciting, don't you?

Natalie Not particularly. (*She flicks his hand affectionately.*) But if they knew, they would be surprised. (*Warm smile.*) That's true, isn't it?

Natalie *eating the sandwiches.*

Richard You broke the rules.

Natalie What rules? There were no rules.

Richard I did everything you asked.

Natalie There was no agreement between us, Richard, you know that, my love. (*Casually reaching for another sandwich.*) You can always visit, pop across.

Richard Pop across?

Natalie The ocean. I want you so much as a friend still.

Richard Still?

Richard *is looking down at the table, he seems near to tears.*

Natalie (*not taking this too seriously, warm*) What is this? Richard, come on . . .

Richard I'm asking you very simply, please, don't go yet. I've helped you constantly, after all. So many times. Gave you advice, *which you took*, got you out of depression. Please do this for me.

Natalie (*affectionately*) Look at you – come on, Richard. (*Gently, lightly.*) My love. What's happened. Just lost your inner confidence a little bit . . . that's all. Mid-life crisis at thirty! (*She smiles.*) Maybe they're getting earlier and earlier . . . Come on. (*Knowing smile.*) You could do anything if you put your mind to it. You know that.

Richard (*not looking up*) I'll ask you one more time. (*Powerfully.*) Please.

He looks up, tears are streaming down his face, the pianist picking out a twinkling tune, the old ladies munching sandwiches glancing in surprise, atmosphere of unease spreading across the tea rooms, music jauntily continuing.

Natalie (*calmly*) I should never have let it happen.

She then softens, leans towards **Richard** *sisterly, taking his wrist.*

Richard (*pushing her away*) Stop it –

Natalie (*firm*) I don't believe you're this hooked, you're trying to turn it into some fantasy of your own – this is self-dramatisation.

Richard *still crying, the tears pouring.*

Natalie It's not *that* serious, Richard. (*Touching him.*) This is my beautiful brother here . . . who was funny and not afraid of anything. Just let it go, Richard. (*Touching his hand.*) I've managed it, you can do it, I know you can.

Richard's *tears have stopped. The pianist playing, old ladies watching.*

Richard That won't happen. I'm not going to let you go away.

Natalie Oh really? So how you going to stop me?

Richard I *will* stop – and you're not safe here. (*Dangerous.*) You thought you could handle me here – but you were wrong.

Sinclair *is by the table, staring down at them.*

Sinclair Hello, you two. You didn't say Richard would be here as well.

Richard *looks down at table, to mask his red face.*

Sinclair English tea, I'm really going to miss these,

cucumber sandwiches, maybe the last ones we'll see for a while.

Interior: Lobby: Day:

Sinclair *and* **Richard** *stand next to each other,* **Porter** *eyeing them,* **Richard** *blowing his nose, turning away from* **Sinclair.**

Natalie Just got to phone work – check on a couple of things.

Sinclair (*watching* **Natalie** *go*) We're having a great time being lazy, saying goodbye to London, going to shows, and to tourist attractions we'd never seen! (*Sharp smile.*) Keeps Natalie occupied. (*He indicates hotel noticeboard.*) These noticeboards are often surprisingly interesting, you can see what's going on elsewhere in the hotel – conference for Cable TV, you see, meeting of FAX manufacturers, share-holders' meeting, all kinds of boardroom struggles going on in this genteel place.

As **Sinclair** *is saying this,* **Richard** *moving away, towards* **Natalie** *in phone booth, he pushes into booth startling* **Natalie.**

Richard (*very strong*) Natalie, I promise, I'm not kidding, you cannot go.

Natalie *holding phone,* **Richard** *pressed up to her.*

Natalie Get out of here!

Close-up of **Richard.**

Natalie Richard, I told you, there's no going back.

Richard I can't answer for what will happen – if you do try to leave.

Natalie Stop being so melodramatic – you're determined to make something happen –

Richard (*holding her, kissing the side of her face*) This is *me*

Natalie. You know I'm never desperate about anything. I never expected this to happen, either. BUT IT HAS. Come with me . . . Just to talk. Get rid of Sinclair. Come to my flat! You know. *You've got to.* You must.

Porter *knocking on glass,* **Natalie** *twisting her head round, manages to open door.*

Porter Is the lady all right?

Natalie Yes – this is only my brother. (*She moves off, furious whisper to* **Richard**.) For Chrissake – stop it.

They emerge out of phone booth, **Porter** *watching them.* **Sinclair** *is at end of the corridor.*

Sinclair What on earth happened? Where did you go?

Richard (*calling*) She just wanted some change. (*Whispered.*) You *will* come Natalie. By 5.30. You must.

Natalie *moving off.*

I'm waiting for you.

Interior: **Richard**'s *room: Day:*

Richard *alone, the clock showing it's 6.20, golden evening light.*

Noise of somebody on the stairs. Close-up of **Richard**. *They pass his door and go up.* **Richard**'s *face very tense and determined.*

Richard Jesus – how did this happen?

Interior: **Richard**'s *bathroom: Day:*

Richard *goes into the bathroom. Very casually and haphazardly he starts taking all the pills that are there. We see bottle of sleeping pills. He takes everything in the bathroom, pouring them down his*

*throat, very matter-of-fact. They all go down. Empty bottles
clinking into the bath.*

Exterior: Building site: Day:

We cut to **Richard** *wandering down into the great building site,
the dust, the machines, the great hole in the ground, moving among
the workmen, a hallucinatory feeling, the plastic sheeting swirling,
men in goggles staring at him, scaffolding moving overhead, people
looking at him strangely, the cranes towering into the sky. He
wanders further and further into the site, the sounds getting
distorted, the images more vivid, enveloping him, the tremendous size
of the site and* **Richard** *in the middle of it.*

Interior: **Richard**'s *bedroom: Day:*

Cut to **Richard**'s *face hitting his pillow. His eyes closing, his
face strange. His eyes flicker open. Then his body is wracked with
vomiting, his body spinning over, off bed.*

Natalie *is standing over him, pulling him up.*

Natalie (*calm*) Come on, come here. (*Pulling him toward the
bathroom.*)

Interior: **Richard**'s *bathroom: Day:*

Natalie *holds* **Richard** *as he retches.*

Natalie Silly boy, you took vitamin pills as well, more
vitamin pills than sleeping pills it looks like. (*Affectionate
smile, touching him.*) Not the best way to kill yourself.

Interior: **Richard**'s *bedroom: Day:*

Cut to **Richard** *curled up on bed.* **Natalie** *stroking his hair. It is dark now.*

Natalie I came back for the tie actually. (*Smiles.*) Partly for that.

He is still wearing it. She takes it off.

Natalie It's rather a good one. You've messed it up. (*Stroking his hair.*) You wanted to frighten me, did you? You half managed it. (*Calm.*) You're precious to me Richard, don't want you to hurt yourself, but I'm not going to let you destroy us both. Come on pull yourself together – I don't love you when you look like this, all messy and –

Richard (*quiet*) Please, whatever you do, don't tell me to pull myself together.

Natalie OK, OK . . . now if you behave yourself, and if you're brave enough – you can come to our going away party, do you want to do that?

Richard (*looking at her*) I'll see Natalie.

Natalie (*staring invitingly from door*) I think you'll manage it somehow.

Interior: 'Urban Alert' offices: Day:

Office empty except for **Jessica** *and* **Richard**. *Three others including the pudgy girl just leaving for the day.* **Jessica** *is wearing black.* **Richard** *watching her across the whole expanse of the big office.*

Colin's *belongings, his clothes, several pairs of shoes and socks are in neat stacks on a table in the corner. The inky thriller is staring back at* **Richard**.

Jessica Stop staring at them – they'll be going soon.

Richard It's OK – I don't mind. (*He can't keep his eyes off them.*) I think we should keep them here. In memory.

Jessica (*warm smile*) You don't sound too sure.

Richard (*very firm*) No. I am. We should.

Richard *watching* **Jessica**, *formidable behind her desk.*

Richard You'll do well, running this place.

Jessica (*slight smile*) High praise. Thank you.

Richard Come with me tomorrow, please.

Exterior: Gardens of large house near river: Day:

The formal gardens of a house, like Ham House, near river.
Sinclair *and* **Natalie** *have hired a part of the gardens for their farewell party. Groups of people in summer dresses,* **Philippa** *looking beautiful with her children. Champagne and food, a band in red and white playing on gold banqueting chairs on the grass, a microphone on a platform by a summer house, a rich valedictory atmosphere.*

Sinclair *in his element, moving round, joking with people, dazzling people. He takes the microphone.*

Sinclair Just to say the food is not being eaten with sufficient ferocity. There'll be no speeches of any kind, but quite often I will be grabbing the microphone to urge you to eat and drink. *Also* anything that you've been longing to say to us for years and felt you never could, *now* is the time, don't hold back, anything that is insulting, shocking, spiteful, gross, this is turning itself into a speech, definitely forcing itself into a speech, so the only way to stop myself –

Sinclair *walks sharply away from the mike in mid-sentence.*

Richard *and* **Jessica** *together moving among the Surrey people*

and the formal gardens. **Richard** *staring at* **Natalie** *and*
Sinclair *conducting the party.*

Richard Look at them, they are like presiding royalty,
saying goodbye and good riddance to all of us.

Jessica Why do you mind so much?

Richard *watching* **Natalie** *all the time. In a series of stronger
and stronger images he sees* **Natalie** *with* **Sinclair**. *She's teasing
him, ordering him about, behaving with a real confidence with him,
effortless and relaxed.*

Natalie (*teasing* **Sinclair** *in front of others*) No he's hopeless
with modern appliances – trust a business analyst to be
helpless with machines! (*Moving with* **Sinclair** *through
party.*) No, you've never seen Sinclair's table manners!
They are X certificate – frighten children off eating for
days. (*She laughs, touching* **Sinclair**.) He loves being teased.

Richard *watching her, her confidence. She turns and stares at him,
gives him a seemingly secret look, a look saying 'it is over', then
turns away back to friends.*

Exterior: Edge of garden/road near party: Day:

Richard *filling with fury. He follows her round the party,
watches her all the time. Suddenly grabs her when she is for a
moment on the edge of the party, pulling her away, through the
grass and trees, further and further from the guests.*

Natalie (*shouts, yelling*) Stop it Richard – what are you
doing? Please – please, stop it.

Richard God, I want to kill you, you know that?

*He pulls her through the apple trees, as she yells and shouts, trying
to fight him off.*

Richard It's so easy for you. *Easy*. I hate you.

They come out of the trees, rolling down a bank of grass on top of each other, onto a narrow road. They lie in the middle of the long straight road. **Richard** *on top of her, pulling her arms back.*

Richard You used me – didn't you.

Natalie (*fighting back*) Used you.

Richard To get a little excitement into your marriage, make it take fire again – make you feel strong, (*Strange, mocking.*) help you 'find yourself' – a little bored were you in your wonderful house – just play with this shall we – (*Strange, mocking.*) now we're all refreshed again, are we!

Natalie Richard, please.

Richard And now you think, no longer need him, let's throw him away – WHAT ABOUT ME? WHAT HAS HAPPENED TO ME? I hate you . . . I *won't* allow you to . . .

Natalie (*furious*) Stop this Richard, I'm warning you, I'm warning . . .

Richard (*twisting* **Natalie***'s head around*) What if you were pregnant?

Natalie But I'm not. (*Strong.*) I'm not . . .

Richard The child would have an enormous head probably, wouldn't it! . . .

Natalie Richard – you're going to stop this.

A lorry nearly mows them down as they fight, rolling out of its path. A cathartic fight, **Richard***'s rage pouring over her,* **Natalie** *is crying, fighting him away, tears roll down her,* **Richard** *begins to stop, they both collapse onto each other, exhausted and bleeding.*

They lie on top of each other by the road, oblivious of any passing cars.

Natalie (*touching him, curling his hair*) I'm sorry . . . I didn't mean to use you . . . maybe I did use you. (*Running her fingers down his nose.*) Now we're even.

Richard Are we? (*Pause.*)

Natalie I love you . . . (*Lightly.*) I knew you'd want this to end with one of us dying, trust you to get both of us nearly killed.

A car full of daytrippers, passing this strange couple on top of each other.

Natalie I'll tell you a secret . . .

Richard What secret?

Natalie Is it over? Not going to erupt again?

Richard Not for the moment. What is it?

Natalie We're not going away, Sinclair's deal fell through. But we still wanted to have the party.

Richard, *slight smile.*

Natalie Serves me right doesn't it.

Exterior: Gardens of house: Day:

We cut back to the party. The evening light. Slowly on the edge of the frame **Natalie** *and* **Richard** *move towards us, badly cut from the road, bedraggled, their clothes torn, but they move nonchalantly through the guests, who part in front of them, looking startled, forming a path for them, as the guests back away.*

Richard *and* **Natalie** *sit down at a table – the white tablecloth flapping.* **Sinclair** *staring at them.* **Natalie** *casually pours herself an orange juice.* **Sinclair** *moves up to the table.*

Sinclair Something tells me it's the end of the party.

Sinclair *sits, staring from* **Natalie** *to* **Richard** *and back. People watching all three of them as they sit at the table.* **Jessica**

looking very startled. Bewildered guests begin to melt away. The musicians play on, as the party empties. Till only the three and the musicians are left.

Interior: **Sinclair** *and* **Natalie**'s *house: Sitting room: Day:*

We see **Sinclair** *alone, staring into a mirror, deeply pensive, trying to retain control, quietly stunned.*

Interior: **Sinclair** *and* **Natalie**'s *house: Evening:*

Natalie *lying on sofa in hallway.* **Sinclair** *gently wiping cream on her legs, and folding a bandage.* **Richard** *is sitting watching,* **Natalie**'s *eyes half closed. A late summer evening, sound of woodpigeons, dreamy, quiet.*

Sinclair Does that feel all right?

Natalie (*quiet*) Yes.

Sinclair You look like you've been in mortar fire you two.

Natalie (*lying in profile*) We have.

Richard You know don't you – you know everything.

Sinclair Know what?

Richard About me and Natalie.

Sinclair (*simply*) I know a few things, I know there was something extraordinary between you two, something that had to be purged. (*Holds up his hand in case* **Richard** *tells him more,* **Sinclair**'s *face pale but controlled.*) I don't want to know any more, there is a limit beyond which I can't go, I don't want to hear. (*Slight pause.*) It's enough that the worst is over.

Richard (*quiet*) You think so?

Sinclair Yes. I believe that – yes. (*Staring at* **Richard**.) Getting less intense . . . isn't it?

Richard (*quiet*) You're being so . . . calm Sinclair. It's amazing.

Sinclair I'm amazed myself. Somebody had to be calm around here. (*Self-mocking smile, pause.*) I mean I could start screaming . . . maybe I will. Delayed shock. Who knows? . . . (*Quiet.*) *I don't think so.* I hope not.

Natalie (*half opens her eyes, warm*) I told you he was wise, didn't I.

Richard (*quiet*) So Sinclair – you know everything. (*Pause, the sounds of the summer evening.*) What's going to happen then?

Sinclair To us or the human race?

Richard (*lightly*) Both.

Sinclair (*pause*) I haven't a clue.

Exterior: River: Evening:

They are walking along the river bank, the three of them, dusk just falling. A couple of bonfires in people's gardens sending smoke across the water and into the evening sky.

They walk away from the camera.

Sinclair Bonfires! Look. That's autumn! (*Looks across at bonfires, the smoke wafting.*) Those fires, always the typical English end to summer.

Natalie (*gently*) I certainly wouldn't call this summer typical . . .

Richard (*pulling at the leaves by the river, quiet*) No . . .

They move on along the bank.

Sinclair (*glancing at the river*) It could be a good idea we're not going away after all. (*Waves at the view.*) I might have begun to miss this.

They move away from us along the river. Slowly a wipe starts at the top of the screen, turning the final image into a drawing, catching them there, in the distance on the river bank, as they have instantaneously moved into the past, and this summer has already become a memory, of the early nineties.

Methuen Contemporary Dramatists
include

Peter Barnes (three volumes)
Sebastian Barry
Edward Bond (six volumes)
Howard Brenton
  (two volumes)
Richard Cameron
Jim Cartwright
Caryl Churchill (two volumes)
Sarah Daniels (two volumes)
David Edgar (three volumes)
Dario Fo (two volumes)
Michael Frayn (two volumes)
Peter Handke
Jonathan Harvey
Declan Hughes
Terry Johnson
Bernard-Marie Koltès
Doug Lucie

David Mamet (three volumes)
Anthony Minghella
  (two volumes)
Tom Murphy (four volumes)
Phyllis Nagy
Philip Osment
Louise Page
Stephen Poliakoff
  (three volumes)
Christina Reid
Philip Ridley
Willy Russell
Ntozake Shange
Sam Shepard (two volumes)
David Storey (three volumes)
Sue Townsend
Michel Vinaver (two volumes)
Michael Wilcox

Methuen Modern Plays
include work by

Jean Anouilh
John Arden
Margaretta D'Arcy
Peter Barnes
Sebastian Barry
Brendan Behan
Edward Bond
Bertolt Brecht
Howard Brenton
Simon Burke
Jim Cartwright
Caryl Churchill
Noël Coward
Sarah Daniels
Nick Dear
Shelagh Delaney
David Edgar
Dario Fo
Michael Frayn
John Godber
Paul Godfrey
David Greig
John Guare
Peter Handke
Jonathan Harvey
Iain Heggie
Declan Hughes
Terry Johnson
Sarah Kane
Charlotte Keatley
Barrie Keeffe
Robert Lepage
Stephen Lowe

Doug Lucie
Martin McDonagh
John McGrath
David Mamet
Patrick Marber
Arthur Miller
Mtwa, Ngema & Simon
Tom Murphy
Phyllis Nagy
Peter Nichols
Joseph O'Connor
Joe Orton
Louise Page
Joe Penhall
Luigi Pirandello
Stephen Poliakoff
Franca Rame
Mark Ravenhill
Philip Ridley
Reginald Rose
David Rudkin
Willy Russell
Jean-Paul Sartre
Sam Shepard
Wole Soyinka
C. P. Taylor
Theatre de Complicite
Theatre Workshop
Sue Townsend
Judy Upton
Timberlake Wertenbaker
Victoria Wood

Methuen World Classics
include

Printed in the United Kingdom
by Lightning Source UK Ltd.
122187UK00001B/106/A

9 780413 723208